Law and Politics

Readings in Legal and Political Thought

Edited with introduction and essay by

Shadia B. Drury

Associate Editor

Rainer Knopff

Detselig Enterprises Ltd.
Calgary, Alberta

Shadia Drury, *Editor*
Rainer Knopff, *Associate Editor*

Canadian Cataloguing in Publication Data

Main entry under title:

Law and Politics

ISBN 0 - 920490 - 12 - 3

1. Law and politics - Addresses, essays, lectures.
2. Natural law - Addresses, essays, lectures.
I. Drury, Shadia, 1950-
II. Knopff, Rainer, 1948-
K487.P65L38 340 C81 - 091030 - 6

6147 Dalmarnock Cr. N.W.
Calgary, Alberta T3A 1H3

Printed in Canada ISBN 0 - 920490 - 12 - 3

TABLE OF CONTENTS

Sources and Acknowledgements

Chapter 2: From *The Dialogues of Plato,* translated by Benjamin Jowett, (New York: Oxford University Press, 1892, 1920). Reprinted by permission of the publisher. Jowett's footnotes have been inserted by the editors in square brackets in the text.

Chapter 3: From *The Summa Theologica of St. Thomas Aquinas,* (New York: Benziger, 1948). Reprinted by permission of the publisher. Aquinas' footnotes have been inserted by the editors in square brackets in the text.

Chapter 4: From *The English Works of Thomas Hobbes,* 7 vols. Collected and edited by Sir William Molesworth, 1839, Vol. 3.

Chapter 5: From John Locke, *The Second Treatise of Government,* (New York: Bobbs-Merrill Co. Inc., 1952). Reprinted by permission of the publisher.

Chapter 6: from John Austin, *The Province of Jurisprudence Determined,* (New York: Lenox Hill Publishing & Distributing, 1861).

Chapter 7: From Hans Kelsen, *Pure Theory of Law,* translated by Max Knight, (Berkeley: University of California Press, 1967). Reprinted by permission of the publishers.

And from Hans Kelsen, "Natural-Law Doctrine Before the Tribunal of Science," *Western Political Quarterly,* 1949. Reprinted by permission of the University of Utah, copyright holder.

Chapter 8: From Lon L. Fuller, *The Morality of Law,* revised edition. (New Haven: Yale University Press, 1969). Reprinted by permission of the publisher.

Introduction

More than any other, the debate between natural law and legal positivism in the history of western thought illustrates the close connection between law and politics. Today political theorists tend to leave the question "what is law?" to legal philosophers, as if it were of no concern to them. Yet political theorists are concerned with the nature of the good political order. In particular, they attempt to discover the ends to which the good political order ought to be directed. Since law is the most fundamental way in which the state seeks to accomplish its ends, the question of the ends of political order cannot be kept separate from the question concerning the ends towards which law ought to be directed.

At first blush, the debate between natural law and legal positivism appears to be a debate about the nature of law. The two schools provide different definitions of what law is. This certainly seems to be a very academic and fruitless debate about the proper signification of the word "law". Yet so much has been written with so much passion and zeal on this apparently academic question that one must become suspicious that more is at stake than a mere definition of law.

The debate revolves around the relationship of law to morality. The questions involved include the following: Can law be understood independently of moral concepts? Can we understand law apart from justice? Is it possible for a law to be valid and yet be morally evil? Is it possible for a legal system to exist and yet be completely or almost completely devoid of justice? Are law and goodness necessarily related or are they separate?

The school of natural law insists on the necessary connection of law with moral goodness and justice. It maintains that a law is valid if and only if it is morally good or at least not morally evil. A valid law is not simply a law that has been enacted by due process. It is a law that deserves our respect and obedience. Laws enacted by the proper authorities do not deserve our respect or obedience if they are morally pernicious, nor are they properly speaking laws. But surely, we may object that there have been many laws in the past and many in the present that are unjust. Norwould the advocate of natural law deny this. He would add that such laws only have the appearance of laws but are not genuinely speaking laws. Laws properly understood must be morally good. One may object that the connection between law and morality may be necessary for law to be good, but is it necessary for it to be law? The advocate of natural law would reply in the affirmative. According to him, law cannot be understood independently of its function because law is not a thing, but a human activity directed towards an end which is good. Different theorists of natural law attribute different ends or purposes to law, but all are agreed that the ends of law are moral ones. For example, Plato maintained that the rule of law is meant to accomplish the same function in the state that reason accomplishes within the *psyche* of the individual -- that is, create a condition of inner harmony and justice. Aquinas believed that the function of law is to contribute to the moral perfection of man. Locke held that the function of law was to attach known human sanctions to the law of nature and so insure obedience. Unless law were good, it could not hope to fulfill its moral function in political society.

The theory of natural law has several implications. It implies that there is an objective and universal standard by which all law can be evaluated. It implies further than men can readily distinguish between good and evil, just and unjust, and that the former is preferable to the latter. It also has important political implications. It tends to justify political resistance in cases where law is deemed unjust. We find Aquinas, however, extremely cautious when recommending legal disobedience. Locke is much more candid about the doctrine's implications for political resistance.Generally speaking natural law tends to place the love of justice above that of peace, order and survival.

In contrast to natural law, legal positivism insists on the separation of law and morality. From its perspective, insisting on the close affinity of law and morality may have undesirable consequences. It could imply that all laws are by definition good and therefore beyond reproach. This would have the effect of depriving us of the language that makes the moral criticism of law possible. Secondly, it may be interpreted as an invitation to anarchy and chaos since it can be taken to mean that one may disobey whatever laws one does not like. Moral concepts are therefore not only dangerous when closely associated with the understanding of law, they are most definitely unnecessary. For the legal positivist, law is a command issuing from the sovereign in political society according to the proper and accepted law-making procedures in that society. Not all legal positivists, however, would agree with Kelsen that law can have *any* content and still be valid law, but all of them agree that law could be considered by some or even the majority of citizens to be morally pernicious and still be valid law. But how, we may ask, can morally pernicious law achieve the end of law in political society? How can it hope to uphold justice? The legal positivist replies that upholding justice or any of those other exalted moral ends attributed to law are not the proper functions of law in society. The function of law is simply to maintain order. And this it can do without any relation to morality. There may be good and bad order, but that is a separate question from the question about law. Although legal positivist theories are agreed about the separation between law and morality, they do not all agree on its philosophical and political implications. For example, not all legal positivists consider themselves relativists who believe that there exists no objectively valid set of moral standards by which law can be evaluated. And even if such standards existed, they are not according to the relativist knowable. In the absence of moral knowledge, it makes sense to allow positive law to define what is morally acceptable and what is not. Both Hobbes and Kelsen are relativists (or non-cognitivists) of this variety. Others like Austin would deny that moral standards are relative or dependent on arbitrary legal decrees. Austin believed that utility can provide a standard by which law can be evaluated. Good law maximizes utility or the greatest happiness of the greatest number. Even though it is not entirely clear that this position does not collapse into relativism, it is important to note that Austin's own self-understanding is not relativistic.

Another important point of disagreement among legal positivists concerns the question of the legitimacy of legal disobedience. Hobbes, for example, wants to maintain that law is the command of the sovereign, and since we have by virtue of being in political society agreed to obey the sovereign regardless of his commands (unless he commands us to give up our life), we never have any justification for disobeying the law. Hobbes' positivism has an extremely conservative flavour and finds the traditional natural law view threatening precisely because it is far too radical. Austin, on the other hand, does not rule out all disobedience. Under severe circumstances, governmental resistance may be justified on utilitarian grounds.

The selected readings from Plato, Aquinas, Hobbes, Locke, Austin and Kelsen contribute to the proper understanding of the debate between natural law and legal positivism. Only when this debate is understood as a debate about the *function* of law in political society, will its importance for politics be recognized. Far from being a quibble about the definition of law, this debate has important political implications. It is as much a political as a legal concern. By concentrating on an issue that is central to both law and politics, it is hoped that these readings will serve as an introduction to legal as well as political thought.

I

The Resilient Core Of Natural Law

S.B. Drury

"Natural law" refers to the broad outlines of a philosophy of law and politics that has been remarkably persistent throughout the history of legal and political thought. In our time natural law is very much under attack. It has been accused of encouraging anarchy and political radicalism on one hand, and political absolutism and conservatism on the other.[1] Democrats have accused it of promoting intolerance and oppression at the expense of democratic tolerance and equality.[2] Philosophers have rejected it as a theory wrought with confusion and contradition.[3] It still remains very much a part of legal and political debate in our time.[4] Nor is it as unpopular as it may seem. On the contrary, it is experiencing a revival.[5] But despite many defenders, natural law remains shrouded in mystery. Some of its defenders are converts from legal positivism. They are men who have been awakened from their positivistic slumber by their experience in Nazi Germany. They are like men who have been to hell and have come back to reveal to us new truths.[6] This approach can hardly aid the cause of natural law, and not surprisingly, leaves its skeptical critics unmoved. Its more lucid defenders are willing to defend only a very attenuated version of it.[7] And those who have attempted to understand the theory in the context of legal and political thought have done little to clarify it. Some have defined it so broadly that it has become coeval with legal and political thought itself.[8] Others have defined it so narrowly as to exclude authors not to their liking.[9]

''Natural law'' is not a term whose meaning has remained unchanged through the ages. It does not refer to a homogeneous doctrine in legal and political thought. Nevertheless, it is erroneous to assume that natural law has no resilient core designating a remarkably persistent conception of the foundations of the legal and political order. In this essay I will not dwell on the historical variations and transformations of natural law; some of these the reader can discover in the forthcoming selections. Instead, I will set out clearly the set of ideas that together constitute what I believe to be the resilient core of natural law. By this, I mean the set of ideas which together form the outlines of a theory of law and politics that can be described as a natural law theory. The resilient core of natural law is therefore the set of ideas that make up the permanent features of diverse theories of natural law. Many, although not all the criticisms of natural law, rest on misunderstandings. In this essay I hope to elucidate the meaning of natural law in order to make a fair evaluation of it possible.

It is my contention that there are at least seven main claims that constitute the resilient core of natural law. With the exception perhaps of the last, all are necessary constituents of any theory that can be described as a natural law theory of law and politics. I will begin by briefly listing these seven claims, and then discussing each at greater length below.

The resilient core of natural law consists of the following claims:

a. When used in a narrow sense, ''natural law refers to a universal, trans-historical, moral order that is independent of human volition, convention of political decree.[10] This means that it is an objective moral standard. Furthermore, it is (to some degree) accessible to man through reason.

b. The knowledge of natural law or natural justice is *practical* in the sense that it directs or guides action, unlike purely theoretical knowledge.

c. Natural law is a deonotolgical ethic. The term ''deontology'' derives from the Greek words *deon* (duty) and *logos* (science) and so literally means the science of duty. In modern usage, a deontological ethic is one that regards moral duties as fundamental and intrinsically valuable. Nor is their value derived from their success or failure in achieving ideal ends. The natural law requires us to act rightly, but this is not the same as requiring us to perform actions that produce the best results. Natural law is not only deontological but more importantly, it is act deontological. This means that natural law is not a set of rules. An act deontological ethic regards certain actions under certain circumstances to be intrinsically right. But right actions or actions in harmony with the law of nature cannot be captured in advance and enshrined in a set of rules that are always binding regardless of circumstances or consequences.

d. There is necessary connection between law and morality. Law is not properly speaking law unless it has a moral content. Positive laws or the laws of the state are valid if and only if they are in harmony with the law of nature.

e. The law of nature is forever transcendent. It is an ideal to aspire towards; but it can never be completely realized in any given historical political order. The distinction between natural and positive law can never give way to their identity.

f. The most modest degree of everyday justice will fail to be realized by law alone. Not even the best set of laws can guarantee a modestly just society. Without just individuals to administer the law, the best legal systems are almost of no avail. While elevating the function of law in society, natural law also harbours a deep pessimism about what law alone can achieve.

g. Natural law presupposes a particular view of nature and of human nature. That view explains why nature can be a source of moral and legal norms.

Natural Law and Moral Objectivity

When not used broadly to designate a philosophy of law and politics, "natural law" is more strictly speaking a legal metaphor referring to a universal and trans-historical moral order that is "natural" in the sense of being uncreated by man and therefore independent of human volition, convention or political decree. It is discovered by human reason as the ultimate standard with which positive law and morality must conform. The idea is probably coeval with human thought itself. But one of its earliest, most eloquent and most familiar expressions can be found in Sophocles' *Antigone*. Here is the reason Antigone gives the tyrant Creon for disobeying his orders:

> That order did not come from God, Justice,
> That dwells with the gods below, knows no such law.
> I did not think your edicts strong enough
> To overrule the unwritten unalterable laws
> Of God and heaven, you being only a man.
> They are not of yesterday or to-day, but everlasting.
> Though where they came from, none of us can tell.
> Guilty of their transgression before God
> I cannot be, for any man on earth.
> I knew that I should have to die, of course,
> With or without your order. If it be soon,
> So much the better . . . .[11]

The central idea is that justice is not a human artifact that can be arbitrarily defined by human law or decree. This means that it is an objective standard by which positive law is to be evaluated and to which it must conform. What is meant by the objectivity of justice is difficult to explain, but it is something like this: what is objective has a reality that is independent of us, it exists whether we recognize it or not. To say that justice (or morality as a whole for that matter) is objective is to say that it can be understood, but not altered. And furthermore, our lack of understanding of it or our lack of desire to recognize it does not diminish its truth or reality in the least. All this means that moral statements are not altogether unlike mathematical statements. That four 4's are sixteen is true whether I or anyone wishes to believe it is. Besides, I may believe that four 4's are sixteen because I've been taught this at school and have taken it on trust. But at some point I may come to see that it must be so. The same experience is applicable to moral knowledge. I may believe that truth is good and that selfishness is bad because I have been brought up to think so, and have taken it on trust. But some day, I may come to see that it must be so.[12]

To talk of moral or mathematical ideas as having objective reality is not to say that they possess location in space and time. It means rather that they are part of the very nature of things, are eternally valid and have a universal appeal to reason (i.e. that all rational men must see it to be so). Problems arise when we ask what the status of ideas that have never been thought by rational men is? What kind of reality could they have apart from having been thought? Objectivists maintain that moral and mathematical ideas "exist" even if no human being thinks of them.[13] Others postulate that they exist for a Mind or more specifically for the mind of the Great Architect.[14] However, it is important note that the objectivity of moral ideas does *not* depend on the belief in God or the existence of a Great Architect who is responsible for the physical as well as the moral order men discover in the universe. On the contrary, the human discovery of a physical and moral order in the universe has led some to acknowledge the reasonableness of such a belief.

Natural law refers to the moral order inherent in the universe. Referring to the moral order as "natural" emphasizes the fact that it is independent of human making or belief. Using the term "natural law" is meant to indicate that the moral order is no less real than the natural order. However, the term is somewhat unfortunate since it has been a source of confusion. The physical order may well be manifest in the physical laws of nature like the laws of gravity and the laws of thermodynamics. But many who maintain that the universe has a moral as well as a physical order, do not think that the former can be summed up in a set of rules or laws valid for all time.[15] Therefore, the term natural law or law of nature is not meant to indicate that morality can be summarized in a set of all inclusive, comprehensive and eternally valid rules. Natural law is only a legal metaphor referring to the objective moral order permeating the universe. I will attempt to explain later why the metaphor has so much appeal.

Natural Law and Moral Knowledge

If man were totally incapable of acquiring knowledge of the objective moral order, then declaring its existence is of little or no significance. A philosophy of natural law must maintain not only that there exists a moral order, but that it is to some extent at least knowable. Furthermore, the knowledge of natural law must be different from that of other things. It must be different from knowing the laws of planetary motion for example, since it must have consequences for action. More than a purely theoretical knowledge of natural law is necessary if it is to influence human conduct. Knowledge of natural law must therefore be practical rather than purely theoretical.

The distinction between practical and theoretical reason was made by Aristotle.[16] Simply stated, the distinction is as follows. Theoretical reason is directed towards knowledge of things that are necessary and unchanging. For example, understanding the laws of planetary motion is a proper subject for theoretical reason. The laws of planetary motion are invariable and cannot be influenced or changed by human action. The function of theoretical reason is to understand. Practical reason differs from theoretical reason in an important way. Its function is not simply to understand things that are necessary and unchanging, but to direct action. The proper subjects for practical reason are those things that are not necessary or unchanging, but are contingent and can be changed by human action. Politics, for example, is a proper subject for practical reason.[17] Unlike the universe, the political domain is not impervious to change as a result of human action. On this view, it is as much the function of reason as a whole to understand as to direct or guide action.

Aquinas develops this distinction explicitly in relation to natural law.[18] Even though practical and theoretical reason direct themselves towards different subject matters, they share an important similarity. Both theoretical and practical reason begin their reasoning processes from certain self-evident indemonstrable principles. As Aquinas puts it, "being" is the first idea to fall under the apprehension of theoretical reason, whereas "good" is the first to fall under that of practical reason.[19] It is not surprising then that the first principle of theoretical reason is that something cannot both be and not be or (and this is to say the same thing), "to affirm and to deny simultaneously is excluded".[20] The first principle of practical reason on the other hand is that "good is to be done and evil avoided".[21] The difference between these two principles is that one tells us about what *is* or can be whereas the other tells us about what *ought* to be done. Practical reason does not only give us information, it is concerned with directing action towards the good. Interestingly, Aquinas identifies the first principle of practical reason with the first precept of natural law from which all others are derived.[22] To say that the first principle is self-evident and underived means that if anyone were to ask why good is to be done instead of evil, we could no more give him an answer than we could give someone who asks why something cannot both be and not be. Accepting the first principles is part of what it means to be rational.

This account raises two issues. First, what is the nature of "good" and how can we recognize it? Could not the most brutal and depraved beings assent to the first principle of practical reason and define good in any way they find suitable? Is Aquinas' theory of natural law as the first principle of practical reason eloquent only at the price of utter vacuity?[23] Second, is practical reason capable of motivating man to action? Is everyone motivated by practical reason or are only a few so motivated? Does everyone possess practical reason? If so, does everyone then share equally in the knowledge of the law of nature? I do not hope to answer these questions satisfactorily, but only to indicate ways in which theories of natural law could respond or have responded to them.

Can "good" be arbitrarily defined? Any theorist of natural law must answer this question in the negative. For Aquinas, as for any theorist of natural law, "good" is a definite intelligible quality that cannot be arbitrarily defined. If this is so, then how can we distinguish "good" from "evil"? I believe that it is impossible to answer this question without relying to some extent on "intuition". To say that something is known by intuition is to say that it is self-evident and known to be so directly and without demonstration. This is in part what Aquinas claims for the idea of "good". It is my contention that any theory of natural law that attempts to answer the question regarding the nature of good will have to rely to *some extent* on intuition. Unfortunately, the latter has been very much discredited in our time because advocates of "intuitionism" in twentieth century ethics have attributed to intuition more than it can withstand.[24] H. A. Prichard, for example, maintained that the concepts of "right" and "good" are immediately intuited properties in any given situation. Furthermore, these properties, being unique, are irreducible to any others. This means that the question "why is this good?" or "is this really my duty?" cannot be answered apart from saying that if you are face to face with a particular instance you will simply *see* (not literally of course) that it is right or good.[25] The stark simplicity of this position leaves no place for reasoning in difficult situations or when confronted with a conflict of duties. It also makes it impossible to say anything about the nature of goodness or rightness since they are unique simple properties that cannot be reduced to any other.[26] Certainly, no such doctrine is a necessary part of any account of natural law. Nor is such radical intuitionism part of Aquinas' account of natural law.

Despite its shortcomings, intuitionism does contain a grain of truth. Goodness is a property that is unique. It cannot be reduced to other properties such as being pleasant, producing the greatest happiness for the greatest number, furthering self-interest, contributing to self-realization, or involving benevolent intentions. One can agree with the intuitionists that goodness is a property distinct from all of the above, without maintaining that nothing can be said about the relationship of goodness to these other properties.[27]

When Aquinas maintains that "good is to be done and evil avoided" is a self-evident first principle of practical reason, he does not imply that all moral truths are self-evident and can be simply seen to be true or known to be true by intuition. On his view, a very special class of moral judgements are self-evident, the rest are not. In cases where good and evil are clearly distinguishable, then it is self-evident that good is to be done and evil avoided. But in many cases, we will find ourselves in doubt about what is good in a given situation. In such cases, reasoning, not intuition, is important. But in all our moral reasoning we must rely to some degree on what Aquinas calls the "intelligibility of good". We may never by able to explain *completely* why something is good; but contrary to the claims of some intuitionists, we can come a long way in doing this. Just because we acknowledge our reliance on intuition in knowing the good does not mean that we need to be fanatical and insist on maintaining a bleak silence on the matter.

Turning now to the second issue raised above. Is practical reason capable of motivating man to action? Does everyone possess practical reason? And if so, does everyone share equally in the knowledge of the law of nature? These are related but not identical questions. Let me turn first to whether practical reason can move man to action. Aristotle's response to this seems to be in the affirmative. The practical intellect consists of true reasoning and right desire.[28] Therefore action has its origin in what Aristotle calls "desiderative reason" or "ratiocinative desire".[29] For Aristotle, having practical wisdom consists not only in knowing what is right and good, but in being able to act accordingly.[30] This is why the same person cannot have practical wisdom and be incontinent. The incontinent person is someone who "knows" what is right but does not act upon it. Socrates had maintained that this is impossible. If a person really knew what is good he could not act otherwise. This is part of what Socrates meant by saying that virtue is wisdom and ignorance is vice. But the difference between Socrates and Aristotle may not be as great as the latter believes it to be. It is apparent in Plato's *Republic* that when Plato, following Socrates speaks about knowing the Good, he does not refer to a cold and indifferent apprehension of an idea. On the contrary, knowing the Good is also finding it to be beautiful, attractive and desirable. It is a knowledge overwhelmed by desire.[31] It does not therefore differ a great deal from what Aristotle refers to as "ratiocinative desire" which he attributes to the man of practical wisdom. The incontinent man has a "knowledge" of the good that is less than what Plato and Socrates considered true or full-bodied knowledge, and something other than the kind of knowledge Aristotle attributes to the man of practical wisdom.

And wisdom, Socrates, Plato and Aristotle are agreed, is a virtue of the few.

Aquinas' views of the matter are a subject of controversy among scholars. Nevertheless, Aquinas seems to think the knowledge of natural law binds man because it is practical and not purely theoretical. This means that it urges man to pursue his duty and the excellence for which he is fitted; hence the appropriateness of the legal metaphor. Natural law understood as a legal metaphor for what is good and right by nature makes sense only because the good is not just there to be coldly apprehended or even admired. It is experienced as imperative. The metaphor draws on the resemblance of the experience of being impelled towards one's duty to that of physical objects impelled by physical laws. What is unclear is whether Aquinas believes that everyone experiences or knows the law of nature in this forceful way. At times he implies that everyone knows the first precept of natural law. But does that mean that all men are equally inclined towards the good?[32]

The question of whether all men have equal knowledge of the law of nature is not one that is answered homogeneously by philosophers of natural law. It is a question that in my view has important political ramifications. If only a few are capable of moral knowledge as Plato and Aristotle maintain, then a well ordered society would be one where those with superior moral wisdom govern and direct other citizens towards the good. If, on the other hand, all men are equal with regards to moral knowledge, then a democratic rather than an aristocratic society would be more reasonable. This shift occurs in Locke's christianized theory of natural law.

According to Locke, revelation is an indispensable aid to those who lack the wisdom of the great philosophers. Although in principle the law of nature is knowable by the unaided human understanding, not all men have the intellectual capacity to come to know it in this way. Revelation is therefore indispensable for the greater number. It is our good fortune that the laws of nature have been revealed to us in scripture. The laws of nature are simply those divine laws which can be known by the unaided human understanding. In a post-christian world they are widely known as a result of revelation. Furthermore, they are generallyobeyed not simply out of appreciation for their intrinsic excellence (although that is important) but also (and for many) out of fear of eternal damnation. In His wisdom, God has attached to his law the reward of eternal bliss and the sanction of eternal damnation.[33] The laws of nature are therefore known to the greater number and experienced as obligatory in the severest sense of that term since they are grounded in the Will of God. [34] Christian revelation makes the law of nature known to the many and experienced as obligatory on their conduct.

The equality of moral knowledge lays the foundations for an egalitarian or democratic politics just as the disparity of moral knowledge gave Plato reasons for attacking democratic politics. After all, if it is admitted that moral knowledge and moral integrity are essential ingredients for political leadership, and that they are possessed only by the few, then not all citizens are equally fit to rule as the friends of democracy advocate. This is what Plato argued. Locke appears to accept the Platonic premise that moral knowledge is the essential ingredient of political order. However, Plato's aristocratic politics is no longer necessary after the advent of Christian revelation which removes the disparities of moral knowledge. But the differences between the Platonic and Lockian positions may not be as great as it seems if it is remembered that it is not the wise or the many who rule, but the law. Both positions share the faith in the rule of law as the best political order known to man.

Needless to say, an egalitarian politics can be grounded in the equality of moral ignorance as much as in the equality of moral knowledge. Indeed, critics of natural law often argue that relativism and non-cognitivism are more compalible with tolerance and democracy than is natural law.[35]

In conclusion, what is important to note is that every theory of natural law must not only maintain that there exists an objective moral order, but also that man must be capable of coming to know it either through reason alone or through a combination of reason and revelation. If the objective moral order is not accessible to human understanding, then it would be of little significance for human life. Furthermore, the knowledge of natural law must be practical, that is, it must include the motivation for action. In other words, natural law must be understood to be imperative on human conduct, if not because of its intrinsic worth and beauty, then out of fear of God's wrath.

The Deontological Character of Natural Law

Since our knowledge of natural law is practical, it is not independent of experience. However, what the law of nature requires of us is not simply a summary of those acts that experience tells us have the best results or consequences (or tend to have the best results or consequences under most circumstances). Natural law is a deontological rather than a consequential ethic. This means that it rejects the consequentialist separation of the Right and the Good and insists on their unity. The consequentialist may or may not believe that the Good can be arbitrarily defined. But he certainly thinks that whatever the Good is, the Right is that which produces, maximizes or brings about the Good. Utilitarianism is one type of consequentialism. The classical utilitarians like Bentham and Austin maintained that the Good is the greatest happiness for the greatest number, and they understood happiness as being synonymous with pleasure. More contemporary utilitarians define the Good as maximum satisfaction of desire, or of "rational" desire, which means those desires that it is possible to satisfy, not desires to be a unicorn or a mermaid. But the classical and modern utilitarians are agreed that the Right, or right action, is action that produces the greatest amount of Good as defined. Right is therefore conceived as being instrumental to the Good, which is primary. The Good, is usually conceived of as a state of affairs, a desirable condition or situation, and the Right refers to action or activity intended to bring about the desired state of affairs. Problems in the theory emerge when human happiness is recognized to consist in *activity* rather than in a particular condition. If this is so, then it becomes increasingly difficult to maintain the separation of Right (activity) and Good (state of affairs).[36] In saying that natural law is deontological, I mean that it insists on the unity of the Right and the Good. Indeed it understands the good life for man as a life where man's moral and rational capacities can be exercised. The good life for man is a life lived according to reason and in harmony with the law of nature. The good state of affairs for man is one where a certain type of activity (i.e. moral and intellectual) is possible. Human activity is not independent of or instrumental to the good life. The good life for man depends on the nature of human activity.

In a natural law theory, acts that have or tend to have good results are not necessarily sanctioned by the law of nature. The moral goodness of actions (or their rightness) does not depend exclusively on the results or consequences of those actions. Moral actions are actions with intrinsic moral worth that is independent of their results or consequences. Does this mean that there are certain acts that are specified in advance to be good regardless of their results in particular circumstances? And if this is so, can these intrinsically worthy acts not be summarized in a set of rules valid for all time? After all, it would be possible to make rules valid for all time and in all circumstances if the moral worth of actions were independent of their results in any particular set of circumstances. Is this what a deontological theory and particularly a natural law theory involves?

And if so, is it possible to take an ethical theory seriously if it ignores consequences altogether?

There is a difference between *rule* and *act* deontological theories.[37] A rule deontologist maintains that there are certain rules specifying particular actions that are always under any circumstances morally obligatory. These moral rules are often regarded as the expressions of God's will or God's commands revealed in scripture. Whether the rules have a religious origin or not, the rule deontologist considers them fundamental and worthy of obedience in their own right. Some advocates of natural law (like Locke) identify the law of nature with God's laws revealed in scriptures. Those philosophers attempt to compile authoritative sets of rules to illustrate the actions required by the law of nature. But such attempts invariably fail. It is always possible to show that a set of predetermined rules cannot be binding at all times in all circumstances. Indeed, the attempt to reduce the law of nature to a set of rules led to the understandable criticism of natural law as a rigid ahistorical theory insensitive to the variability of historical circumstances.

Act deontologists, unlike rule deontologists, do not consider rules as fundamental. They believe that there are actions which in particular circumstances are intrinsically right or at least morally preferable to all others; but the rightness or a given action is not perceived to be linked to the conformity of that action with one of the fundamental rules of morality. In other words, the moral goodness of actions is not independent of things like the circumstances in which the action takes place, the intentions of the actor and the foreseeable results of that action. The moral goodness of the action therefore depends neither exclusively on its results as the consequentialist holds nor on its conformity with a rule as the rule deontologist maintains. This means that the same action may be right in some circumstances but wrong in others. Needless to say, such variability makes our moral tasks difficult and our attempts to define natural law complex.

The first book of Plato's *Republic* is still one of the best illustrations of the inevitable failure of defining the just in terms of a set of rules. When Socrates asks his interlocutors what justice is, they tend to reply that it consists of doing this or that action -- telling the truth or paying back one's debt. As Socrates illustrates, circumstances invariably arise in which following the rule or doing that particular action is not the right thing to do under the circumstances. He gives an example of one who has borrowed weapons from a friend who has since become deranged and perhaps is bent on destroying himself and others. There is little doubt that returning what is borrowed is under those circumstances not the right thing to do.[38]

Just as Plato did not think that justice can be summarized in a set of required actions valid for all time and in all circumstances, so Aquinas did not think of the natural law as a set of rules. Both Plato and Aquinas are act deontologists as I understand the latter. This view may well have its difficulties, but it is fair to say that it is more faithful to the complexity of our moral experience. Theories of natural law worth consideration are act rather than rule deontological. It is not that theories that identify the law of nature with the will of God, as Locke does, are not properly speaking part of the tradition of natural law. The theories that *are* antithetical to the proper understanding of natural law are *not* those that ground the latter in a Divine Will understood as rational and bound by what is good as Locke maintained,[39] but those that ground the law of nature in a Divine Will that is arbitrary, capricious and inscrutable.

To say that natural law has a deontological character is to say that it conceives of what is right and obligatory as unchanging in its essence and intimately related to, if not identical with, the good and not instrumental to it. Furthermore, the Good and the Right are fundamental and independent of the capriciousness of Divine Will as well as the arbitrariness of human desire. A rule deontological theory that identifies the law of nature with the will of a capricious and inscrutable God, is antithetical to the proper understanding of natural law. To say further that natural law has an act deontological character is to say that the law of nature cannot be reduced to a set of absolutely inflexible rules that are obligatory at all times and in all circumstances.

The Necessary Connection Between Law and Morality

The most important thing that follows from maintaining the existence and knowledge of a universal moral order is the claim that positive law is *valid* only when it partakes of or participates in the natural law. For law to participate in or partake of natural law it must be just or at least not unjust. The meaning of *validity* is significant for understanding the legal and political implications of natural law. A *valid* law is not simply a law that has been duly enacted by the powers that be. Just because a law has been accepted by the House of Commons and ratified by the Senate (as in our own Canadian system) and administered by the courts does not mean it is a valid law. Not that due process is irrelevant to the validity of law. Due process alone, however is not sufficient to insure the validity of law. The validity of law depends rather on its moral content. A valid law is a law that is just (or at least not unjust) and as a result deserves our respect and obedience. A valid law is one that is morally obligatory, or as Aquinas put it, one that is binding on the rational conscience. Only good law can succeed in obligating *inforo interno*. In other words, the connection between law and morality is necessary for law to be good and as a result capable of binding the conscience of its citizens.

It is clear that the connection between law and morality is necessary if law is to be good, but is it necessary for law to be law? Interestingly this is precisely the claim involved in natural law. To say that the connection between law and morality is *necessary* for law to be *valid* amounts to saying that it is necessary for law to be properly speaking law. A law that is unjust is not really a law, or is only a law in a manner of speaking. But surely, one can object, that it is meaningful to speak of an unjust law. Since this is so obviously true, it is worth inquiring why denying the label "law" to unjust laws is a persistent claim of natural law thinking.

I would like to suggest that the persistent claim that unjust laws are not really laws is partly a way of taking into account the honorific use of the term law in ordinary discourse. Imagine, for example, a law that is commanded by the powers that be, and backed by threat of punishment upon disobedience; however, this law is secret or contradictory and incoherent. It is not inconceivable, indeed it is perfectly meaningful to say of that law, "this is hardly a law at all." But no one would misconstrue this statement to mean (as some of the critics of natural law have) that bad or unjust laws do not exist. On the contrary, the statement is pointing to a law that is so bad that it does not deserve to be called a law. The statement is meaningful because of what I have called the honorific use of the word "law" in ordinary discourse. This means that we use the word law to refer to something that deserves respect and obedience. When we refer to a law as "not really a law at all" we mean to say that it does not deserve respect, indeed, we mean to encourage others to disregard and disobey it. In view of this usage of the term law, it is understandable that when legal positivists like Austin deny that international law is really law (on the ground that it is not commanded by a sovereign or superior who can enforce it by the use of sanctions) there is an outcry. To deprive international law of the status involved in the label "law" amounts to undermining its authority and encouring sovereign states to disregard it. This honorific use of the word law, which explains why definitions of law are such emotionally charged issues, is not peculiar to law.

There are other words that are used in an honorific sense in ordinary discourse. Human activities such as dancing and making music are particularly illustrative. For example, if upon hearing some adolescents strumming their electric guitars, I say "this is not music", I doubt very much that my listener would be confused or think I was contradicting myself. Likewise, I may see a girl wearing a tutu and walking on her toes and still say, "this is not ballet". All this means is that there is more to music than notes emerging from instruments and more to ballet than walking on one's toes. The same is true of the word "human". If someone says, "Hitler was hardly human", no one would think Hitler may have had webbed feet or a long tail. There is no mistake about the meaning of the statement since it is generally recognized that there is more to being human than is entailed in a purely biological description. The same is true of law and lawmaking. To say of a bad or unjust law that "it is hardly a law at all" has the same force as saying "Hitler was hardly human". These statements do not deny that unjust laws and unjust persons exist; rather, they are meant to indicate that there is more to law than an arbitrary command issued by the authorities, just as there is more to being human than a purely biological description would allow.

The reason that such figures of speech make sense is because music, ballet, law and human beings cannot be understood apart from some conception of their peculiar excellence. This is not meant to preclude disagreement about the characteristics of good music, good dancing, good human beings or good law. It is simply meant to indicate that some conception of the peculiar *excellence* of these things is entailed in the understanding of what they *are*. Lon Fuller has argued for the necessary connection of law and morality along these lines. Fuller maintains that where purposive human activities like lawmaking are involved, there exists an intimate connection between what they are and what they aim at or ought to be.[40] The reason that what law *is* is inseparable from what law ought to be, is because law is not a thing but a purposive human activity directed towards an end. If it completely fails to achieve that end, it fails *qua* law. But to what end does law exist?

The tradition of natural law in legal thought has tended to elevate the status and function of law within political order. Locke, for example, thought that positive law had the effect of attaching to natural law known human sanctions that would better insure justice was upheld among men. Such a view of law stands in marked contrast to the claim that law serves merely to uphold the interests of those in power.

Plato provides a further example of the extent to which the tradition of natural law has elevated the function of law in political society. According to Plato, one of the important functions of law is to lead or guide society rather than simply follow it, or reflect its positive morality.[41] Therefore, in a case where the positive morality has gone astray, the function of law is to redirect it and set it right. Law can therefore be an instrument of social change. Nor would law be a gentle reformer; but in an age where terrorism is the most common mode of political change, the power (and perhaps even beauty) of law deserves to be reconsidered.

The moral perfection of man is yet another grandiose role attributed to law by exponents of natural law.[42] Plato and Aquinas both believed that what men may first do only out of fear of punishment, they may eventually learn to do even when it is unlikely for their disobedience to be found out. Moral education begins with good habits. Law seeks to establish these good habits as the first but necessary step in the perfection of man. This view of law stands in marked contrast to the view according to which the function of law is to maximize the satisfaction of human desires.[43]

When the debate between natural law and legal positivism is understood as a debate about what law ought to achieve (i.e., what function or purpose it is to play in political society) then it will not appear to be a quibble about terms. The debate about what law is, has been inseparable from the debate about what law ought to be or ought to achieve. On one hand, exponents of natural law give law grandiose functions like upholding true justice, promoting the moral perfection of man, guiding human action, redirecting a society that has gone astray, or all of the above. On the other hand, advocates of legal positivism hold that the function of law is primarily to maintain order and to promote human survival (especially where the latter is seen as contributing to the cause of order).[44] The differences between these two conceptions of the ends of law lead to significant differences in their attempts to define law. It is not difficult to see that the kinds of roles natural law advocates expect law to play require that it have a moral content -- hence their insistence that law and morals are necessarily connected. On the other hand, what legal positivists wish law to accomplish does not require that it be intimately connected with morality. As H. L. A. Hart has argued, law need not be moral or good to promote human survival and to achieve a respectable degree of order.[45]

If we abandon those ends of law that appear to necessitate its connection with morality, and accept the modest end of law as the source of order, can we then deny that law, understood as the source of social order, need have no necessary connection with morality? Lon Fuller denies that this is the case. He accepts the modest positivist claim that the function of law is to maintain order. But he denies that there is no connection between order and goodness. If law hopes to maintain order, Fuller argues, it cannot afford to abandon its intimate connection with goodness. Indeed, he maintains that order has a greater affinity with good than evil. He does not hope to prove this, but gives us reasons for thinking it plausible. Before giving a hint of Fuller's argument, let me pause briefly in order to emphasize what is *not* meant by a necessary connection between law and morality.

Many contemporary authors who are unsympathetic with the claims of natural law, nevertheless acknowledge that there is an intimate connection between law and morality. By this they do not mean that there exists a *necessary* connection between law and morality as such, but only that there exists a *historical* connection between law and positive morality.[46] A historical connection is not necessary, it is merely contingent, indicating that law often reflects the moral views held by the majority in the society.[47] This is a far cry from what is meant by insisting on the necessary connection between law and morality. The latter means that law cannot have a morally iniquitious content and still be law. Law must partake of objective (not merely positive) morality if it is to succeed as law.

The originality of Lon Fuller's ideas rest primarily in his claim that law cannot succeed in its most elementary functions (and hence cannot succeed as law) without a certain moral content. According to Fuller there is a certain "morality that makes law possible" which he refers to as "the internal (or, inner) morality of law".[48] Commands, even when backed by sufficient force, cannot be laws unless they fulfill the following requirements: (1) cases cannot be decided on an *ad hoc* basis,there must be rules; (2) these rules must be promulgated or publicized;(3) the rules can't be retroactive except on rare occasions; (4) the rules must be clear and comprehensible, not obscure; (5) the rules must not be contradictory; (6) the rules must not require the impossible; (7) the rules must be stable and not in a permanent state of flux; (8) there must be congruence between the rules announced and their administration. On Fuller's view, failure in *any* of the above"does not simply result in a bad system of law; it results in something that is not properly called a legal system at all."[49] It is understandable that a law that is obscure, contradictory, secret or changing from minute to minute is impossible to obey. If law is to create any semblance of order, it must direct human action. It cannot hope to do this if it does not conform to what Fuller calls the "internal morality of law".

All this may be granted, yet it may be objected that morally iniquitous laws can be formulated that conform to the ''internal morality'' of law, and therefore, what is required for law to succeed as law is not so much moral content, as principles of good craftsmanship.[50] It does not appear to me that Fuller has adequately responded to this criticism. Nevertheless, something needs to be said on his behalf. It is essential to distinguish between formal and substantive justice in order to appreciate what Fuller is trying to say. The principles contained in the ''internal morality'' or law can be described as principles of formal justice. Although Fuller does not himself use this terminology, I don't think I am distorting his position by describing it this way. Formal justice requires that no one be found guilty for disobeying a law that was impossible for him to know because it was secret, extremely obscure or self-contradictory. Formal justice requires that no one be punished for not doing what is impossible for human beings to do given their limitations -- for example, appear before the court ten seconds after receiving a summons in the mail. Formal justice requires that like cases be treated alike or that equals are treated equally. The latter is a moral obligation that administrators of the law must fulfill if the legal system is to boast the smallest pretentions of order. Substantive justice, on the other hand, refers to the actual content of the law. A law that insists on the death penalty for traffic violations is substantively unjust (the punishment does not fit the crime). It may be clearly promulgated and impartially administered, and so, satisfy the requirements of formal justice and still be substantively unjust. Fuller does not speak of formal and substantive justice, rather he speaks of the internal (formal) and external (substantive) moralities of law.

Fuller is not maintaining that formal justice exhausts the whole of legal justice. The requirements of formal justice succeed only in eliminating the most blatant injustices from being any part of a legal system. He has not to my mind demonstrated that moral goodness is an essential ingredient of law. However, his achievement is not to be undermined. He has come a long way in showing that certain blatant injustices are imcompatible with the very existence of law.

There is in Fuller's account of law the assumption that formal and substantive justice are closely connected and that one necessarily implies the other. The claim is not simply that formal justice is a necessary prerequisite for the existence of substantive justice, but that where formal justice exists, at least a modest amount of substantive justice is also to be found or that injustice has, to a considerable extent, been minimized. Fuller puts it this way:

> . . . these external and internal moralities of law reciprocally influence one another; a deterioration of the one will almost inevitably produce a deterioration in the other.[51]

Fuller's critics are unconvinced. A legal system that completely satisfies the demands of formal justice but whose substantive aims are morally pernicious is plausible. Fuller does not adequately defend his claim, but there is something important that he says on the matter that has been largely overlooked.

Fuller's critics point to the plausibility of a well crafted and fairly administered legal system that is devoted to the most morally perverse ends. Fuller wishes to deny the logical plausibility of such a system and insists on the fact that goodness has a close affinity with order and evil with disorder. Therefore a legal system devoted to the most pernicious ends cannot hope to create the modest degree of order required by the internal morality of law. Fuller admits that he does not adequately defend this claim. But there is another claim (which is not usually distinguished from the above claim even by Fuller himself) that I believe Fuller does successfully maintain. This is the claim that injustice has rarely taken the form of the legal system described above -- namely, a clearly promulgated set of laws directed towards evil ends. According to Fuller, men have throughout history been reluctant to write clearly and unambiguously evil intentions in the law. This is simple prudence -- they are likely to be far more successful in accomplishing their evil ends if they keep them secret rather than exposing them to the public scrutiny of a clearly promulgated law. In this way, much mischief can be accomplished before many of the citizens have any idea of what is happening. Besides, is it realistic to expect that those without moral scruples will worry their heads about the fair administration of law? In other words, men who have little regard for substantive principles of justice are unlikely to behave with irreproachable integrity where the requirements of formal justice are concerned. Fuller's account of Nazi law illustrates the form which injustice usually takes.

Fuller points out that the injustice of Nazi laws rested not so much in the content of those laws, but in the manner in which they were crafted and subsequently administered. For example, the Nazi regime used retroactive law not as a curative measure for legal irregularities, but to bestow legality on their own murderous acts after the fact. The murder of Nazis by fellow Nazis during the "Roehm purge" of July 3,1934 were later declared to be lawful executions. The killings of innocent persons in concentration camps were likewise made legal retroactively. Many

Nazi laws were secret, others were obscure or had secret and outrageous interpretations that effectively destroyed the letter of the published law. Nor is all this surprising. It would be far more surprising to find the Nazi regime so rash as to enshrine their aims in bold letters in the law. On the contrary, those in power went to great lengths to keep the ugliness from public view. They excelled in the use of euphemisms. On Fuller's view, the Nazi laws were not just bad laws; they failed as laws altogether. They did not succeed in creating the smallest degree of order, they merely institutionalized disorder. It is therefore not surprising that the German courts after the war saw fit to declare them not laws and rejected the defense of the grudge informers who argued that what they did was lawful at the time they acted.[52]

The Nazi example illustrates that in the absence of substantive justice, formal justice is not likely to exist, and vice versa. The internal and external moralities of law (formal and substantive justice) are interconnected. Fuller does not wish to say only that the connection is historical; that they have tended to be found together. He wishes to make a logical claim as well. He wants to say that evil and the most modest degree of order guaranteed by the internal morality of law are in some sense logically incompatible. Order and goodness on Fuller's view have a great affinity to one another. This amounts to saying that it is impossible to create general, clearly promulgated, non-contradictory, and fairly administered laws if they are substantively evil in their content. This may well be so, but Fuller has not adequately explained why. He has successfully argued that such a situation is highly unlikely. This is not the way in which injustice has historically manifested itself. Besides, it is so highly imprudent that it is unlikely to be adopted by anyone for whom success is of any concern. In other words, Fuller's stronger claim is not so much the logical as the historical one. But even though Fuller has not succeeded in showing that there is a necessary (in the sense of logical) connection between law and morality,[53] he has shown that law, even when understood as having the modest end of order, cannot be completely separated from morality. Indeed, the very existence of law is incompatible with the kinds of blatant injustices that result from disregarding any part of the internal morality of law.

In conclusion, the insistence on the connection of law and morality characteristic of natural law has important political ramifications. Politically, it provides a moral justification for disobedience. If we say that "law is law" regardless of how poorly crafted it is and how inequitably administered, then we are unlikely to justify disobedience. The claim that law is not really law if it is unjust implies that unjust laws ought not to be obeyed and that those who disobey them are not morally culpable. Aquinas is reluctant to draw these political implications of natural law and so tends to emphasize that the disobedience is justified only when the injustice caused by the law is far greater than the mischief caused by disobedience. In Locke, natural law takes a much more politically radical character. Locke uses it to justify the overthrow of government.[54] But on the whole, natural law is not so much a philosophy of political radicalism as a philosophy of civil disobedience. Radical politics is characterized by its tendency to overestimate what men can achieve. As we shall see in the sections to come, natural law is characterized by an excessive sobriety regarding what lies within human capabilities. Its high ideals are therefore moderated by its sober expectations. It therefore contains within it a certain conservatism, but it should never be mistaken for a politics of acquiescence.

The Transcendence of Natural Law

By the "transcendence of natural law" I mean to say that despite the best conditions and intentions, the law of nature could never be fully realized in history or in the positive law of any particular political community. Even the best political order known to man will fall short of the ideal of natural justice. The gap between natural and positive law will never be bridged as long as man will live. Natural law is a transcendent ideal for positive law. Its transcendence is necessary if it is to fulfill its function, which is not only to *evaluate* but to *inspire* positive law.

There are those that deny the transcendence of natural law but insist on using the term to describe their philosophies. Hegel and Otto Gierke are examples.[55] Hegel believed that the philosophical distinctions between the ideal and the actual or Being and Becoming describe only a particular moment in the development of the world. If we apply this claim to the distinction between natural and positive law, we would conclude that the distinction between them is not, as I suggested above, permanent. On the contrary, the distinction between natural and positive law reflects a historical moment characterized by alienation, unhappiness and political unrest. History was for Hegel a dialectic between the immanent (here and now) and the transcendent ideal. The end of history is the culmination of this dialectical process which heralds the end of the alienation and separation of these two domains of existence. What emerges at the end of this dialectical process is a matter of great controversy among Hegelian scholars. What is difficult to understand is that Hegel held, on one hand, that only the transcendent eternal is real and, on the other hand, that the transcendent cannot be distinct from the immanent, finite and particular. Hegel did not think these views incompatible, but it has been argued that the second is a denial of all transcendence. Even if Hegel did not intend such an outcome, it is difficult to escape.

Otto Gierke's philosophy of natural law in my view illustrates the total perversion of the theory that results when the Hegelian conception of history is applied to the distinction between natural and positive law. A brief excursus into Gierke's ideas will illustrate what I mean.

Gierke was one of the leading members of the historical school of law as well as a distinguished student of the tradition of natural law in the history of political thought.[56] According to the historical school, law does not have its foundation in abstract universal reason. On the contrary, law, like language, is distinctive of each national character. To understand the law of a nation one must study its history. Law is therefore immanent in the historical process, and is of no need of a transcendent, trans-historical moral order to explain its source and sanction. The sanction of law depends on custom and not on some abstraction like its inherent justice. Nor can law emanate from the mind of a single individual like Lycurgus or Solon. The historical school rejected the idea of the great lawgiver. Instead, the historical school maintained that law developes out of and is part of the spirit of the people or *Volksgeist*.

Just as Hegel was disturbed by the separation of the transcendent or eternal and the immanent or finite, so Gierke was disturbed by the separation of natural and positive law. Just as Hegel understood the separation of the transcendent and the immanent as an undesirable condition of alienation, so Gierke understood the separation of natural and positive law as a condition that cannot be tolerated.

What Gierke found intolerable about the traditional account of natural law (as a transcendent ideal that can never be fully actualized in the positive law of the state), is its damaging effect on both natural and positive law. On the one hand, it has the effect of depriving natural law of "reality", which in Gierke's view is intimately related to historical existence. On the other hand, it damages the positive law of the state by denying that it is an expression of the *Volksgeist* or folkspirit of the people and maintains instead that law has its foundation in an abstract, ahistorical rational principle indifferent to the spirit of the people and their will.

It is generally believed that the historical school of law developed primarily as a reaction to the rationalism and universalism of natural law. However, Gierke's own self-understanding testifies that he was not so much surrendering natural law but fulfilling it by welding it with his own historical understanding of law. Here is how he describes his own enterprise:

> The idea of Law has won real and permanent conquests from the development of Natural Law; we can see that the historical point of view, far from surrendering those conquests has only generalized and diffused them; . . . the sovereign independence of the idea of Justice, secured before by the old conception of Natural Law, will continue to be firmly secured by our new conception of Law as something thoroughly positive. . . .[57]

I will not dwell here on the details of Gierke's position. I simply want to raise doubt about the possibility of providing a meaningful understanding of natural law while denying its transcendence. It is difficult to understand how it is possible to maintain the ''sovereign independence'' of justice within a conception of law that is ''thoroughly positive''. Despite Gierke's belief that he is fulfilling rather than surrendering the idea of natural law, I think his attempt fails to be true to the essential core of natural law. The evidence for its failure is in its results.

The results of denying the transcendence of natural law are manifest in Gierke's conclusions. First, law and the state (understood as the embodiment of the *Volksgeist* or folkspirit) become impossible to distinguish:

> We shall no longer ask whether the State is prior to Law or Law to the State. We shall regard them both as inherent functions of the common life which is inseparable from the idea of man.[58]

Secondly, Might and Right become one and are indistinguishable. Nor did Gierke think this result unfortunate:

> The human conscience cannot permanently endure the separation of the two. Right which cannot establish itself vanishes at last from the common conscience, and thereby ceases to be Right. Might which exists without Right, if it succeeds in maintaining itself, is felt at last by the general conscience to exist as of right, and is thus transformed into Right.[59]

Gierke did not seem to realize that welding the law of nature to the positive social order had the effect of destroying it. Natural law cannot retain its meaning or its function unless it is distinct from the positive order. The distinction between the ideal or transcendent and the actual or historical domains is in my view essential to natural law. If it is to serve its critical purpose, natural law must transcend the positive political order.

Despite his errors, Gierke is not to be condemned entirely. His critique of the natural law tradition is somewhat justified. Natural law theories generally take little notice of the historical and developmental aspects of law. Gierke is right in maintaining that law has a close affinity with social beliefs and customs. Indeed law tends to reflect the developments of the *Volksgeist*. However, law may well be capable of being other than the simple reflection of the *Volksgeist*. It may be capable of leading, directing, and even rescuing the *Volksgeist* from decay and degeneration. For this a great legislator may be needed. And even though the inspired legislator is a rare figure in human history, he is not a fictitious one. Even though law tends to follow and reflect the *Volksgeist*, it can at times lead it. And therein lies its true greatness. To admit this is to acknowledge that what is socially acceptable is not always good; and that is why the *Volksgeist* cannot be the only standard of legal excellence. An ideal that transcends the *Volksgeist* is necessary not only to evaluate positive law but to inspire it.

Gierke teaches us two important lessons. The first, and one he did not intend to teach us, is that natural law cannot be made totally immanent without being utterly destroyed and completely meaningless. The second,and one he intended to teach us, is that natural law is equally meaningless and entirely impotent if it is kept in an air-tight compartment of transcendence. Gierke is right in warning us against placing too much emphasis on the transcendence of natural law. He is right in thinking that it is unwholesome to leave the ideal and the actual completely unrelated. Indeed, it frustrates the very purpose of natural law and perverts its meaning.

The radical transcendence of natural law is no part of the proper understanding of the theory. It has the effect of perverting its meaning as much as does its complete immanence. Let me illustrate what I mean by using an extreme example from Ernst Troeltsch. In his *Social Teaching of the Christian Churches,* Troeltsch describes a philosophy of natural law held by the early church Fathers. According to Troeltsch, the Fathers distinguished between a "primary" or absolute and a "secondary" or relative natural law.[60] The primary natural law was relevant to man prior to the fall. The secondary natural law was applicable to man after the fall. The difference between these two natural laws was considerable.

The primary natural law expressed an ideal completely beyond the reach of fallen man. It prohibited slavery, patriarchalism, tyranny and even government. The secondary natural law, appropriate to man's fallen capacities, sanctioned slavery, patriarchalism, government and even tyranny.

The ideal or "primary" natural law is so radically transcendent that man could not hope to participate or partake of it in the least. Its radical transcendence keeps it so completely out of reach for man that it is of no relevance whatsoever to his life on earth. It cannot serve as a source of inspiration for the legal or political order. It represents a golden age that has been lost forever. Any attempt to try and duplicate it amounts to attempting the impossible and is simply madness. The primary natural law is irretrievable to fallen humanity. An ideal that so radically transcends the human condition is of no significance to man's political life.

The secondary natural law is all that is left to man in his fallen condition. But when it is examined it turns out not to be an idea towards which one could aspire. On the contrary, it is a blueprint of an existing social and political order, and not a very good one at that. Whereas the primary natural law is radically transcendent, the secondary natural law is completely immanent. The most unjust legal and political order is not likely to fall short of it. The result of both the radical transcendence and the complete immanence of natural law is to leave us without any ideal that could be used to evaluate (or to inspire) the positive legal and political order.

I am not concerned here about the historical accuracy of the theory described above. I am using it simply as an illustration to show the kind of theory that must be excluded by any proper understanding of what natural law is. Both radical transcendence and complete immanence must be excluded from a meaningful account of natural law. The theory attributed to the early church Fathers illustrates the danger which Gierke sought to alert us to. Gierke's own theory is equally unacceptable.

Natural law cannot be conceived as being so radically transcendent that the positive political order cannot partake of it, without becoming utterly meaningless as a standard for human excellence. By the same token, it cannot be conceived as fully immanent within the political order without being destroyed.

A theory of natural law must combine a certain degree of optimism regarding man's capacity to know what the law of nature requires of him with a certain degree of pessimism regarding his capacity to put it into practice. Too great a pessimism, however, could be as damaging as too great an optimism. Too great a pessimism leads to extreme political conservatism and quietism. Too great an optimism can have the same effect if the identity of the actual and the ideal is seen as a *fait accompli*. Of course if the identity of the actual and the ideal is seen as an event to be achieved by human efforts in the fullness of time, then it could lead to extreme political radicalism, which, in its attempt to realize the ideal, wreaks havoc and destruction on the political order. What T. S. Eliot said of a good Catholic is equally applicable to a theory of natural law. A good Catholic, he said, is someone with high ideals and moderate expectations.

The Need For Just Persons

The aspect of natural law that I am about to discuss is not one that has been explicitly articulated by any of the exponents of natural law. It is nevertheless of some importance because it sets theories of natural law apart from other legal and political theories. It explains why theories of natural law consider the paramount political problem to be a moral one.

Theories of natural law do not focus on the importance of planning, organization, technical skills, wealth or even legal institutions as having much importance in the making of a good political order. Indeed, They put very little faith in what legal institutions alone can contribute to the making of a just political order. Interestingly, they combine a very grandiose account of what law can and ought to accomplish with a deep pessimism about what law alone can achieve. This means that even the best set of laws will not guarantee a modestly just society if no just individuals can be found to administer them. In other words, a political society is only as good as its individual components, especially those in positions of power.

The myth of Promytheus as told by Protagoras in one of Plato's dialogues illustrates what I mean by saying that the paramount political problem is moral, and that just persons are indispensable for the existence of a just political order. According to Protagoras, there was once a time when no mortal creatures existed. Then, the gods formed the mortal creatures. When they were ready to bring them into the light, they charged Prometheus and Epimetheus with the task of allotting to them powers and equipping them with the means of survival. Epimetheus begged Prometheus to allow him to make the distribution. It was then agreed that Epimetheus would complete the task and Prometheus would inspect it.

Epimetheus insured the survival of each species by giving it either strength or speed or fertility. He also provided each species with furs, feathers or thick skin to protect it from the elements. Epimetheus however, made a grave error. He distributed all the available powers to the brutes and forgot the needs of man.

When Prometheus came to inspect the work, he found man "naked, unshod, unbedded and unarmed".[61] To save him from complete annihilation, Prometheus stole fire and with it the gift of skill in the arts from the dwelling of Athena and Hephaestus. Consequently, man was able to develop a sufficient amount of "technical skill" to provide himself with nurture. However, lacking strength, men continued to be devoured, and so their continued survival was endangered. Realizing that they could not be self-sufficient, men attempted to come together in cities. This attempt, however, proved unsuccessful.

Protagoras explains that men injured one another and so were unable to live in society "for want of political skill."[62] As it became evident that technical skill alone was not sufficient to prevent the total destruction of the race, Zeus resolved to give man the highest gift he could offer -- namely, the art of politics.

> Zeus therefore, fearing the total destruction of our race, sent Hermes to impart to men the qualities of respect for others and a sense of justice, so as to bring order to our cities and create a bond of friendship and union.[63]

Being a skeptic about the gods, Protagoras could not make fear of the gods a viable motivation for embracing justice. Yet Protagoras believed justice was the essential element without which community is impossible. A social order devoid of justice, cannot insure the continued survival of men in cities.

Werner Jaeger's interpretation of myth explains that:

> The civilization which could be produced by Promethean man by subduing the elementary forces of nature was a mere technical civilization. It resulted in violence and destruction and humanity seemed about to perish miserably through its own inventions.[64]

In other words, the social order that is the result of technical knowledge is insufficient to insure the continued survival of mankind. Unless technical ability is governed and hence restrained by knowledge of right, it threatens to devour its own creators. The myth teaches a lesson that is invaluable in our own technological age.

What is true of technical skill is also true of law. Like good technical skills, good laws are not sufficient to insure a just society. Just persons are needed. Just persons are those who refrain from disobeying the law not just out of fear of punishment, but because they are persuaded by the goodness and rationality of the law. Neither the goodness of the law, nor its coersive power are sufficient to insure that it will be respected by citizens. Yet unless citizens respect the law, injustice will prevail. Where citizens have no respect for the law, the state is doomed to the neverending task of enacting and amending one law after another hoping to eliminate the loopholes of the previous law. In Plato's opinion this endless task accomplishes as little as "cutting off a hydra's head."[65] Following Plato, Aristotle and Aquinas also recognized that the best laws were of no avail unless they were inscribed in the hearts of citizens.[66] They therefore believed that law must become a moral educator if it hopes to succeed.

Good law may fail to provide us with a modestly just political society for more than one reason. It may fail because legislation, like any other technical skill is not enough to save man from self-annihilation. Good laws that are not respected by citizens are of no avail. The justice of a political order rests not only on its laws but on its citizens. There is another reason that good law may fail to insure justice. This failure has to do with the inadequacy of law itself. Because of its generality,law cannot take into account the infinite variety of human situations and circumstances. Many cases will arise where following the letter of the law will not insure that justice is done. Only equitable administrators can compensate for this shortcoming of law. As Aristotle explained, equity is a correction of legal justice owing to the generality of law on one hand, and the indefinite nature of practical affairs on the other.[67] Aristotle's point is not that there exists an error in the law or in the legislator that needs correction, but that good laws are in need of equitable individuals to execute them properly, since laws cannot possibly account for every case before it arises. From this we must conclude that individuals of moral integrity (both citizens and administrators) are as important to a just political order as are good laws.

Philosophers of natural law tended to follow Plato and Aristotle in assuming that the paramount political problem is moral, and that without at least a few good individuals in power a good political order is impossible to achieve. Even where the aristocratic ideas of Plato were abandoned or replaced by democratic ones, as they were by John Locke, the justification of the new order was given in Platonic terms. A democratic political order is justified in view of the fact that the majority of individuals have, by the grace of God, a knowledge of the law of nature, and so, are rational moral agents capable of playing a significant role in political life. Individuals whose actions reveal that they are unfamiliar with the law of nature, citizens and sovereigns alike, forfeit their political rights and ought to be excluded from civilized society. For Locke, no less than for Plato, the state has no character of its own, divorced from that of the individuals within it.[68]

That our society is only as good as ourselves is a hard truth to swallow; and political thinkers have tried to avoid it. Today we tend to think that the paramount political problems are economic rather than moral. We attribute social disorder not to the moral corruption of our politicians but to their want of technical skills. It is not at all clear to us what the relevance of individuals of moral integrity is to a prosperous and well-ordered political society. The poet Bernard Mandeville was the first to recognize and articulate the phenomenon I am attempting to describe in political thought. I cannot hope to describe this trend in political thought as well as Mandeville has. Let me therefore resort to his own account of it in his poem *The Fable of the Bees*.

In the preface to his poem, Mandeville denies that what makes man a social animal is his desire for company, pity, affability and such graces. On the contrary, he maintains that it is man's

> vilest and most hateful Qualities that are the most necessary Accomplishments to fit him for the largest, and according to the World,happiest and most flourishing Societies.[69]

Mandeville paints a picture of a society held together by greed, self-indulgence and the basest instincts of mankind. He offers us a vision of social order that functions like a machine, not despite, but because of, the lack of moral rectitude among the individuals within it:

> Thus every Part was full of Vice,
> Yet the whole Mass a Paradise;
> . . .
> Such were the Blessings of that State;
> Their Crimes conspir'd to make them great:
> And Virtue, who from Politicks
> Had learn'd a Thousand Cunning Tricks,

> Was, by their happy influence,
> Made Friends with Vice: And ever since,
> The worst of all the Multitude
> Did something for the Common Good.[70]

Mandeville's poem may be considered a satire on a socio-economic *milieu* where self-interest, egoism and the love of luxury are necessary to maintain an economy flourishing on continuous and varied production.[71] The necessity for constant and ever-growing production makes perpetual and excessive consumption a social virtue. Given the nature of the economic order, it is not surprising to find in "private vices, public benefits" as Mandeville appropriately subtitled his poem.

Contempory technology may have given us the means of satisfying our greed, but the age of Mandeville, as he suspected, gave us a philosophy that made greed and the uncompromising pursuit of wealth respectable. I would be inclined to attribute this accomplishment to Adam Smith. Contrary to the mercantalists who deplored the selfishness of the merchant and insisted that it must be subject to rigorous controls if it is to be prevented from plunging the nation into ruins, Adam Smith was confident that a providential harmony insured that the general welfare was best served when each individual pursued his own interests. In pursuit of his own private interest, the individual is "led by an invisible hand to promote an end which was no part of his intention."By substituting for Mandeville's paradox, a harmony between personal vice and social well-being, Smith succeeded in making egoism respectable, and Mandevillian ideas palatable.

For Plato, it is inconceivable that a society can thrive despite the proliferation of private vices and the uncompromising pursuit of wealth. The reason is not simply that he regarded wealth with suspicion (which he did), but that he considered virtue and self-restraint necessary in making up a good political order. In my view, political philosophies in which natural law plays a dominant role, tend to take this Platonic belief for granted.

The modern study of politics suggests that Mandevillian ideas continue to charm the students of political order. Jürgen Habermas is among those who have noted the trend in recent political analysis to assume that individual morality plays no significant role in politics. Habermas observes that the conception of order changes as the domain being ordered shifts from the individual *psyche* to the external conditions. The result is that "the order of virtuous conduct is changed into the regulation of social intercourse":

> . . . the engineers of the correct order can disregard the categories of ethical social intercourse and confine themselves to the construction of conditions under which human beings, just like objects within nature, will necessarily behave in a calculable manner. [72]

Karl Popper's concern with "social engineering" is is one example. The social engineer is charged with the improvement of society, but he has none of the characteristics of the great legislators, who are said to have the ability of writing their laws on people's hearts.[73] It is taken for granted today that the political problem *par excellence* is organization, not moral.

Thinking that private vices do not endanger, but rather enhance a political paradise is seductive because it implies the possibility of achieving excellence without effort. This is not unlike advertisements that promise a healthy trim figure without diet or exercise. Sheldon Wolin is yet another writer who finds the modern study of politics preoccupied with miraculous cures. In particular, he notes that "method" and "organization" are:

> . . . the salvation of puny men, the compensatory device for individual foibles, the gadget which allows mediocrity to transcend its limitation.[74]

Even though it is true that individual men can only attain excellence or be the best they can be, in a social context, it is not true that society can make them into what they cannot be. I suspect that Wolin's antipathy to the contemporary preoccupation with method and organization stems from the unrealistic expectations it fosters. But this is true of the trend recognized by Mandeville in general. It not only facilitates the separation of ethics and politics, but also propagates high and often unrealistic expectations since it divorces the political order from its components. It undermines the need for just persons and relies on external organization alone. But even the most ingenious social organization will not allow the state to transcend the limitations of its human material. To think otherwise is to make the error Prometheus made in thinking that a civilization can thrive on technical skill alone.

The Idea of Nature

Natural law has been associated with a particular view of nature. Even though this view of nature may not be an essential ingredient in every theory of natural law, it is nevertheless part of the most well known and perhaps most interesting theories of natural law.[75] Exploring this view of nature is significant because it enables us to make sense of "natural law" as a legal metaphor referring to a transcendent universal moral order.

The term "natural law" is perhaps a very unfortunate metaphor that has been the source of much confusion. For one thing it is easily confused with the physical laws of nature. Much of the criticism of the concept has revolved around the claim that it involves a confusion of moral and physical laws.[76]

The term "natural law" also tends to imply that the universal principles of justice can be neatly summarized into a set of rules. Mortimer Adler has rightly pointed out that the term is a Roman distortion of the Greek analysis of natural justice.[77] The Greeks found it difficult to speak of nature *(physis)* and law *(nomos)* at once because they took for granted the opposition between *nomos* and *physis*. *Nomos* signified not only law, but convention; and convention and nature were opposites. Plato and Aristotle therefore preferred to speak of natural justice rather than of natural law. Nevertheless, it is Plato and Aristotle that provide us with the view of nature that enables us to make sense of describing the moral law as "natural".

Much of the obscurity that has surrounded the idea of natural law has been a result of thinking that the Stoic philosophers are the founders of this idea in western legal thought.[78] The Stoic philosophers are indeed responsible for having popularized the term "natural law". But this fact alone is no indication that the ideas required to make sense of the term are an innovation of their own. It is surprising that so few scholars have recognized Plato's contribution to understanding natural law.[79] The fact that Plato never coined or used the phrase 'law of nature' except as a paradox,[80] is not a sufficient reason to believe that he did not provide the earliest and most sophisticated account of the ideas behind the term.

It was Plato who argued that law and justice are natural. In the *Republic* he argued that justice is a condition of the human *psyche* that is particularly fitting to the nature of man. In the *Laws,* Plato set out to show that law has a foundation in nature, and is not, contrary to the claims of the Sophists, a product of arbitrary human conventions. Plato's arguments can be properly understood only in the context of his debate with the Sophists.

The Sophists emphasized the opposition of nature *(physis)* and convention *(nomos).* In the second book of Plato's *Republic,* Glaucon and Adeimantus describe to Socrates the prevalence of this view among the Sophists of their time. The Sophists believed that human conventions had no resemblance to nature whatsoever. Being part of convention, law and justice are also highly unnatural. In nature, might is right, and wronging another is naturally good. But most men are too weak and cowardly to declare the truth openly as did Callicles when he said,

> . . . what in truth could be worse and more shameful than temperance and justice?[81]

In the opinion of Callicles and other Sophists, most men are hypocrites who are led by their cowardice to praise law and justice. This is not surprising in view of the fact that most men are weak and so would find themselves at a disadvantage in the condition of nature. In the condition of nature, the weak are constantly being victimized by the strong without being able to take their revenge. The majority therefore find it to their advantage to come together and agree not to inflict injury upon one another. They establish laws and attach penalties to them. They also spend a great deal of time extoling the greatness of justice. But this is merely a means to their self-interest; they do not really believe that justice is a good thing. They know that it is a compromise between the best of all possible worlds and the worst. The best of all possible worlds is to be able to benefit from the spoils of one's own injustice while avoiding any harm as a result of the injustice of others. The worst of all possible worlds is suffering harm and being unable to inflict it. Law and justice are therefore a good bargain for the weak but not so advantageous to the strong who find themselves restrained by the united strength of the weak. The origin of law and justice is therefore to be found in human compact, agreement and artifice. Law and justice are not only foreign to nature, they are supremely unnatural.

The Sophists apparently have a particular conception of nature that leads them to believe that law and justice are unnatural. The Sophists think of what is natural as having three distinctive qualities. First, what is natural is primary, in the sense of being there from the beginning. For them, matter (earth, air and fire) are primary. Law is not there from the beginning, it is a product of human artifice. Secondly, what is natural is fixed and unchanging. Nature, they maintain, has everywhere the same force, just as fire burns both here and in Persia, but laws differ from place to place.[82] Thirdly, what is natural is good and wholesome and is to be preferred to the artificial. Law and justice are artificial, and *real* men are not cowardly enough or hypocritical enough to praise them. The use of the term "natural" to refer to what is good and wholesome is still very much part of our own use of the term. The proliferation of advertisements for "natural cereals" is a case in point.

In the tenth book of the *Laws,* Plato sets out to show that (contrary to the claims of the Sophists) law is "natural". He uses the term "natural" in the same sense as his opponents to mean primary, unchanging and good. First, he tries to show that law is primary in the universe, and precedes the existence of matter. Secondly, he tries to show that law contains a fixed and unchanging element that cannot be arbitrarily changed by human artifice or convention. If he can show that law is natural in those two senses, he would be well on his way to convincing his opponents that it is good; (since they are all agreed that what is natural is good and is to be preferred to the artificial). Here is a brief account of how he goes about it.

Plato concedes to his adversaries that law is a product of human art or *techne*. But *techne* is possible only where there is reason and intelligence. If we observe nature, we will discover that reason and *techne* are not foreign to it. The Sophists maintained that matter, not mind, was primary in the universe. Plato explains that matter alone is not capable of accounting for the order that is manifest in the universe. The universe is an ordered whole or *cosmos*. Order has a greater affinity with intelligence than does disorder. Arbitrariness and chance can only result in chaos and disorder. The *cosmos* must therefore be a product of mind or intelligence rather than chance as the Sophists believed. In the *Timaeus* Plato uses a myth to explain what he means. Timaeus is an astronomer who is concerned with the nature and origin of the universe. He tells his audience a highly probable tale about how the universe might have come into being. His story is as follows. In the beginning there was matter in a state of "primal chaos", a condition that one may expect to find in the absence of intelligence. All the elements, fire, air, water and earth were in a state of confusion with none of the consistent properties with which we now associate them. They were in such a condition of disorder as to be unrecognizable as distinct elements. Then there came upon the scene, the "fairest of causes", a perfect and timeless creator or Master-Craftsman.

> Being free of jealousy he desired
> that all things should be as like
> himself as they could be.[83]

The Master-Craftsman turns the "primal chaos" into a *cosmos*. The creation is not *ex nihilo*. Intelligence endeavors to make things as good as possible given disorderly and imperfect material. The Master-Craftsman is not the creator of matter. He is a mythical figure representing mind or intelligence. The latter has access to perfect models or forms that are the ideas in accordance with which it orders matter. This is art or *techne*. Without *techne* there would be no *cosmos*. In this way Plato argues that to acknowledge that law is a product of human *techne* is not to concede that it is unnatural. On the contrary, as a product of reason and intelligence,law shares in what is most primary in the *cosmos*.

Plato's second argument sets out to show that law is natural in the sense of having within it an element that is fixed and unchanging. Plato makes the familiar distinction between the objects of sense that partake of motion, change, perishing and becoming, and the ideas that are apprehended by intelligence. Unlike the former, the latter do not partake of becoming, which involves birth, change and decay. Not being in need of generation, the intelligible never comes to be, but has always been.[84] On Plato's account in the *Republic, Timaeus* and *Laws,* craftsmanship requires knowledge of perfect, intelligible and unchanging models or ideas. The relationship of the latter to the products of *techne* is that of originals to copies.[85] The art of legislation, like any art involves the imitation of perfect models or ideas. If the legislator is to create good laws he must imitate the perfect and unchanging models of justice and goodness. This does not mean that the positive laws created by the art of legislation are themselves perfect, fixed and unchanging. Rather it means that positive laws (if they are the products of the legislative art and not just a facade for self-interest) must be fashioned in the likeness of what is just by nature. The art of legislation is therefore the art that tries to capture the likeness of the eternal and unchanging ideas of justice and goodness. Law is not itself eternal and unchanging, but it contains within it an element of the latter. It cannot therefore be dismissed on the ground that it is unnatural in the sense of containing no fixed and unchanging elements.

Plato and his opponents are agreed that what is natural is good and wholesome and is to be preferred to the artificial. This is why it is so important for Plato to convince his listeners that law is natural. If they could be convinced that law has a foundation in nature and in human nature, then they would have to acknowledge that it is good. To do this, Plato has to challenge the materialistic conception of the universe current among the Sophists. It is not possible to find in nature a source of moral and legal norms if it is understood as matter in motion, a product of arbitrary chance, not intelligence. Plato therefore introduces a conception of nature as permeated with Reason and Goodness. Only in the light of this Platonic conception of nature does it make sense to refer to nature as a source of legal norms.

Law not only has a foundation in nature, but in human nature. Man shares in the intelligence that permeates the *cosmos*. In man, as in the *cosmos,* reason is the source of order and lawfulness. It orders, directs and sets limits to the unlimited and disorderly appetites, portrayed imaginatively as a "multiform beast with many heads."[86] The just man subordinates the beastlike part of his nature to the human, or more properly, the divine.[87] In so doing, he replaces chaos by a *cosmos* within.[88] In the state, law has the same function as does reason in the *psyche*. It is the source of order and justice. It insures harmony between competing interests and promotes the good of the whole. Like reason it must be gentle; it must attempt to govern from within by persuasion, not from without by force. Because the human *psyche* is a microcosm of the universe, law can be said to have a foundation in human nature as well as in nature.

The appropriateness or fittingness of the moral law for human nature later became a fundamental claim of "teleological" theories of natural law like that of St. Thomas Aquinas. These theories rely on the view of nature advocated by Plato and later developed by Aristotle.

Plato equates the perfect models, forms or ideas with nature. In the *Republic* he claims that the ideas exist "by nature".[89] In the *Timaeus,* he writes that the ideas are the essential attributes of intelligence, and hence, are like the latter also "natural".[90] This is not a surprising use of the term nature since the ideas embody all the attributes that both Plato and the Sophists associated with nature. They are primary (i.e., have always been without becoming), they are fixed and unchanging, and most importantly, their excellence is unsurpassed. Given this Platonic use of the term nature, it is not surprising to find Aristotle referring to the nature of a thing as its most perfect form, -- its condition of excellence. When the nature of anything is understood as its most perfect form, the Stoic dictum ''follow nature'' becomes a meaningful prescription when addressed to man. It means follow that which is best; follow the divine within.

Aristotle continues to use nature in the same senses as Plato. He talks of nature as that which is primary,[91] as that which is fixed and unchanging[92] and as that which is contrary to chance.[93] Aristotle adds yet another sense to the term ''nature'' -- that of a developmental motion towards an end, final form or purpose.[94] This is meant to be particularly applicable to living things. This last sense of ''nature'' may appear to be in conflict with nature as that which is fixed and unchanging. But as A. D. Nelson puts it, the two ideas are ''reconciled in the conception of fixed potentialities and ends or goals associated with variable actualizations, fulfillments or degrees of attainment of the goals''.[95] The nature of a thing refers therefore to a fixed and predetermined end or goal *(telos)* that constitutes its optimum condition of development and to which it is directed by nature. The nature of a thing is its form or given potentiality. It is taken for granted that what is natural is good. It is therefore good for things to fulfill their given potentialities.

Like other living things, man has a given potentiality or *telos*. The object of law and the state is to direct man towards that end or at least, to create the conditions under which he can best fulfill his *telos*. If law is to succeed, it must be compatible with the nature of man. This is the view adopted by Aquinas. This view of nature is closely associated with natural law in the minds of its critics.

J. S. Mill was one of the earliest to attack the view that nature can be a source of moral norms. His assault on those who find nature a source of norms deserves to be quoted at length.

> In sober truth, nearly all the things which men are hanged or imprisoned for doing to one another are nature's everyday performances. Killing, the most criminal act recognized by human laws, nature does once to every being that lives, . . . Nature impales men, breaks them as if on the wheel, casts them to be devoured by wild beasts, burns them to death, crushes them with stones like the first Christian martyr, starves them with hunger, freezes them with cold, poisons them by the quick

> or slow venom of her exhalations, and has hundreds of other hideous deaths in reserve . . . All this nature does with the most supercilious disregard both of mercy and of justice, . . . Everything, in short, which the worst men commit either against life or property is perpetrated on a larger scale by natural agents . . . Either it is right that we should kill because nature kills, torture because nature tortures, ruin and devastate because nature does the like, or we ought not to consider at all what nature does, but what it is good to do. . . The physical government of the world being full of the things which when done by men are deemed the greatest enormities, it cannot be religious or moral in us to guide our actions by the analogy of the course of nature.[96]

The view of nature expressed by J. S. Mill stands in marked contrast to the Platonic, Aristotelian and Thomistic views of nature. Nature, understood as it is by J. S. Mill cannot possibly be a source of moral norms for the guidance of human action.

What modern critics find most objectionable in theories of natural law is their tendency to think of nature as a source of norms. The modern critics contend that natural law involves a logical error known as the "naturalistic fallacy".[97] The latter consists of an erroneous deduction of normative or "ought" statements from factual or "is" statements. Needless to say, from the fact that something is the case, it does not follow that it ought to be the case. From the fact that concentration camps for the innocent exist, it does not follow that they ought to exist. Supposedly, theories of natural law make the error of deriving moral and legal norms from facts about human nature. And, it goes without saying, the fact that men have certain desires or inclinations is no reason to think that they ought to be satisfied.

If natural law theories began from a conception of nature in which there are only facts, then the assertion that the theory is an example of the naturalistic fallacy would be justifiable. But as we have seen above, this is not the case. The conception of nature with which teleological theories of natural law begin is one where reason, order and goodness are primary. If Timaeus were to speak to J. S. Mill, he probably would explain that the "evil" he sees in nature is the residue of the "primal chaos" that could not be completely subdued by the Master-Craftsman because of the disorderly and generally imperfect nature of matter itself.

There is however some truth to the claim that theories of natural law tend to derive their moral and legal norms from facts about human nature. In response to this, several things ought to be said. First, human nature does not consist of a set of inert facts. It contains tendencies and potentialities towards the good. It is these latter that are to be exploited as the source of moral and legal norms. Secondly, from the potentialities inherent in the nature of man, moral and legal norms are not arrived at by a process of logical deduction. But what man is, and what potentialities he is given cannot be unrelated to what he ought to do. In Kantian language, "Ought" implies "Can". Man can be morally required to do something only if it is possible (i.e., within his given potentialities) to do it; nor do I mean simply physical possibility. Laws that frustrate the most urgent human needs and tendencies cannot be just. For example, laws cannot require men to sacrifice themselves, forbid women from having children, prohibit sexual intercourse or command men to live in total isolation without any intercourse with other human beings. This is part of what Aquinas meant when he said that self-preservation,sexual intercourse, care of offspring, living in society and knowing God were part of the natural law on which the positive law must be modelled. The relation between human nature and moral and legal norms is not one of logical deduction; rather it is one of appropriateness and fittingness.

Conclusion

In conclusion, natural law is (i) a legal metaphor referring to an objective moral order that is (to some degree) accessible to human reason. (ii) Knowledge of this moral order is not purely theoretical, but practical, and so is capable of moving (at least some) men to action. (iii) Furthermore, the moral law is not consequential but deontological; more particularly, it is act deontological and so cannot be summarized in a set of rules. (iv) Advocates of natural law insist that positive law must conform to the natural law if it is to be valid and properly speaking "law". (v) In politics natural law is a philosophy of moderation that combines high ideals with moderate expectations. On one hand, it rejects the political radicalism that is often the result of believing that the natural law can be made completely immanent in the political order and insists instead on the eternal transcendence of the natural law. On the other hand, it rejects the political quietism that is often the result of maintaining the radical transcendence of natural law according to which no part of the latter is realizable in human life. (vi) Natural law also involves the claim that the paramount political problem is moral, and that even the best laws cannot succeed in insuring a modestly just society apart from just persons. (vii) Natural law has often been associated with a particular conception of nature that explains why nature has for so long been considered a source of moral norms, and hence the appeal of "natural law" as a metaphor referring to the moral law that must govern both the state and the individuals within it.

All of the above claims consitute what I have described as the resilient core of natural law. With perhaps the exception of the last, they are all necessary parts of any theory of natural law. Because theories of natural law are not homogeneous and because they are surrounded with so much obscurity, it is important to clarify the central core of the doctrine. Only when properly understood can it be fairly evaluated.

Notes

1 Bentham, *A Fragment on Government*, in 1 *Works* 221, 287, 294 (Bowring ed. 1859) (c. iv, 19th para.). See also Bentham *A Comment on the Commentaries* 49 (1928) (c.iii) where Bentham criticizes Blackstone. See also Blackstone, *Commentaries*, (London, 1826) Vol. 1, Ch2, 41.

2 Felix E. Oppenheim, *Moral Principles in Political Philosophy*, (New York, 1975).

3 S. Hook (ed.), *Law and Philosophy*, (New York, 1964), see especially Kai Nielsen, "The Myth of Natural Law".

4 H. L. A. Hart, "Positivism and the Separation of Law and Morals," *Harvard Law Review*, 71 (1958) pp. 593 ff. and Lon L. Fuller, "Positivism and Fidelity to Law -- A Reply to Professor Hart," *Harvard Law Review*, 71 (1958) pp. 630 ff.

5 Lon L. Fuller, *The Morality of Law*, (London, 1964); Leo Strauss, *Natural Right and History*, (Chicago, 1950); John Wild, *Plato's Modern Enemies and the Theory of Natural Law*, (Chicago, 1953); John Finnis, *Natural Law and Natural Rights*, (Oxford, 1980).

6 See Vonder Heydte, "Natural Law Tendencies in Contemporary German Jurisprudence," *Natural Law Forum*, 1 (1956) pp. 116 ff.

7 Lon L. Fuller, *The Morality of Law*, (London, 1964) and *The Law In Quest of Itself*, (Chicago, 1940).

8 M. B. Crowe, *The Changing Profile of the Natural Law*, (The Hague, 1977), see especially Chapter X.

9 John Wild, *Plato's Modern Enemies and the Theory of Natural Law*, (Chicago, 1953). Wild excludes Kant and Locke from the tradition of natural law. He considers the teleological view of nature (discussed in the last section) to be central to the theory.

10 I have so far used the term "natural law" broadly to refer to a philosophy of law and politics (the broad outlines of which I will set out below). But I will also use the term natural law in a narrow sense as a metaphor referring to natural justice or the objective moral order. I will also use the terms "natural law" and "law of nature" interchangeably.

11 Sophocles, *The Theban Plays*, trans. by E. F. Watling, (London, 1947), p. 138.

12 The difference between knowledge and belief is described by Plato in *Republic*, Bk. V, 476 c ff.

13 Plato, *Republic*, Bk. V.

14 Plato, *Timaeus*, 29 A-B; Hastings Rashdall, *Theory of Good and Evil*, (Oxford, 1907), Vol. 2, p. 212.

15 Bk. 1 of Plato's *Republic* seems to make this point. It is also important to note that Aquinas does not provide us with a list of rules that are contained in the natural law. Locke, unfortunately, could not resist the temptation; but there is no indication that the examples of rules he gives as part of the natural law are ironclad.

16 Aristotle, *Nicomachean Ethics*, Bk. VI, 1139A5 ff.

17 *Ibid.*, Bk. VI, 1141B22.

18 *Summa Theologica*, I-II, Q. 94.

19 *Ibid.*, I-II, Q. 94 A2.

20 *Loc. cit.*

21 *Loc. cit.*

22 The derivation is to be understood as contingent on particular situations and circumstances -- see discussion of act deontology below. It is important to note that the first precept of natural law is underived. Defenders of Aquinas have argued that this is an indication that he was well aware of the impossibility of deriving "ought" from "is". See Germain G. Grisez, "The First Principle of Practical Reason,", *Aquinas: a collection of critical essays*, A. Kenny (ed.), (London, 1969). Grisez argues that it is important to note that the first principle of natural law is self-evident and underived and that therefore the obligatory character of natural law is not derived from the fact that men have appetites or inclinations any more than from the fact that the universe is huge.

23 Kai Nielsen, "The Myth of Natural Law," *Law and Philosophy*, Sidney Hook (ed.), *Op. cit.*

24 I have in mind H. A. Prichard in particular. Other intuitionists like G. E. Moore and W. D. Ross are in my view less fanatical but not altogether unblameworthy for the illrepute of intuition today. See H. A. Prichard, "Does Moral Philosophy Rest on a Mistake?" *Mind*, 1912, also reprinted in his *Moral Obligation*, (Oxford, 1949).

25 H. A. Prichard, *Loc. cit.*

26 Unlike H. A. Prichard, G. E. Moore thought only the good can be apprehended by intuition; the right however is an object of rational calculation since it is the means for maximizing the good.

27 W. D. Ross concedes this point. See *The Right and the Good*, (Oxford, 1930).

28 *Nicomachean Ethics*, 1139 A24.

29 *Ibid.*, 1139 B4.

30 *Ibid.*, 1152 A8.

31 *Republic*, at 508e -- Plato describes how the philosopher is overwhelmed by the extraordinary beauty of the form of Good; at 475c he speaks of those who "love the spectacle of truth," G. M. A.Grube's translations, (Indianapolis, 1974).

32 I cannot give a satisfactory answer to this controversial aspect of Aquinas' theory of natural law. I can only refer the reader to the following treatments of it: D. J. O'Connor, *Aquinas and Natural Law*, (Toronto, 1967); M. B. Crowe, *The Changing Profile of the Natural Law*, (The Hague, 1977), esp. Chs. 6 & 7; H. V. Jaffa, *Thomism and Aristotelianism*, (Chicago, 1954), esp. Ch. 8.

33 Locke, *The Reasonableness of Christianity*, *Works of John Locke*, (London, 1823), 10 Vols., Vol. 7, p. 150.

34 See my "John Locke: Natural Law and Innate Ideas," *Dialogue*, (December, 1980).

35 Felix Oppenheim, *op. cit.*

36 This criticism of consequentialism is developed further by Bernard Williams in J. J. C. Smart and Bernard Williams, *Utilitarianism: for and against*, (Cambridge, 1973).

37 A similar difference exists between rule and act utilitarian theories. See John Rawls, "Two Concepts of Rules," *The Philosophical Review*, Vol. 64 (January, 1955) pp. 3-32. See also Austin's defense of his utilitarianism in Lecture II of *The Province of Jurisprudence Determined*, (New York, 1861), reproduced below. Austin maintains that the utilitarianism he is defending is a rule utilitarianism (even though he does not use these modern terms), however in certain pressing situations his rule utilitarianism seems to collapse into act utilitarianism (as his example of governmental resistance illustrates).

38 *Republic*, 331c.

39 Locke, *An Essay Concerning Human Understanding*, J. W. Yolton (ed.), (London, 1961), 2 vols., Bk I, Ch. 3, sec. I.

40 Lon L. Fuller, *Law in Quest of Itself;* and "Human Purpose and Natural Law," *Journal of Philosophy*, 53 (1956) pp. 697-705, reprinted in *Natural Law Forum*, Vol. 3, No. 1 (1958), pp. 68-76.

41 The view that law tends to follow or reflect the positive morality is expressed by Patrick Devlin in *The Enforcement of Morals*, (Oxford, 1965).

42 *Laws*, 632B, 963A. This view assumes that man has a peculiar excellence to which he is fitted. See last section below for further discussion.

43 This view was expressed by Roscoe Pound in *An Introduction to the Philosophy of Law*, (New Haven, 1922), Ch. 2.

44 H. L. A. Hart, *The Concept of Law*, (Oxford, 1961), Ch. 9.

45 *Loc. cit.*

46 H. L. A. Hart, *Law, Liberty and Morality*, (Stanford, 1963).

47 Patrick Devlin, *op. cit.*

48 Lon L. Fuller, *The Morality of Law, op. cit.;* and "Positivism and Fidelity to Law -- A Reply to Professor Hart," *op. cit.*

49 Lon L. Fuller, *The Morality of Law, op. cit.*, p. 39.

50 H. L. A. Hart, "Book Review: The Morality of Law by Lon L. Fuller," *Harvard Law Review*, 78(1965), p. 1281.

51 Lon L. Fuller, "Positivism and Fidelity to Law -- A Reply to Professor Hart," *op. cit.*, Section III.

52 Lon L. Fuller, *The Morality of Law*, "Appendix: The Problem of the Grudge Informer", pp. 245-253.

53 Philip Mullock, "The Inner Morality of Law," *Ethics*, Vol. 84 (1973-74) pp. 327-331. Mullock argues that Fuller's connection between law and morality is *practical* rather than *logical*. I take this to mean that it is necessary for law to be moral if it hopes to achieve the good end that Fuller understands law to be directed towards. Mullock's argument is plausible. But it is puzzling why Fuller would describe his claim in epistemological terms if all he intended was a practical connection between law and morality. Surely he also wishes to maintain an epistemological connection between order and goodness as such.

54 Locke, *Two Treatises of Government*, second treatise, Ch. 19, reprinted below.

55 Hegel, *Natural Law*, T. M. Knox, transl., (Pennsylvania, 1975); Otto Gierke *Das deutche Genossenschaftsrecht*, part of the fourth volume has been translated by Ernest Barker as *Natural Law and the Theory of Society, 1500-1800*, (Cambridge, 1934, 1959).

56 Otto Gierke, *loc. cit.*

57 *Ibid.*, p.224.

58 *Loc. cit.*

59 *Ibid.*, p. 226.

60 Many historians have followed Troeltsch's account even though there is little evidence of this particular terminology in the sources. See A. P. d'Entreves, *Natural Law*, (London, 1951, 1970), p. 41, footnote 1.

61 *Protagoras*, 321, trans. by W. K. C. Guthrie.

62 *Ibid., 3326.*

63 Ibid., 322c.

64 Werner Jaeger, "Praise of Law: The Origins of Philosophy and the Greeks," *Interpretations of Modern Legal Philosophies*, Paul Sayre (ed.), (New York, 1947), p. 362.

65 *Republic*, 426e-427. A hydra is a mythical monster with many heads. If one head was cut off, several others grew in its place.

66 *Politics*, 1310A12.

67 *Nicomachean Ethics*, 1137B, 10-29.

68 *Republic*, Bk. VIII.

69 *Fable of the Bees*, F.B. Kaye (ed.), (London, 1924), Vol. I, p. 4.

70 *Ibid.*, Vol. I, p. 24. Part of this passage is also quoted by Arthur O. Lovejoy in his *Reflections on Human Nature*, (Baltimore, 1961), p. 41. Lovejoy points out that Mandevillian ideas gained popularity at a time when despairing of human nature was rampant. Naturally, the possibility of constructing an ideal political order out of flawed human material appealed to those who had little faith in human nature. Lovejoy claims that Mandevillian ideas rather than Lockian ones, were the source of the genius of the Fathers of the American Constitution and shows explicit restatements of these ideas in the work of early American figures like James Madison.

71 See J.H. Tufts, *The Individual and his Relation to Society as Reflected in British Ethics*, (Chicago, 1898), part II, p. 13ff.

72 Jürgen Habermas, *Theory and Practice*, (Boston, 1973), p. 43. It is important to note that Habermas is not an advocate of natural law. However, he shares the sentiment I find implicit in natural law theories that a good political order is not simply a matter of engineering.

73 R. Jordan, "The Revolt Against Philosophy: The Spell of Popper," in John Wild (ed.), *Return to Reason*, (Chicago, 1953). Jordan has noted that the social engineer is charged with the improvement of society, but has no power to improve people's characters.

74 Sheldon Wolin, *Politics and Vision*, (Boston, 1960), p. 383.

75 For example, it is not part of Kant's theory, yet I would be reluctant to exclude Kant from the tradition of natural law.

76 Karl Popper, *The Open Society and Its Enemies*, (London, 1945), Vol. I, p. 61.

77 Mortimer Adler, "A Question About Law," in Robert E. Brennan (ed.), *Essays in Thomism*, (New York, 1942), p. 235.

78 See George H. Sabine, *A History of Political Theory*, 4th ed., (Hindal, Illinois, 1973), ch. 9; R. W. Carlyle and A. J. Carlyle, *A History of Medieval Political Theory in the West*, (Edinburgh, 1963), 6 vols.; Richard Wollheim, "Natural Law," *The Encyclopedia of Philosophy*, Paul Edwards (ed.), (London, 1964); Leo Strauss, "Natural Law," *International Encyclopedia of the Social Sciences*, (New York, 1968) 17 vols., vol. II, pp. 80-85.

79 See John Wild, *Plato's Modern Enemies and the Theory of Natural Law*, *op. cit.* Joseph P. Maguire's "Plato's Theory of Natural Law," *Yale Classical Studies*, (1947), pp. 151-178. I find Maguire's definition too broad to distinguish natural law from any other kind of moral standard. An excellent article on the subject is by Glenn R. Morrow, "Plato and the Law of Nature," *Essays in Political Theory Presented to George Sabine*, Milton R. Konvitz and Arthur E. Murphy (eds.), (New York, 1948).

80 *Gorgias*, 483c, trans. by W. D. Woodhead.

81 *Ibid.*, 492b.

82 Aristotle, *Nicomachean Ethics*, Bk. VI, ch. 7, 1134B25. Aristotle is here making the distinction between two aspects of political justice, one "natural" and everywhere the same, another "legal" and differing from place to place (e.g., that a prisoner's ransom shall be a mina, or that a goat and not two sheep shall be sacrificed). The

"legal" part of justice, as opposed to the "natural" part is determined by convention.

83 *Timaeus*, 29E-30A, Benjamin Jowett, trans.

84 *Ibid.*, 28A; *Republic*, 478d.

85 *Timaeus*, 29A-B; *Republic*, 596b ff.

86 *Republic*, 588c.

87 *Ibid.*, 589d.

88 *Ibid.*, 590d.

89 *Ibid.*, 501b, 597b, 597c.

90 *Timaeus*, 29B.

91 Aristotle, *Metaphysics*, Bk. V, ch. 4, 1014B27.

92 *Ibid.*, 1014B28.

93 Aristotle's *Physics*, Bk. II, ch. 8, 199A 1-8.

94 *Ibid.*, Bk II, ch. 1, 192B 10-35; *Metaphysics*, Bk. V, ch. 4, 1014B 16-30 and 1015Al-20.

95 A. D. Nelson "'Nature' in Behavioralist Explanations of Politics," a paper presented to the fiftieth annual meeting of the Canadian Political Science Association, London, Ontario, 1978, p. 12.

96 J. S. Mill, essay on "Nature" in *Essays on Ethics, Religion and Society*, Vol. X of Mill's *Collected Works*, J. M. Robinson (ed.), (Toronto, 1963).

97 The expression was introduced by G. E. Moore in his *Principia Ethica*, (Cambridge, 1971), but the idea is commonly supposed to originate with Hume. The account of the naturalistic fallacy I have given is not exhaustive, to say the least. There is more than one account of what constitutes this logical fallacy. See *The Is-Ought Question*, W. D. Hudson, (London, 1969); see also W. K. Frankena, "The Naturalistic Fallacy," *Mind*, 48 (1939), pp. 464-77.

2

Plato

On Justice

The Republic

Book I

Persons of the Dialogue

SOCRATES, who is the narrator

GLAUCON

ADEIMANTUS

CEPHALUS

THRASYMACHUS

CLEITOPHON

POLEMARCHUS

And others who are mute auditors

THE SCENE is laid in the house of Cephalus at the Piraeus; and the whole dialogue is narrated by Socrates the day after it actually took place to Timaeus, Hermocrates, Critias, and a nameless person, who are introduced in the Timaeus.

I went down yesterday to the Piraeus with Glaucon the son of
327 Ariston, that I might offer up my prayers to the goddess [Bendis, the Thracian Artemis]; and also because I wanted to see in what manner they would celebrate the festival, which was a new thing. I was delighted with the procession of the inhabitants; but that of the Thracians was equally, if not more, beautiful. When we had finished our prayers and viewed the spectacle, we turned in the direction of the city; and at that instant Polemarchus the son of Cephalus chanced to catch sight of us from a distance as we were starting on our way home, and told his servant to run and bid us wait for him. The servant took hold of me by the cloak behind, and said: Polemarchus desires you to wait.

I turned round, and asked him where his master was.

There he is, said the youth, coming after you, if you will only wait.

Certainly we will, said Glaucon; and in a few minutes Polemarchus appeared, and with him Adeimantus, Glaucon's brother, Naceratus the son of Nicias, and several others who had been at the procession.

Polemarchus said to me: I perceive, Socrates, that you and your companion are already on your way to the city.

You are not far wrong, I said.

But do you see, he rejoined, how many we are?

Of course.

And are you stronger than all these? for if not, you will have to remain where you are.

May there not be the alternative, I said, that we may persuade you to let us go?

But can you persuade us, if we refuse to listen to you? he said.

Certainly not, replied Glaucon.

Then we are not going to listen; of that you may be assured.

328 Adeimantus added: Has no one told you of the torch-race on horseback in honour of the goddess which will take place in the evening?

With horses! I replied: That is a novelty. Will horsemen carry torches and pass them one to another during the race?

Yes, said Polemarchus, and not only so, but a festival will be celebrated at night, which you certainly ought to see. Let us rise soon after supper and see this festival; there will be a gathering of young men, and we will have a good talk. Stay then, and do not be perverse.

Glaucon said: I suppose, since you insist, that we must.

Very good, I replied.

Accordingly we went with Polemarchus to his house; and there we found his brothers Lysias and Euthydemus, and with them Thrasymachus the Chalcedonian, Charmantides the Paeanian, and Cleitophon the son of Aristonymus. There too was Cephalus the father of Polemarchus, whom I had not seen for a long time, and I thought him very much aged. He was seated on a cushioned chair, and had a garland on his head, for he had been sacrificing in the court; and there were some other chairs in the room arranged in a semicircle, upon which we sat down by him. He saluted me eagerly, and then he said: --

You don't come to see me, Socrates, as often as you ought: If I were still able to go and see you I would not ask you to come to me. But at my age I can hardly get to the city, and therefore you should come oftener to the Piraeus. For let me tell you, that the more the pleasures of the body fade away, the greater to me is the pleasure and charm of conversation. Do not then deny my request, but make our house your resort and keep company with these young men; we are old friends, and you will be quite at home with us.

I replied: There is nothing which for my part I like better, Cephalus, than conversing with aged men; for I regard them as travellers who have gone a journey which I too may have to go, and of whom I ought to enquire, whether the way is smooth and easy, or rugged and difficult. And this is a question which I should like to ask of you who have arrived at that time which the poets call the 'threshold of old age' -- Is life harder towards the end, or what report do you give of it?

I will tell you, Socrates, he said, what my own feeling is. Men of 329
my age flock together; we are birds of a feather, as the old proverb says; and at our meetings the tale of my acquaintance commonly is -- I cannot eat, I cannot drink; the pleasures of youth and love are fled away: there was a good time once, but now that is gone, and life is no longer life. Some complain of the slights which are put upon them by relations, and they will tell you sadly of how many evils their old age is the cause. But to me, Socrates, these complainers seem to blame that which is not really in fault. For if old age were the cause, I too being old, and every other old man, would have felt as they do. But this is not my own experience, nor that of others whom I have known. How well I remember the aged poet Sophocles, when in answer to the question, How does love suit with age, Sophocles, -- are you still the man you were? Peace, he replied; most gladly have I escaped the thing of which you speak; I feel as if I had escaped from a mad and furious master. His words have often occurred to my mind since, and they seem as good to me now as at the time when he uttered them. For certainly old age has a great sense of calm and freedom; when the passions relax their hold, then, as Sophocles says, we are freed from the grasp not of one mad master only, but of many. The truth is, Socrates, that these regrets, and also the complaints about relations, are to be attributed to the same cause, which is not old age, but men's characters and tempers; for he who is of a calm and happy

nature will hardly feel the pressure of age, but to him who is of an opposite disposition youth and age are equally a burden.

I listened in admiration, and wanting to draw him out, that he might go on -- Yes, Cephalus, I said; but I rather suspect that people in general are not convinced by you when you speak thus; they think that old age sits lightly upon you, not because of your happy disposition, but because you are rich, and wealth is well known to be a great comforter.

You are right, he replied; they are not convinced: and there is something in what they say; not, however, so much as they imagine. I might answer them as Themistocles answered the Seriphian who was
330 abusing him and saying that he was famous, not for his own merits but because he was an Athenian: 'If you had been a native of my country or I of yours, neither of us would have been famous.' And to those who are not rich and are impatient of old age, the same reply may be made; for to the good poor man old age cannot be a light burden, nor can a bad rich man ever have peace with himself.

May I ask, Cephalus, whether your fortune was for the most part inherited or acquired by you?

Acquired! Socrates; do you want to know how much I acquired? In the art of making money I have been midway between my father and grandfather: for my grandfather, whose name I bear, doubled and trebled the value of his patrimony, that which he inherited being much what I possess now; but my father Lysanias reduced the property below what it is at present: and I shall be satisfied if I leave to these my sons not less but a little more than I received.

That was why I asked you the question, I replied, because I see that you are indifferent about money, which is characteristic rather of those who have inherited their fortunes than of those who have acquired them; the makers of fortunes have a second love of money as a creation of their own, resembling the affection of authors for their own poems, or of parents for their children, besides that natural love of it for the sake of use and profit which is common to them and all men. And hence they are very bad company, for they can talk about nothing but the praises of wealth.

That is true, he said.

Yes, that is very true, but may I ask another question? -- What do you consider to be the greatest blessing which you have reaped from your wealth?

One, he said, of which I could not expect easily to convince others. For let me tell you, Socrates, that when a man thinks himself to be near death, fears and cares enter into his mind which he never had before; the tales of a world below and the punishment which is exacted there of

deeds done here were once a laughing matter to him, but now he is tormented with the thought that they may be true: either from the weakness of age, or because he is now drawing nearer to that other place, he has a clearer view of these things; suspicions and alarms crowd thickly upon him, and he begins to reflect and consider what wrongs he has done to others. And when he finds that the sum of his transgressions is great he will many a time like a child start up in his sleep for fear, and he is filled
with dark forebodings. But to him who is conscious of no sin, sweet 331
hope, as Pindar charmingly says, is the kind nurse of his age:

> 'Hope,' he says, 'cherishes the soul of him who lives in justice and holiness, and is the nurse of his age and the companion of his journey; -- hope which is mightiest to sway the restless soul of man.'

How admirable are his words! And the great blessing of riches, I do not say every man, but to a good man, is, that he has had no occasion to deceive or to defraud others, either intentionally or unintentionally; and when he departs to the world below he is not in any apprehension about offerings due to the gods or debts which he owes to men. Now to this peace of mind the possession of wealth greatly contributes; and therefore I say, that, setting one thing against another, of the many advantages which wealth has to give, to a man of sense this is in my opinion the greatest.

Well said, Cephalus, I replied; but as concerning justice, what is it? -- to speak the truth and to pay your debts -- no more than this? And even to this are there not exceptions? Suppose that a friend when in his right mind has deposited arms with me and he asks for them when he is not in his right mind, ought I to give them back to him? No one would say that I ought or that I should be right in doing so, any more than they would say that I ought always to speak the truth to one who is in his condition.

You are quite right, he replied.

But then, I said, speaking the truth and paying your debts is not a correct definition of justice.

Quite correct, Socrates, if Simonides is to be believed, said Polemarchus interposing.

I fear, said Cephalus, that I must go now, for I have to look after the sacrifices, and I hand over the argument to Polemarchus and the company.

Is not Polemarchus your heir? I said.

To be sure, he answered, and went away laughing to the sacrifices.

Tell me then, O thou heir of the argument, what did Simonides say, and according to you truly say, about justice?

He said that the re-payment of a debt is just, and in saying so he appears to me to be right.

I should be sorry to doubt the word of such a wise and inspired man, but his meaning, though probably clear to you, is the reverse of clear to me. For he certainly does not mean, as we were just now saying, that I ought to return a deposit of arms or of anything else to one who asks for it when he is not in his right senses; and yet a deposit cannot
332 be denied to be a debt.

True.

Then when the person who asks me is not in his right mind I am by no means to make the return?

Certainly not.

When Simonides said that the repayment of a debt was justice, he did not mean to include that case?

Certainly not; for he thinks that a friend ought always to do good to a friend and never evil.

You mean that the return of a deposit of gold which is to the injury of the receiver, if the two parties are friends, is not the repayment of a debt, -- that is what you would imagine him to say?

Yes.

And are enemies also to receive what we owe to them?

To be sure, he said, they are to receive what we owe them, and an enemy, as I take it, owes to an enemy that which is due or proper to him -- that is to say, evil.

Simonides, then, after the manner of poets, would seem to have spoken darkly of the nature of justice; for he really meant to say that justice is the giving to each man what is proper to him, and this he termed a debt.

That must have been his meaning, he said.

By heaven! I replied; and if we asked him what due or proper thing is given by medicine, and to whom, what answer do you think that he would make to us?

He would surely reply that medicine gives drugs and meat and drink to human bodies.

And what due or proper thing is given by cookery, and to what?

Seasoning to food.

And what is that which justice gives, and to whom?

If, Socrates, we are to be guided at all by the analogy of the preceding instances, then justice is the art which gives good to friends and evil to enemies.

That is his meaning then?

I think so.

And who is best able to do good to his friends and evil to his enemies in time of sickness?

The physician.

Or when they are on a voyage, amid the perils of the sea?

The pilot.

And in what sort of actions or with a view to what result is the just man most able to do harm to his enemy and good to his friend?

In going to war against the one and in making alliances with the other.

But when a man is well, my dear Polemarchus, there is no need of a physician?

No.

And he who is not on a voyage has no need of a pilot?

No.

Then in time of peace justice will be of no use?

I am very far from thinking so.

You think that justice may be of use in peace as well as in war? 333

Yes.

Like husbandry for the acquisition of corn?

Yes.

Or like shoemaking for the acquisition of shoes, -- that is what you mean?

Yes.

And what similar use or power of acquisition has justice in time of peace?

In contracts, Socrates, justice is of use.

And by contracts you mean partnerships?

Exactly.

But is the just man or the skilful player a more useful and better partner at a game of draughts?

The skilful player.

And in the laying of bricks and stones is the just man a more useful or better partner than the builder?

Quite the reverse.

Then in what sort of partnership is the just man a better partner than the harp-player, as in playing the harp the harp-player is certainly a better partner than the just man?

In a money partnership.

Yes, Polemarchus, but surely not in the use of money; for you do not want a just man to be your counsellor in the purchase or sale of a horse; a man who is knowing about horses would be better for that, would he not?

Certainly.

And when you want to buy a ship, the shipwright or the pilot would be better?

True.

Then what is that joint use of silver or gold in which the just man is to be preferred?

When you want a deposit to be kept safely.

You mean when money is not wanted, but allowed to lie?

Precisely.

That is to say, justice is useful when money is useless?

That is the inference.

And when you want to keep a pruning-hook safe, then justice is useful to the individual and to the state; but when you want to use it, then the art of the vine-dresser?

Clearly.

And when you want to keep a shield or a lyre, and not to use them, you would say that justice is useful; but when you want to use them, then the art of the soldier or of the musician?

Certainly.

And so of all the other things; -- justice is useful when they are useless, and useless when they are useful?

That is the inference.

Then justice is not good for much. But let us consider this further point: Is not he who can best strike a blow in a boxing match or in any kind of fighting best able to ward off a blow?

Certainly.

And he who is most skilful in preventing or escaping from a disease is best able to create one?

True.

And he is the best guard of a camp who is best able to steal a march
334 upon the enemy?

Certainly.

Then he who is a good keeper of anything is also a good thief?

That, I suppose, is to be inferred.

Then if the just man is good at keeping money, he is good at stealing it.

That is implied in the argument.

Then after all the just man has turned out to be a thief. And this is a lesson which I suspect you must have learnt out of Homer; for he, speaking of Autolycus, the maternal grandfather of Odysseus, who is a favourite of his, affirms that.

> He was excellent above all men in theft and perjury.

And so, you and Homer and Simonides are agreed that justice is an art of theft; to be practised however 'for the good of friends and for the harm of enemies,' -- that was what you were saying?

No, certainly not that, though I do not now know what I did say; but I still stand by the latter words.

Well there is another question: By friends and enemies do we mean those who are so really, or only in seeming?

Surely, he said, a man may be expected to love those whom he thinks good, and to hate those whom he thinks evil.

Yes, but do not persons often err about good and evil: many who are not good seem to be so, and conversely?

That is true.

Then to them the good will be enemies and the evil will be their friends?

True.

And in that case they will be right in doing good to the evil and evil to the good?

Clearly.

But the good are just and would not do an injustice?

True.

Then according to your argument it is just to injure those who do no wrong?

Nay, Socrates; the doctrine is immoral.

Then I suppose that we ought to do good to the just and harm to the unjust?

I like that better.

But see the consequence: -- Many a man who is ignorant of human nature has friends who are bad friends, and in that case he ought to do harm to them; and he has good enemies whom he ought to benefit; but, if so, we shall be saying the very opposite of that which we affirmed to be the meaning of Simonides.

Very true, he said; and I think that we had better correct an error into which we seem to have fallen in the use of words 'friend' and 'enemy.'

What was the error, Polemarchus? I asked.

We assumed that he is a friend who seems to be or who is thought good.

And how is the error to be corrected?

We should rather say that he is a friend who is, as well as seems,
335 good; and that he who seems only, and is not good, only seems to be and
is not a friend; and of an enemy the same may be said.

You would argue that the good are our friends and the bad our enemies?

Yes.

And instead of saying simply as we did at first, that it is just to do good to our friends and harm to our enemies, we should further say: It is just to do good to our friends when they are good and harm to our enemies when they are evil?

Yes, that appears to me to be the truth.

But ought the just to injure any one at all?

Undoubtedly he ought to injure those who are both wicked and his enemies.

When horses are injured, are they improved or deteriorated?

The latter.

Deteriorated, that is to say, in the good qualities of horses, not of dogs?

Yes, of horses.

And dogs are deteriorated in the good qualities of dogs, and not of horses?

Of course.

And will not men who are injured be deteriorated in that which is the proper virtue of man?

Certainly.

And that human virtue is justice?

To be sure.

Then men who are injured are of necessity made unjust?

That is the result.

But can the musician by his art make men unmusical?

Certainly not.

Or the horseman by his art make them bad horsemen?

Impossible.

And can the just by justice make men unjust, or speaking generally, can the good by virtue make them bad?

Assuredly not.

Any more than heat can produce cold?

It cannot.

Or drought moisture?

Clearly not.

Nor can the good harm any one?

Impossible.

And the just is the good?

Certainly.

Then to injure a friend or any one else is not the act of a just man, but of the opposite, who is the unjust?

I think that what you say is quite true, Socrates.

Then if a man says that justice consists in the repayment of debts, and that good is the debt which a man owes to his friends, and evil the debt which he owes to his enemies, -- to say this is not wise; for it is not true, if, as has been clearly shown, the injuring of another can be in no case just.

I agree with you, said Polemarchus.

Then you and I are prepared to take up arms against any one who attributes such a saying to Simonides or Bias or Pittacus, or any other wise man or seer?

I am quite ready to do battle at your side, he said.

Shall I tell you whose I believe the saying to be? 336

Whose?

I believe that Periander or Perdiccas or Xerxes or Ismenias the Theban,or some other rich and mighty man, who had a great opinion of his own power, was the first to say that justice is 'doing good to your friends and harm to your enemies.'

Most true, he said.

Yes, I said; but if this definition of justice also breaks down, what other can be offered?

Several times in the course of the discussion Thrasymachus had made an attempt to get the argument into his own hands, and had been put down by the rest of the company, who wanted to hear the end. But when Polemarchus and I had done speaking and there was a pause, he could no longer hold his peace; and, gathering himself up, he came at us like a wild beast, seeking to devour us. We were quite panic-stricken at the sight of him.

He roared out to the whole company: What folly, Socrates, has taken possession of you all? And why, sillybillies, do you knock under to one another? I say that if you want really to know what justice is, you should not only ask but answer, and you should not seek honour to yourself from the refutation of an opponent, but have your own answer; for there is many a one who can ask and cannot answer. And now I will not have you say that justice is duty or advantage or profit or gain or interest, for this sort of nonsense will not do for me; I must have clearness and accuracy.

I was panic-stricken at his words, and could not look at him without trembling. Indeed I believe that if I had not fixed my eye upon him, I should have been struck dumb: but when I saw his fury rising, I looked at him first, and was therefore able to reply to him.

Thrasymachus, I said, with a quiver, don't be hard upon us. Polemarchus and I may have been guilty of a little mistake in the argument, but I can assure you that the error was not intentional. If we were seeking for a piece of gold, you would not imagine that we were 'knocking under to one another,' and so losing our chance of finding it. And why, when we are seeking for justice, a thing more precious than many pieces of gold, do you say that we are weakly yielding to one another and not doing our utmost to get at the truth? Nay, my good friend, we are most willing and anxious to do so, but the fact is that we cannot. And if so, you people who know all things should pity us and not be angry with us.

337 How characteristic of Socrates! he replied, with a bitter laugh; -- that's your ironical style! Did I not foresee -- have I not already told you, that whatever he was asked he would refuse to answer, and try irony or any other shuffle, in order that he might avoid answering?

You are a philosopher, Thrasymachus, I replied, and well know that if you ask a person what numbers make up twelve, taking care to prohibit him whom you ask from answering twice six, or three times four, or six times two, or four times three, 'for this sort of nonsense will not do for me,' -- then obviously, if that is your way of putting the question, no one can answer you. But suppose that he were to retort, 'Thrasymachus, what do you mean? If one of these numbers which you interdict be the true answer to the question, am I falsely to say some other number which is not the right one? -- is that your meaning?' -- How would you answer him?

Just as if the two cases were at all alike! he said.

Why should they not be? I replied; and even if they are not, but only appear to be so to the person who is asked, ought he not to say what he thinks, whether you and I forbid him or not?

I presume then that you are going to make one of the interdicted answers?

I dare say that I may, notwithstanding the danger, if upon reflection I approve of any of them.

But what if I give you an answer about justice other and better, he said, than any of these? What do you deserve to have done to you?

Done to me! -- as becomes the ignorant, I must learn from the wise -- that is what I deserve to have done to me.

What, and no payment! a pleasant notion!

I will pay when I have the money, I replied.

But you have, Socrates, said Giaucon: and you, Thrasymachus, need be under no anxiety about money, for we will all make a contribution for Socrates.

Yes, he replied, and then Socrates will do as he always does -- refuse to answer himself, but take and pull to pieces the answer of some one else.

Why, my good friend, I said, how can any one answer who knows, and says that he knows, just nothing; and who, even if he has some faint notions of his own, is told by a man of authority not to utter them? The natural thing is, that the speaker should be some one like yourself who 338
professes to know and can tell what he knows. Will you then kindly answer, for the edification of the company and of myself?

Glaucon and the rest of the company joined in my request and Thrasymachus, as any one might see, was in reality eager to speak; for he thought that he had an excellent answer, and would distinguish himself. But at first he affected to insist on my answering; at length he consented to begin. Behold, he said, the wisdom of Socrates; he refuses to teach himself, and goes about learning of others, to whom he never even says Thank you.

That I learn of others, I replied, is quite true; but that I am ungrateful I wholly deny. Money I have none, and therefore I pay in praise, which is all I have; and how ready I am to praise any one who appears to me to speak well you will very soon find out when you answer; for I expect that you will answer well.

Listen, then, he said; I proclaim that justice is nothing else than the interest of the stronger. And now why do you not praise me? But of course you won't.

Let me first understand you, I replied. Justice, as you say, is the interest of the stronger. What, Thrasymachus, is the meaning of this? You cannot mean to say that because Polydamas, the pancratiast, is stronger than we are, and finds the eating of beef conducive to his bodily strength, that to eat beef is therefore equally for our good who are weaker than he is, and right and just for us?

That's abominable of you, Socrates; you take the words in the sense which is most damaging to the argument.

Not at all, my good sir, I said; I am trying to understand them; and I wish that you would be a little clearer.

Well, he said, have you never heard that forms of government differ; there are tyrannies, and there are democracies, and there are aristocracies?

Yes, I know.

And the government is the ruling power in each state?

Certainly.

And the different forms of government make laws democratical, aristocratical, tyrannical, with a view to their several interests; and these laws, which are made by them for their own interests, are the justice which they deliver to their subjects, and him who transgresses them they punish as a breaker of the law, and unjust. And that is what I mean when I say that in all states there is the same principle of justice, which is the interest of the government; and as the government must be supposed to
339 have power, the only reasonable conclusion is, that everywhere there is one principle of justice, which is the interest of the stronger.

Now I understand you, I said; and whether you are right or not I will try to discover. But let me remark, that in defining justice you have yourself used the word 'interest' which you forbade me to use. It is true, however, that in your definition the words 'of the stronger' are added.

A small addition, you must allow, he said.

Great or small, never mind about that: we must first enquire whether what you are saying is the truth. Now we are both agreed that justice is interest of some sort, but you go on to say 'of the stronger'; about this addition I am not so sure, and must therefore consider further.

Proceed.

I will; and first tell me, Do you admit that it is just for subjects to obey their rulers?

I do.

But are the rulers of states absolutely infallible, or are they sometimes liable to err?

To be sure, he replied, they are liable to err.

Then in making their laws they may sometimes make them rightly, and sometimes not?

True.

When they make them rightly, they make them agreeably to their interest; when they are mistaken, contrary to their interest; you admit that?

Yes.

And the laws which they make must be obeyed by their subjects, -- and that is what you call justice?

Doubtless.

Then justice, according to your argument, is not only obedience to the interest of the stronger but the reverse?

What is that you are saying? he asked.

I am only repeating what you are saying, I believe. But let us consider: Have we not admitted that the rulers may be mistaken about their own interest in what they command, and also that to obey them is justice? Has not that been admitted?

Yes.

Then you must also have acknowledged justice not to be for the interest of the stronger, when the rulers unintentionally command things to be done which are to their own injury. For if, as you say, justice is the obedience which the subject renders to their commands, in that case, O wisest of men, is there any escape from the conclusion that the weaker are commanded to do, not what is for the interest, but what is for the injury of the stronger?

Nothing can be clearer, Socrates, said Polemarchus.

Yes, said Cleitophon, interposing, if you are allowed to be his 340
witness.

But there is no need of any witness, said Polemarchus, for Thrasymachus himself acknowledges that rulers may sometimes command what is not their own interest, and that for subjects to obey them is justice.

Yes, Polemarchus, -- Thrasymachus said that for subjects to do what was commanded by their rulers is just.

Yes, Cleitophon, but he also said that justice is the interest of the stronger, and, while admitting both these propositions, he further acknowledged that the stronger may command the weaker who are his subjects to do what is not for his own interest; whence follows that justice is the injury quite as much as the interest of the stronger.

But, said Cleitophon, he meant by the interest of the stronger what the stronger thought to be his interest, -- this was what the weaker had to do; and this was affirmed by him to be justice.

Those were not his words, rejoined Polemarchus.

Never mind, I replied, if he now says that they are, let us accept his statement. Tell me, Thrasymachus, I said, did you mean by justice what the stronger thought to be his interest, whether really so or not?

Certainly not, he said. Do you suppose that I call him who is mistaken the stronger at the time when he is mistaken?

Yes, I said, my impression was that you did so, when you admitted that the ruler was not infallible but might be sometimes mistaken.

You argue like an informer, Socrates. Do you mean, for example, that he who is mistaken about the sick is a physician in that he is mistaken? or that he who errs in arithmetic or grammar is an arithmetician or grammarian at the time when he is making the mistake, in respect of the mistake? True, we say that the physician or arithmetician or grammarian has made a mistake, but this is only a way of speaking; for the fact is that neither the grammarian or any other person of skill ever makes a mistake in so far as he is what his name implies; they none of them err unless their skill fails them, and then they cease to be skilled artists. No artist or sage or ruler errs at the time when he is what his name implies;

though he is commonly said to err, and I adopted the common mode of speaking. But to be perfectly accurate, since you are such a lover of accuracy, we should say that the ruler, in so far as he is a ruler, is
341 unerring, and, being unerring, always commands that which is for his own interest; and the subject is required to execute his commands; and therefore, as I said at first and now repeat, justice is the interest of the stronger.

Indeed, Thrasymachus, and do I really appear to you to argue like an informer?

Certainly, he replied.

And do you suppose that I ask these questions with any design of injuring you in the argument?

Nay, he replied, 'suppose' is not the word -- I know it; but you will be found out, and by sheer force of argument you will never prevail.

I shall not make the attempt, my dear man; but to avoid any misunderstanding occurring between us in future, let me ask, in what sense do you speak of a ruler or stronger whose interest, as you were saying, he being the superior, it is just that the inferior should execute -- is he a ruler in the popular or in the strict sense of the term?

In the strictest of all senses, he said. And now cheat and play the informer if you can; I ask no quarter at your hands. But you never will be able, never.

And do you imagine, I said, that I am such a madman as to try and cheat Thrasymachus? I might as well shave a lion.

Why, he said, you made the attempt a minute ago, and you failed.

Enough, I said, of these civilities. It will be better that I should ask you a question: Is the physician, taken in that strict sense of which you are speaking, a healer of the sick or a maker of money? And remember that I am now speaking of the true physician.

A healer of the sick, he replied.

And the pilot -- that is to say, the true pilot -- is he a captain of sailors or a mere sailor?

A captain of sailors.

The circumstance that he sails in the ship is not to be taken into account; neither is he to be called a sailor; the name pilot by which he is distinguished has nothing to do with sailing, but is significant of his skill and of his authority over the sailors.

Very true, he said.

Now, I said, every art has an interest?

Certainly.

For which the art has to consider and provide?

Yes, that is the aim of art.

And the interest of any art is the perfection of it -- this and nothing else?

What do you mean?

I mean what I may illustrate negatively by the example of the body. Suppose you were to ask me whether the body is self-sufficing or has wants, I should reply: Certainly the body has wants; for the body may be ill and require to be cured, and has therefore interests to which the art of medicine ministers; and this is the origin and intention of medicine, as you will acknowledge. Am I not right?

Quite right, he replied.

But is the art of medicine or any other art faulty or deficient in any 342
quality in the same way that the eye may be deficient in sight or the ear fail of hearing, and therefore requires another art to provide for the interests of seeing and hearing -- has art in itself, I say, any similar liability to fault or defect, and does every art require another supplementary art to provide for its interests, and that another and another without end? Or have the arts to look only after their own interests? Or have they no need either of themselves or of another? -- having no faults or defects, they have no need to correct them, either by the exercise of their own art or any other; they have only to consider the interest of their subject-matter. For every art remains pure and faultless while remaining true -- that is to say, while perfect and unimpaired. Take the words in your precise sense, and tell me whether I am not right.

Yes, clearly.

Then medicine does not consider the interest of medicine, but the interest of the body?

True, he said.

Nor does the art of horsemanship consider the interests of the art of horsemanship, but the interests of the horse; neither do any other arts care for themselves, for they have no needs; they care only for that which is the subject of their art?

True, he said.

But surely, Thrasymachus, the arts are the superiors and rulers of their own subjects?

To this he assented with a good deal of reluctance.

Then, I said, no science or art considers or enjoins the interest of the stronger or superior, but only the interest of the subject and weaker?

He made an attempt to contest this proposition also, but finally acquiesced.

Then, I continued, no physician, in so far as he is a physician, considers his own good in what he prescribes, but the good of his patient;

for the true physician is also a ruler having the human body as a subject, and is not a mere money-maker; that has been admitted?

Yes.

And the pilot likewise, in the strict sense of the term, is a ruler of sailors and not a mere sailor?

That has been admitted.

And such a pilot and ruler will provide and prescribe for the interest of the sailor who is under him, and not for his own or the ruler's interest?

He gave a reluctant 'Yes.'

Then, I said, Thrasymachus, there is no one in any rule who, in so far as he is a ruler, considers or enjoins what is for his own interest, but always what is for the interest of his subject or suitable to his art; to that he looks, and that alone he considers in everything which he says and does.

343 When we had got to this point in the argument, and every one saw that the definition of justice had been completely upset, Thrasymachus, instead of replying to me, said: Tell me, Socrates, have you got a nurse?

Why do you ask such a question, I said, when you ought rather to be answering?

Because she leaves you to snivel, and never wipes your nose: she has not even taught you to know the shepherd from the sheep.

What makes you say that? I replied.

Because you fancy that the shepherd or neatherd fattens or tends the sheep or oxen with a view to their own good and not to the good of himself or his master; and you further imagine that the rulers of states, if they are true rulers, never think of their subjects as sheep, and that they are not studying their own advantage day and night. Oh, no; and so entirely astray are you in your ideas about the just and unjust as not even to know that justice and the just are in reality another's good; that is to say, the interest of the ruler and the stronger, and the loss of the subject and servant; and injustice the opposite; for the unjust is lord over the truly simple and just: he is the stronger, and his subjects do what is for his interest, and minister to his happiness, which is very far from being their own. Consider further, most foolish Socrates, that the just is always a loser in comparison with the unjust. First of all, in private contracts: wherever the unjust is the partner of the just you will find that, when the partnership is dissolved, the unjust man has always more and the just less. Secondly, in their dealings with the State: when there is an income-tax, the just man will pay more and the unjust man on the same amount of income; and when there is anything to be received the one gains nothing and the other much. Observe also what happens when they take an office; there is the just man neglecting his affairs and perhaps

suffering other losses, and getting nothing out of the public, because he is just; moreover he is hated by his friends and acquaintance for refusing
to serve them in unlawful ways. But all this is reversed in the case of the 344
unjust man. I am speaking, as before, of injustice on a large scale in which the advantage of the unjust is more apparent; and my meaning will be most clearly seen if we turn to that highest form of injustice in which the criminal is the happiest of men, and the sufferers or those who refuse to do injustice are the most miserable -- that is to say tyranny, which by fraud and force takes away the property of others, not little by little but wholesale; comprehending in one, things sacred as well as profane, private and public; for which acts of wrong, if he were detected perpetrating any one of them singly, he would be punished and incur great disgrace -- they who do such wrong in particular cases are called robbers of temples, and man-stealers and burglars and swindlers and thieves. But when a man besides taking away the money of the citizens has made slaves of them, then, instead of these names of reproach, he is termed happy and blessed, not only by the citizens but by all who hear of his having achieved the consummation of injustice. For mankind censure injustice, fearing that they may be the victims of it and not because they shrink from committing it. And thus, as I have shown, Socrates, injustice, when on a sufficient scale, has more strength and freedom and mastery than justice; and, as I said at first, justice is the interest of the stronger, whereas injustice is a man's own profit and interest.

Thrasymachus, when he had thus spoken, having, like a bathman, deluged our ears with his words, had a mind to go away. But the company would not let him; they insisted that he should remain and defend his position; and I myself added my own humble request that he would not leave us. Thrasymachus, I said to him, excellent man, how suggestive are your remarks! And are you going to run away before you have fairly taught or learned whether they are true or not? Is the attempt to determine the way of man's life so small a matter in your eyes -- to determine how life may be passed by each one of us to the greatest advantage?

And do I differ from you, he said, as to the importance of the enquiry?

You appear rather, I replied, to have no care or thought about us, Thrasymachus -- whether we live better or worse from not knowing what
you say you know, is to you a matter of indifference. Prithee, friend, do 345
not keep your knowledge to yourself; we are a large party; and any benefit which you confer upon us will be amply rewarded. For my own part I openly declare that I am not convinced, and that I do not believe injustice to be more gainful than justice, even if uncontrolled and allowed to have free play. For, granting that there may be an unjust man who is able to

commit injustice either by fraud or force, still this does not convince me of the superior advantage of injustice, and there may be others who are in the same predicament with myself. Perhaps we may be wrong; if so, you in your wisdom should convince us that we are mistaken in preferring justice to injustice.

And how am I to convince you, he said, if you are not already convinced by what I have just said; what more can I do for you? Would you have me put the proof bodily into your souls?

Heaven forbid! I said; I would only ask you to be consistent; or, if you change, change openly and let there be no deception. For I must remark, Thrasymachus, if you will recall what was previously said, that although you began by defining the true physician in an exact sense, you did not observe a like exactness when speaking of the shepherd; you thought that the shepherd as a shepherd tends the sheep not with a view to their own good, but like a mere diner or banquetter with a view to the pleasures of the table; or, again, as a trader for a sale in the market, and not as a shepherd. Yet surely the art of the shepherd is concerned only with the good of his subjects; he has only to provide the best for them, since the perfection of the art is already ensured whenever all the requirements of it are satisfied. And that was what I was saying just now about the ruler. I conceived that the art of the ruler, considered as ruler, whether in a state or in private life, could only regard the good of his flock or subjects; whereas you seem to think that the rulers in states, that is to say, the true rulers, like being in authority.

Think! Nay, I am sure of it.

Then why in the case of lesser offices do men never take them willingly without payment, unless under the idea that they govern for the
346 advantage not of themselves but of others? Let me ask you a question: Are not the several arts different, by reason of their each having a separate function? And, my dear illustrious friend, do say what you think, that we may make a little progress.

Yes, that is the difference, he replied.

And each art gives us a particular good and not merely a general one -- medicine, for example, gives us health; navigation, safety at sea, and so on?

Yes, he said.

And the art of payment has the special function of giving pay: but we do not confuse this with other arts, any more than the art of the pilot is to be confused with the art of medicine, because the health of the pilot may be improved by a sea voyage. You would not be inclined to say, would you, that navigation is the art of medicine, at least if we are to adopt your exact use of language?

Certainly not.

Or because a man is in good health when he receives pay you would not say that the art of payment is medicine?

I should say not.

Nor would you say that medicine is the art of receiving pay because a man takes fees when he is engaged in healing?

Certainly not.

And we have admitted, I said, that the good of each art is specifically confined to the art?

Yes.

Then, if there be any good which all artists have in common, that is to be attributed to something of which they all have the common use?

True, he replied.

And when the artist is benefited by receiving pay the advantage is gained by an additional use of the art of pay, which is not the art professed by him?

He gave a reluctant assent to this.

Then the pay is not derived by the several artists from their respective arts. But the truth is, that while the art of medicine gives health, and the art of the builder builds a house, another art attends them which is the art of pay. The various arts may be doing their own business and benefiting that over which they preside, but would the artist receive any benefit from his art unless he were paid as well?

I suppose not.

But does he therefore confer no benefit when he works for nothing?

Certainly, he confers a benefit.

Then now, Thrasymachus, there is no longer any doubt that neither arts nor governments provide for their own interests; but, as we were before saying, they rule and provide for the interests of their subjects who are the weaker and not the stronger -- to their good they attend and not to the good of the superior. And this is the reason, my dear Thrasymachus, why, as I was just now saying, no one is willing to govern; because no one likes to take in hand the reformation of evils which are not his concern
without remuneration. For, in the execution of his work, and in giving 347
his orders to another, the true artist does not regard his own interest, but always that of this subjects; and therefore in order that rulers may be willing to rule, they must be paid in one of three modes of payment, money, or honour, or a penalty for refusing.

What do you mean, Socrates? said Glaucon. The first two modes of payment are intelligible enough, but what the penalty is I do not understand, or how a penalty can be a payment.

You mean that you do not understand the nature of this payment which to the best men is the great inducement to rule? Of course you know that ambition and avarice are held to be, as indeed they are, a disgrace?

Very true.

And for this reason, I said, money and honour have no attraction for them; good men do not wish to be openly demanding payment for governing and so to get the name of hirelings, nor by secretly helping themselves out of the public revenues to get the name of thieves. And not being ambitious they do not care about honour. Wherefore necessity must be laid upon them, and they must be induced to serve from the fear of punishment. And this, as I imagine, is the reason why the forwardness to take office, instead of waiting to be compelled, has been deemed dishonourable. Now the worst part of the punishment is that he who refuses to rule is liable to be ruled by one who is worse than himself. And the fear of this, as I conceive, induces the good to take office, not because they would, but because they cannot help -- not under the idea that they are going to have any benefit or enjoyment themselves, but as a necessity, and because they are not able to commit the task of ruling to any one who is better than themselves, or indeed as good. For there is reason to think that if a city were composed entirely of good men, then to avoid office would be as much an object of contention as to attain office is at present; then we should have plain proof that the true ruler is not meant by nature to regard his own interest, but that of his subjects; and every one who knew this would choose rather to receive a benefit from another man than to have the trouble of conferring one. So far am I from agreeing with Thrasymachus that justice is the interest of the stronger. This latter question need not be further discussed at present; but when Thrasymachus says that the life of the unjust is more advantageous than that of the just, his new statement appears to me to be of a far more serious character. Which of us has spoken truly? And which sort of life, Glaucon, do you prefer?

I for my part deem the life of the just to be the more advantageous, he answered.

348 Did you hear all the advantages of the unjust which Thrasymachus was rehearsing?

Yes, I heard him, he replied, but he has not convinced me.

Then shall we try to find some way of convincing him, if we can, that he is saying what is not true?

Most certainly, he replied.

If, I said, he makes a set speech and we make another recounting all the advantages of being just, and he answers and we rejoin, there must be a numbering and measuring of the goods which are claimed on either side, and in the end we shall want judges to decide; but if we proceed in our enquiry as we lately did, by making admissions to one another, we shall unite the offices of judge and advocate in our own persons.

Very good, he said. And which method do I understand you to prefer? I said.

That which you propose.

Well, then, Thrasymachus, I said, suppose you begin at the beginning and answer me. You say that perfect injustice is more gainful than perfect justice?

Yes, that is what I say, and I have given you my reasons.

And what is your view about them? Would you call one of them virtue and the other vice?

Certainly.

I suppose that you would call justice virtue and injustice vice?

What a charming notion! So likely too, seeing that I affirm injustice to be profitable and justice not.

What else then would you say?

The opposite, he replied.

And would you call justice vice?

No, I would rather say sublime simplicity.

Then would you call injustice malignity.

No; I would rather say discretion.

And do the unjust appear to you to be wise and good?

Yes, he said; at any rate those of them who are able to be perfectly unjust, and who have the power of subdoing states and nations; but perhaps you imagine me to be talking of cutpurses. Even this profession if undetected has advantages, though they are not to be compared with those of which I was just now speaking.

I do not think that I misapprehend your meaning. Thrasymachus, I replied; but still I cannot hear without amazement that you class injustice with wisdom and virtue, and justice with the opposite.

Certainly I do so class them.

Now, I said, you are on more substantial and almost unanswerable ground; for if the injustice which you were maintaining to be profitable had been admitted by you as by others to be vice and deformity, an 349
answer might have been given to you on received principles; but now I perceive that you will call injustice honourable and strong, and to the unjust you will attribute all the qualities which were attributed by us before to the just, seeing that you do not hesitate to rank injustice with wisdom and virtue.

You have guessed most infallibly, he replied.

Then I certainly ought not to shrink from going through with the argument so long as I have reason to think that you, Thrasymachus, are speaking your real mind; for I do believe that you are now in earnest and are not amusing yourself at our expense.

I may be in earnest or not, but what is that to you? -- to refute the argument is your business.

Very true, I said; that is what I have to do: But will you be so good as answer yet one more question? Does the just man try to gain any advantage over the just?

Far otherwise; if he did he would not be the simple amusing creature which he is.

And would he try to go beyond just action?

He would not.

And how would he regard the attempt to gain an advantage over the unjust; would that be considered by him as just or unjust?

He would think it just, and would try to gain the advantage; but he would not be able.

Whether he would or would not be able, I said, is not to the point. My question is only whether the just man, while refusing to have more than another just man, would wish and claim to have more than the unjust?

Yes, he would.

And what of the unjust -- does he claim to have more than the just man and to do more than is just?

Of course, he said, for he claims to have more than all men.

And the unjust man will strive and struggle to obtain more than the unjust man or action, in order that he may have more than all?

True.

We may put the matter thus, I said -- the just does not desire more than his like but more than his unlike, whereas the unjust desires more than both his like and his unlike?

Nothing, he said, can be better than that statement.

And the unjust is good and wise, and the just is neither?

Good again, he said.

And is not the unjust like the wise and good and the just unlike them?

Of course, he said, he who is of a certain nature, is like those who are of a certain nature; he who is not, not.

Each of them, I said, is such as his like is?

Certainly, he replied.

Very good, Thrasymachus, I said; and now to take the case of the arts: you would admit that one man is a musician and another not a musician?

Yes.

And which is wise and which is foolish?

Clearly the musician is wise, and he who is not a musician is foolish.

And he is good in as far as he is wise, and bad in as far as he is foolish?

Yes.

And you would say the same sort of thing of the physician?

Yes.

And do you think, my excellent friend, that a musician when he adjusts the lyre would desire or claim to exceed or go beyond a musician in the tightening and loosening the strings?

I do not think that he would.

But he would claim to exceed the non-musician?

Of course.

And what would you say of the physician? In prescribing meats and 350
drinks would he wish to go beyond another physician or beyond the practice of medicine?

He would not.

But he would wish to go beyond the non-physician?

Yes.

And about knowledge and ignorance in general; see whether you think that any man who has knowledge ever would wish to have the choice of saying or doing more than another man who has knowledge. Would he not rather say or do the same as his like in the same case?

That, I suppose, can hardly be denied.

And what of the ignorant? would he not desire to have more than either the knowing or the ignorant?

I dare say.

And the knowing is wise?

Yes.

And the wise is good?

True.

Then the wise and good will not desire to gain more than his like, but more than his unlike and opposite?

I suppose so.

Whereas the bad and ignorant will desire to gain more than both?

Yes.

But did we not say, Thrasymachus, that the unjust goes beyond both his like and unlike? Were not these your words?

They were.

And you also said that the just will not go beyond his like but his unlike?

Yes.

Then the just is like the wise and good, and the unjust like the evil and ignorant?

That is the inference.

And each of them is such as his like is?

That was admitted.

Then the just has turned out to be wise and good and the unjust evil and ignorant.

Thrasymachus made all these admissions, not fluently, as I repeat them, but with extreme reluctance; it was a hot summer's day, and the perspiration poured from him in torrents; and then I saw what I had never seen before, Thrasymachus blushing. As we were now agreed that justice was virtue and wisdom, and injustice vice and ignorance, I proceeded to another point:

Well, I said, Thrasymachus, that matter is now settled; but were we not also saying that injustice had strength; do you remember?

Yes, I remember, he said, but do not suppose that I approve of what you are saying or have no answer; if however I were to answer, you would be quite certain to accuse me of haranguing; therefore either permit me to have my say out, or if you would rather ask, do so, and I will answer 'Very good,' as they say to storytelling old women, and will nod 'Yes' and 'No.'

Certainly not, I said, if contrary to your real opinion.

Yes, he said, I will, to please you, since you will not let me speak. What else would you have?

Nothing in the world, I said; and if you are so disposed I will ask and you shall answer.

Proceed.

Then I will repeat the question which I asked before, in order that
351 our examination of the relative nature of justice and injustice may be carried on regularly. A statement was made that injustice is stronger and more powerful than justice, but now justice, having been identified with wisdom and virtue, is easily shown to be stronger than injustice, if injustice is ignorance; this can no longer be questioned by any one. But I want to view the matter, Thrasymachus, in a different way: You would not deny that a state may be unjust and may be unjustly attempting to enslave other states, or may have already enslaved them, and may be holding many of them in subjection?

True, he replied; and I will add that the best and most perfectly unjust state will be most likely to do so.

I know, I said, that such was your position; but what I would further consider is, whether this power which is possessed by the superior state can exist or be exercised without justice or only with justice.

If you are right in your view, and justice is wisdom, then only with justice; but if I am right, then without justice.

I am delighted, Thrasymachus, to see you not only nodding assent and dissent, but making answers which are quite excellent.

That is out of civility to you, he replied.

You are very kind, I said; and would you have the goodness also to inform me, whether you think that a state, or an army, or a band of robbers and thieves, or any other gang of evil-doers could act at all if they injured one another?

No indeed, he said, they could not.

But if they abstained from injuring one another, then they might act together better?

Yes.

And this is because injustice creates divisions and hatreds and fighting, and justice imparts harmony and friendship; is not that true, Thrasymachus?

I agree, he said, because I do not wish to quarrel with you.

How good of you, I said; but I should like to know also whether injustice, having this tendency to arouse hatred, wherever existing, among slaves or among freemen, will not make them hate one another and set them at variance and render them incapable of common action?

Certainly.

And even if injustice be found in two only, will they not quarrel and fight, and become enemies to one another and to the just?

They will.

And suppose injustice abiding in a single person, would your wisdom say that she loses or that she retains her natural power?

Let us assume that she retains her power.

Yet is not the power which injustice exercises of such a nature that wherever she takes up her abode, whether in a city, in an army, in a
family, or in any other body, that body is, to begin with, rendered 352
incapable of united action by reason of sedition and distraction; and does it not become its own enemy and at variance with all that opposes it, and with the just? Is not this the case?

Yes, certainly.

And is not injustice equally fatal when existing in a single person; in the first place rendering him incapable of action because he is not at unity with himself, and in the second place making him an enemy to himself and the just? Is not that true, Thrasymachus?

Yes.

And O my friend, I said, surely the gods are just?

Granted that they are.

But if so, the unjust will be the enemy of the gods, and the just will be their friend?

Feast away in triumph, and take your fill of the argument; I will not oppose you, lest I should displease the company.

Well then, proceed with your answers, and let me have the remainder of my repast. For we have already shown that the just are clearly wiser and better and abler than the unjust, and that the unjust are incapable of common action; nay more, than to speak as we did of men who are evil acting at any time vigorously together, is not strictly true, for if they had been perfectly evil, they would have laid hands upon one another; but it is evident that there must have been some remnant of justice in them, which enabled them to combine; if there had not been they would have injured one another as well as their victims; they were but half-villains in their enterprises; for had they been whole villains, and utterly unjust, they would have been incapable of action. That, as I believe, is the truth of the matter, and not what you said at first. But whether the just have a better and happier life than the unjust is a further question which we also proposed to consider. I think that they have, and for the reasons which I have given; but still I should like to examine further, for no light matter is at stake, nothing less than the rule of human life.

Proceed.

I will proceed by asking a question: Would you not say that a horse has some end?

I should.

And the end or use of a horse or of anything would be that which could not be accomplished, or not so well accomplished, by any other thing?

I do not understand, he said.

Let me explain: Can you see, except with the eye?

Certainly not.

Or hear, except with the ear?

No.

These then may be truly said to be the ends of these organs?

They may.

353 But you can cut off a vine-branch with a dagger or with a chisel, and in many other ways?

Of course.

And yet not so well as with a pruning-hook made for the purpose?

True.

May we not say that this is the end of a pruning-hook?

We may.

Then now I think you will have no difficulty in understanding my meaning when I asked the question whether the end of anything would be that which could not be accomplished, or not so well accomplished, by any other thing?

I understand your meaning, he said, and assent.

And that to which an end is appointed has also an excellence? Need I ask again whether the eye has an end?

It has.

And has not the eye an excellence?

Yes.

And the ear has an end and an excellence also?

True.

And the same is true of all other things; they have each of them an end and a special excellence?

That is so.

Well, and can the eyes fulfil their end if they are wanting in their own proper excellence and have a defect instead?

How can they, he said, if they are blind and cannot see?

You mean to say, if they have lost their proper excellence, which is sight; but I have not arrived at that point yet. I would rather ask the question more generally, and only enquire whether the things which fulfil their ends fulfil them by their own proper excellence, and fail of fulfilling them by their own defect?

Certainly, he replied.

I might say the same of the ears; when deprived of their own proper excellence they cannot fulfil their end?

True.

And the same observation will apply to all other things?

I agree.

Well; and has not the soul an end which nothing else can fulfil? for example, to superintend and command and deliberate and the like. Are not these functions proper to the soul, and can they rightly be assigned to any other?

To no other.

And is not life to be reckoned among the ends of the soul?

Assured, he said.

And has not the soul an excellence also?

Yes.

And can she or can she not fulfil her own ends when deprived of that excellence?

She cannot.

Then an evil soul must necessarily be an evil ruler and superintendent, and the good soul a good ruler?

Yes, necessarily.

And we have admitted that justice is the excellence of the soul, and injustice the defect of the soul?

That has been admitted.

Then the just soul and the just man will live well, and the unjust man will live ill?

That is what your argument proves.

354 And he who lives well is blessed and happy, and he who lives ill the reverse of happy?

Certainly.

Then the just is happy, and the unjust miserable?

So be it.

But happiness and not misery is profitable.

Of course.

Then, my blessed Thrasymachus, injustice can never be more profitable than justice.

Let this, Socrates, he said, be your entertainment at the Bendidea.

For which I am indebted to you, I said, now that you have grown gentle towards me and have left off scolding. Nevertheless, I have not been well entertained; but that was my own fault and not yours. As an epicure snatches a taste of every dish which is successively brought to table, he not having allowed himself time to enjoy the one before, so have I gone from one subject to another without having discovered what I sought at first, the nature of justice. I left that enquiry and turned away to consider whether justice is virtue and wisdom or evil and folly; and when there arose a further question about the comparative advantages of justice and injustice, I could not refrain from passing on to that. And the result of the whole discussion has been that I know nothing at all. For I know not what justice is, and therefore I am not likely to know whether it is or is not a virtue, nor can I say whether the just man is happy or unhappy.

Book II

With these words I was thinking that I had made an end of the discussion; but the end, in truth, proved to be only a beginning. For
Gaucon, who is always the most pugnacious of men, was dissatisfied at 357
Thrasymachus' retirement; he wanted to have the battle out. So he said to me: Socrates, do you wish really to persuade us, or only to seem to have persuaded us, that to be just is always better than to be unjust?

I should wish really to persuade you, I replied, if I could.

Then you certainly have not succeeded. Let me ask you now: -- How would you arrange goods -- are there not some which we welcome for their own sakes, and independently of their consequences, as, for example, harmless pleasures and enjoyments, which delight us at the time, although nothing follows from them?

I agree in thinking that there is such a class, I replied.

Is there not also a second class of goods, such as knowledge, sight, health, which are desirable not only in themselves, but also for their results?

Certainly, I said.

And would you not recognize a third class, such as gymnastic, and the care of the sick, and the physician's art; also the various ways of money-making -- these do us good but we regard them as disagreeable; and no one would choose them for their own sakes, but only for the sake of some reward or result which flows from them?

There is, I said, this third class also. But why do you ask?

Because I want to know in which of the three classes you would place justice?

In the highest class, I replied, -- among those goods which he who 358
would be happy desires both for their own sake and for the sake of their results.

Then the many are of another mind; they think that justice is to be reckoned in the troublesome class, among goods which are to be pursued for the sake of rewards and of reputation, but in themselves are disagreeable and rather to be avoided.

I know, I said, that this is their manner of thinking, and that this was the thesis which Thrasymachus was maintaining just now, when he censured justice and praised injustice. But I am too stupid to be convinced by him.

I wish, he said, that you would hear me as well as him, and then I shall see whether you and I agree. For Thrasymachus seems to me, like a snake, to have been charmed by your voice sooner than he ought to have been; but to my mind the nature of justice and injustice have not yet been made clear. Setting aside their rewards and results, I want to know what they are in themselves, and how they inwardly work in the soul. If you please, then, I will revive the argument of Thrasymachus. And first I will speak of the nature and origin of justice according to the common view of them. Secondly, I will show that all men who practice justice do so against their will, of necessity, but not as a good. And thirdly, I will argue that there is reason in this view, for the life of the unjust is after all better far than the life of the just -- if what they say is true, Socrates, since I myself am not of their opinion. But still I acknowledge that I am perplexed when I hear the voices of Thrasymachus and myriads of others dinning in my ears; and, on the other hand, I have never yet heard the superiority of justice to injustice maintained by any one in a satisfactory way. I want to hear justice praised in respect of itself; then I shall be satisfied, and you are the person from whom I think that I am most likely to hear this; and therefore I will praise the unjust life to the utmost of my power, and my manner of speaking will indicate the manner in which I desire to hear you too praising justice and censuring injustice. Will you say whether you approve of my proposal?

Indeed I do; nor can I imagine any theme about which a man of sense would oftener wish to converse.

I am delighted, he replied, to hear you say so, and shall begin by speaking, as I proposed, of the nature and origin of justice.

They say that to do injustice is, by nature, good; to suffer injustice,evil; but that the evil is greater than the good. And so when men
359 have both done and suffered injustice and have had experience of both, not being able to avoid the one and obtain the other, they think that they had better agree among themselves to have neither; hence there arise laws and mutual covenants; and that which is ordained by law is termed by them lawful and just. This they affirm to be the origin and nature of justice; -- it is a mean or compromise, between the best of all, which is to do injustice and not be punished, and the worst of all, which is to suffer injustice without the power of retaliation; and justice, being at a middle point between the two, is tolerated not as a good, but as the lesser evil, and honoured by reason of the inability of men to do injustice. For no man who is worthy to be called a man would ever submit to such an agreement if he were able to resist; he would be mad if he did. Such is the received account, Socrates, of the nature and origin of justice.

Now that those who practise justice do so involuntarily and because they have not the power to be unjust will best appear if we imagine something of this kind: having given both to the just and the unjust power to do what they will, let us watch and see whither desire will lead them; then we shall discover in the very act the just and unjust man to be proceeding along the same road, following their interest, which all natures deem to be their good, and are only diverted into the path of justice by the force of law. The liberty which we are supposing may be most completely given to them in the form of such a power as is said to have been possessed by Gyges the ancestor of Croesus the Lydian. According to the tradition, Gyges was a shepherd in the service of the king of Lydia; there was a great storm, and an earthquake made an opening in the earth at the place where he was feeding his flock. Amazed at the sight, he descended into the opening, where, among other marvels, he beheld a hollow brazen horse, having doors, at which he stooping and looking in saw a dead body of stature, as appeared to him, more than human, and having nothing on but a gold ring; this he took from the finger of the dead and reascended. Now the shepherds met together, according to custom, that they might send their monthly report about the flocks to the king; into their assembly he came having the ring on his finger, and as he was sitting among them he chanced to turn the collet of the ring inside his hand, when instantly he became invisible to the rest of the company and they began to speak of him as if he were no longer present. He was astonished at this, and again touching the ring he turned the collet out- 360
wards and reappeared; he made several trials of the ring, and always with the same result -- when he turned the collet inwards he became invisible, when outwards he reappeared. Whereupon he contrived to be chosen one of the messengers who were sent to the court; where as soon as he arrived he seduced the queen, and with her help conspired against the king and slew him, and took the kingdom. Suppose now that there were two such magic rings, and the just put on one of them and the unjust the other; no man can be imagined to be of such an iron nature that he would stand fast in justice. No man would keep his hands off what was not his own when he could safely take what he liked out of the market, or go into houses and lie with any one at his pleasure, or kill or release from prison whom he would, and in all respects be like a God among men. Then the actions of the just would be as the actions of the unjust; they would both come at last to the same point. And this we may truly affirm to be a great proof that a man is just, not willingly or because he thinks that justice is any good to him individually, but of necessity, for wherever any one thinks that he can safely be unjust, there he is unjust. For all men believe in their hearts that injustice is far more profitable to the

individual than justice, and he who argues as I have been supposing, will say that they are right. If you could imagine any one obtaining this power of becoming invisible, and never doing any wrong or touching what was another's, he would be thought by the lookers-on to be a most wretched idiot, although they would praise him to one another's faces, and keep up appearances with one another from a fear that they too might suffer injustice. Enough of this.

Now, if we are to form a real judgment of the life of the just and unjust, we must isolate them; there is no other way; and how is the isolation to be effected? I answer: Let the unjust man be entirely unjust, and the just man entirely just; nothing to be taken away from either of them, and both are to be perfectly furnished for the work of their respective lives. First, let the unjust be like other distinguished masters of craft; like
361 the skilful pilot or physician, who knows intuitively his own powers and keeps within their limits, and who, if he fails at any point, is able to recover himself. So let the unjust make his unjust attempts in the right way, and lie hidden if he means to be great in his injustice (he who is found out is nobody): for the highest reach of injustice is, to be deemed just when you are not. Therefore I say that in the perfectly unjust man we must assume the most perfect injustice; there is to be no deduction, but we must allow him, while doing the most unjust acts, to have acquired the greatest reputation for justice. If he have taken a false step he must be able to recover himself; he must be one who can speak with effect, if any of his deeds come to light, and who can force his way where force is required by his courage and strength, and command of money and friends. And at his side let us place the just man in his nobleness and simplicity, wishing, as Aeschylus says, to be and not to seem good. There must be no seeming, for if he seem to be just he will be honoured and rewarded, and then we shall not know whether he is just for the sake of justice or for the sake of honours and rewards; therefore, let him be clothed in justice only, and have no other covering; and he must be imagined in a state of life the opposite of the former. Let him be the best of men, and let him be thought the worst; then he will have been put to the proof; and we shall see whether he will be affected by the fear of infamy and its consequences. And let him continue thus to the hour of death; being just and seeming to be unjust. When both have reached the uttermost extreme, the one of justice and the other of injustice, let judgment be given which of them is the happier of the two.

Heavens! my dear Glaucon, I said, how energetically you polish them up for the decision, first one and then the other, as if they were two statues.

I do my best, he said. And now that we know what they are like there is no difficulty in tracing out the sort of life which awaits either of them. This I will proceed to describe; but as you may think the description a little too coarse, I ask you to suppose, Socrates, that the words which follow are not mine. -- Let me put them into the mouths of the eulogists of injustice: They will tell you that the just man who is thought unjust will be scourged, racked, bound -- will have his eyes burnt out; and, at last, after suffering every kind of evil, he will be impaled: Then he will understand that he ought to seem only, and not to be, just; the words of
Aeschylus may be more truly spoken of the unjust than of the just. For 362
the unjust is pursuing a reality; he does not live with a view to appearances -- he wants to be really unjust and not to seem only: --

> 'His mind has a soil deep and fertile,
> Out of which spring his prudent counsels.' [Seven against Thebes, 574].

In the first place, he is thought just, and therefore bears rule in the city; he can marry whom he will, and give in marriage to whom he will; also he can trade and deal where he likes, and always to his own advantage because he has no misgivings about injustice; and at every contest, whether in public or private, he gets the better of his antagonists, and gains at their expense, and is rich, and out of his gains he can benefit his friends, and harm his enemies; moreover, he can offer sacrifices, and dedicate gifts to the gods abundantly and magnificently, and can honour the gods or any man whom he wants to honour in a far better style than the just, and therefore he is likely to be dearer than they are to the gods. And thus, Socrates, gods and men are said to unite in making the life of the unjust better than the life of the just.

I was going to say something in answer to Glaucon, when Adeimantus, his brother, interposed: Socrates, he said, you do not suppose that there is nothing more to be urged?

Why, what else is there? I answered.

The strongest point of all has not been even mentioned, he replied.

Well, then, according to the proverb, 'Let brother help brother' -- if he fails in any part do you assist him; although I must confess that Glaucon has already said quite enough to lay me in the dust, and take from me the power of helping justice.

Nonsense, he replied. But let me add something more: There is another side to Glaucon's argument about the praise and censure of justice

and injustice, which is equally required in order to bring out what I
363 believe to be his meaning. Parents and tutors are always telling their sons and their wards that they are to be just; but why? not for the sake of justice, but for the sake of character and reputation; in the hope of obtaining for him who is reputed just some of those offices, marriages, and the like which Glaucon has enumerated among the advantages accruing to the unjust from the reputation of justice. More, however, is made of appearances by this class of persons than by the others; for they throw in the good opinion of the gods, and will tell you of a shower of benefits which the heavens, as they say, rain upon the pious; and this accords with the testimony of the noble Hesiod and Homer, the first of whom says, that the gods make the oaks of the just --

> 'To bear acorns at their summit, and bees in the middle;
> And the sheep are bowed down with the weight of their fleeces,' [Hesiod, Works and Days, 230]

and many other blessings of a like kind are provided for them. And Homer has a very similar strain; for he speaks of one whose fame is --

> 'As the fame of some blameless king who, like a god,
> Maintains justice; to whom the black earth brings forth
> Wheat and barley, whose trees are bowed with fruit,
> And his sheep never fail to bear, and the sea gives him fish.' [Homer, Od. xix. 109]

Still grander are the gifts of heaven which Musaeus and his son [Eumolpus] vouch safe to the just; they take them down into the world below, where they have the saints lying on couches at a feast, everlastingly drunk, crowned with garlands; their idea seems to be that an immortality of drunkenness is the highest meed of virtue. Some extend their rewards yet further; the posterity, as they say, of the faithful and just shall survive to the third and fourth generation. This is the style in which they praise justice. But about the wicked there is another strain; they bury them in a slough in Hades, and make them carry water in a sieve; also while they are yet living they bring them to infamy, and inflict upon them the punishments which Glaucon described as the portion of the just who are reputed to be unjust; nothing else does their invention supply. Such is their manner of praising the one and censuring the other.

Once more, Socrates, I will ask you to consider another way of speaking about justice and injustice, which is not confined to the poets,

but is found in prose writers. The universal voice of mankind is always 364
declaring that justice and virtue are honourable, but grievous and toilsome; and that the pleasures of vice and injustice are easy of attainment, and are only censured by law and opinion. They say also that honesty is for the most part less profitable than dishonesty; and they are quite ready to call wicked men happy, and to honour them both in public and private when they are rich or in any other way influential, while they despise and overlook those who may be weak and poor, even though acknowledging them to be better than the others. But most extraordinary of all is their mode of speaking about virtue and the gods: they say that the gods apportion calamity and misery to many good men, and good and happiness to the wicked. And mendicant prophets go to rich men's doors and persuade them that they have a power committed to them by the gods of making an atonement for a man's own or his ancestor's sins by sacrifices or charms, with rejoicings and feasts; and they promise to harm an enemy, whether just or unjust, at a small cost; with magic arts and incantations binding heaven, as they say, to execute their will. And the poets are the authorities to whom they appeal, now smoothing the path of vice with the words of Hesiod --

> 'Vice may be had in abundance without trouble; the way is smooth and her dwelling-place is near. But before virtue the gods have set toil.' [Hesiod, Works and Days, 287]

and a tedious and uphill road: then citing Homer as a witness that the gods may be influenced by men; for he also says: --

> 'The gods, too, may be turned from their purpose; and men pray to them and avert their wrath by sacrifices and soothing entreaties, and by libations and the odour of fat, when they have sinned and transgressed.' [Homer, Iliad, ix. 493]

And they produce a host of books written by Musaeus and Orpheus, who were children of the Moon and the Muses -- that is what they say -- according to which they perform their ritual, and persuade not only individuals, but whole cities, that expiations and atonements for sin may be made by sacrifices and amusements which fill a vacant hour, and are equally at the service of the living and the dead; the latter sort they call
mysteries, and they redeem us from the pains of hell, but if we neglect 365
them no one knows what awaits us.

He proceeded: And now when the young hear all this said about virtue and vice, and the way in which gods and men regard them, how are their minds likely to be affected, my dear Socrates, -- those of them, I mean, who are quickwitted, and, like bees on the wing, light on every flower, and from all that they hear are prone to draw conclusions as to what manner of persons they should be and in what way they should walk if they would make the best of life? Probably the youth will say to himself in the words of Pindar --

> 'Can I by justice or by crooked ways of deceit ascend a loftier tower which may be a fortress to me all my days?'

For what men say is that, if I am really just and am not also thought just, profit there is none, but the pain and loss on the other hand are unmistakeable. But if, though unjust, I acquire the reputation of justice, a heavenly life is promised to me. Since then, as philosophers prove, appearance tyrannizes over truth and is lord of happiness, to appearance I must devote myself. I will describe around me a picture and shadow of virtue to be the vestibule and exterior of my house; behind I will trail the subtle and crafty fox, as Archilochus, greatest of sages, recommends. But I hear some one exclaiming that the concealment of wickedness is often difficult: to which I answer, Nothing great is easy. Nevertheless, the argument indicates this, if we would be happy, to be the path along which we should proceed. With a view to concealment we will establish secret brotherhoods and political clubs. And there are professors of rhetoric who teach the art of persuading courts and assemblies; and so partly by persuasion and partly by force, I shall make unlawful gains and not be punished. Still I hear a voice saying that the gods cannot be deceived, neither can they be compelled. But what if there are no gods? or, suppose them to have no care of human things -- why in either case should we mind about concealment? And even if there are gods, and they do care about us, yet we know of them only from tradition and the genealogies of the poets; and these are the very persons who say that they may be influenced and turned by 'sacrifices and soothing entreaties and by offerings.' Let us be consistent then, and believe both or neither. If the
366 poets speak truly, why then we had better be unjust, and offer of the
fruits of injustice; for if we are just, although we may escape the vengeance of heaven, we shall lose the gains of injustice; but, if we are unjust, we shall keep the gains, and by our sinning and praying, and praying and sinning, the gods will be propitiated, and we shall not be punished. 'But there is a world below in which either we or our posterity will suffer

for our unjust deeds.' Yes, my friend, will be the reflection, but there are mysteries and atoning deities, and these have great power. That is what mighty cities declare; and the children of the gods, who were their poets and prophets, bear a like testimony.

On what principle, then, shall we any longer choose justice rather than the worst injustice? when, if we only unite the latter with a deceitful regard to appearances, we shall fare to our mind both with gods and men, in life and after death, as the most numerous and the highest authorities tell us. Knowing all this, Socrates, how can a man who has any superiority of mind or person or rank or wealth, be willing to honour justice; or indeed to refrain from laughing when he hears justice praised? And even if there should be some one who is able to disprove the truth of my words, and who is satisfied that justice is best, still he is not angry with the unjust, but is very ready to forgive them, because he also knows that men are not just of their own free will; unless peradventure, there be some one whom the divinity within him may have inspired with a hatred of injustice, or who has attained knowledge of the truth -- but no other man. He only blames injustice who, owing to cowardice or age or some weakness, has not the power of being unjust. And this is proved by the fact that when he obtains the power, he immediately becomes unjust as far as he can be.

The cause of all this, Socrates, was indicated by us at the beginning of the argument, when my brother and I told you how astonished we were to find that of all the professing panegyrists of justice -- beginning with the ancient heroes of whom any memorial has been preserved to us, and ending with the men of our own time -- no one has ever blamed injustice or praised justice except with a view to the glories, honours, and benefits which flow from them. No one has ever adequately described either in verse or prose the true essential nature of either of them abiding in the soul, and invisible to any human or divine eye; or shown that of all the things of a man's soul which he has within him, justice is the greatest good, and injustice the greatest evil. Had this been the universal strain, 367
had you sought to persuade us of this from our youth upwards, we should not have been on the watch to keep one another from doing wrong, but every one would have been his own watchman, because afraid, if he did wrong, of harbouring in himself the greatest of evils. I dare say that Thrasymachus and others would seriously hold the language which I have been merely repeating, and words even stronger than these about justice and injustice, grossly, as I conceive, perverting their true nature. But I speak in this vehement manner, as I must frankly confess to you, because I want to hear from you the opposite side; and I would ask you to show

not only the superiority which justice has over injustice, but what effect they have on the possessor of them which makes the one to be a good and the other an evil to him. And please, as Glaucon requested of you, to exclude reputation; for unless you take away from each of them his true reputation and add on the false, we shall say that you do not praise justice, but the appearance of it; we shall think that you are only exhorting us to keep injustice dark, and that you really agree with Thrasymachus in thinking that justice is another's good and the interest of the stronger, and that injustice is a man's own profit and interest, though injurious to the weaker. Now as you have admitted that justice is one of that highest class of goods which are desired indeed for their results, but in a far greater degree for their own sakes -- like sight or hearing or knowledge or health, or any other real and natural and not merely conventional good -- I would ask you in your praise of justice to regard one point only: I mean the essential good and evil which justice and injustice work in the possessors of them. Let others praise justice and censure injustice, magnifying the rewards and honours of the one and abusing the other; that is a manner of arguing which, coming from them, I am ready to tolerate, but from you who have spent your whole life in the consideration of this question, unless I hear the contrary from your own lips, I expect something better. And therefore, I say, not only prove to us that justice is better than injustice, but show what they either of them do to the possessor of them, which makes the one to be a good and the other an evil, whether seen or unseen by gods and men.

I had always admired the genius of Glaucon and Adeimantus, but on hearing these words I was quite delighted, and said: Sons of an
368 illustrious father, that was not a bad beginning of the Elegiac verses which the admirer of Glaucon made in honour of you after you had distinguished yourselves at the battle of Megara: --

'Sons of Ariston,' he sang, 'divine offspring of an illustrious hero.'

The epithet is very appropriate, for there is something truly divine in being able to argue as you have done for the superiority of injustice, and remaining unconvinced by your own arguments. And I do believe that you are not convinced -- this I infer from your general character, for had I judged only from your speeches I should have mistrusted you. But now, the greater my confidence in you, the greater is my difficulty in knowing what to say. For I am in a strait between two; on the one hand I feel that I am unequal to the task; and my inability is brought home to me by the fact that you were not satisfied with the answer which I made to Thrasymachus, proving, as I thought, the superiority which justice has over injustice. And yet I cannot refuse to help, while breath and speech remain to me; I am afraid that there would be an impiety in being present when justice is evil spoken of and not lifting up a hand in her defence. And therefore I had best give such help as I can.

. . . .

Book IX

Last of all comes the tyrannical man; about whom we have once more
to ask, how is he formed out of the democratical? and how does he live, 571
in happiness or in misery?

Yes, he said, he is the only one remaining.

There is, however, I said, a previous question which remains unanswered.

What question?

I do not think that we have adequately determined the nature and number of the appetites, and until this is accomplished the enquiry will always be confused.

Well, he said, it is not too late to supply the omission.

Very true, I said; and observe the point which I want to understand: Certain of the unnecessary pleasures and appetites I conceive to be unlawful; every one appears to have them, but in some persons they are controlled by the laws and by reason, and the better desires prevail over them -- either they are wholly banished or they become few and weak; while in the case of others they are stronger, and there are more of them.

Which appetites do you mean?

I mean those which are awake when the reasoning and human and ruling power is asleep; then the wild beast within us, gorged with meat and drink, starts up and having shaken off sleep, goes forth to satisfy his desires; and there is no conceivable folly or crime -- not excepting incest or any other unnatural union, or parricide, or the eating of forbidden food -- which at such a time, when he has parted company withall shame and sense, a man may not be ready to commit.

Most true, he said.

But when a man's pulse is healthy and temperate, and when before going to sleep he has awakened his rational powers, and fed them on noble thoughts and enquiries, collecting himself in meditation; after having first indulged his appetites neither too much nor too little, but just enough to lay them to sleep, and prevent them and their enjoyments and
572 pains from interfering with the higher principle -- which he leaves in the solitude of pure abstraction, free to contemplate and aspire to the knowledge of the unknown, whether in past, present, or future: when again he has allayed the passionate element, if he has a quarrel against any one -- I say, when, after pacifying the two irrational principles, he rouses up the third, which is reason, before he takes his rest, then as you know, he attains truth most nearly, and is least likely to be the sport of fantastic and lawless visions.

I quite agree.

In saying this I have been running into a digression; but the point which I desire to note is that in all of us, even in good men, there is a lawless wild-beast nature, which peers out in sleep. Pray, consider whether I am right, and you agree with me.

Yes, I agree.

And now remember the character which we attributed to the democratic man. He was supposed from his youth upwards to have been trained under a miserly parent, who encouraged the saving appetites in him, but discountenanced the unnecessary, which aim only at amusement and ornament?

True.

And then he got into the company of a more refined, licentious sort of people, and taking to all their wanton ways rushed into the opposite extreme from an abhorrence of his father's meanness. At last, being a better man than his corruptors, he was drawn in both directions until he halted midway and led a life, not of vulgar and slavish passion, but of what he deemed moderate indulgence in various pleasures. After this manner the democrat was generated out of the oligarch?

Yes, he said; that was our view of him, and is so still.

And now, I said, years will have passed away, and you must conceive this man, such as he is, to have a son, who is brought up in his father's principles.

I can imagine him.

Then you must further imagine the same thing to happen to the son which has already happened to the father: -- he is drawn into a perfectly lawless life, which by his seducers is termed perfect liberty; and his father and friends take part with his moderate desires, and the opposite party assist the opposite ones. As soon as these dire magicians and tyrant- 573
makers find that they are losing their hold on him, they contrive to implant in him a master passion, to be lord over his idle and spendthrift lusts -- a sort of monstrous winged drone -- that is the only image which will adequately describe him.

Yes, he said, that is the only adequate image of him.

And when his other lusts, amid clouds of incense and perfumes and garlands and wines, and all the pleasures of a dissolute life, now let loose, come buzzing around him, nourishing to the utmost the sting of desire which they implant in his drone-like nature, then at last this lord of the soul, having Madness for the captain of his guard, breaks out into a frenzy; and if he finds in himself any good opinions or appetites in process of formation [Or, 'opinions or appetites such as are deemed to be good.'], and there is in him any sense of shame remaining, to these better principles he puts an end, and casts them forth until he has purged away temperance and brought in madness to the full.

Yes, he said, that is the way in which the tyrannical man is generated.

And is not this the reason why of old love has been called a tyrant?

I should not wonder.

Further, I said, has not a drunken man also the spirit of a tyrant?

He has.

And you know that a man who is deranged and not right in his mind, will fancy that he is able to rule, not only over men, but also over the gods?

That he will.

And the tyrannical man in the true sense of the word comes into being when, either under the influence of nature, or habit, or both, he becomes drunken, lustful, passionate? O my friend, is not that so?

Assuredly.

Such is the man and such is his origin. And next, how does he live?

Suppose, as people facetiously say, you were to tell me.

I imagine, I said, at the next step in his progress, that there will be feasts and carousals and revellings and courtezans, and all that sort of thing; Love is the lord of the house within him, and orders all the concerns of his soul.

That is certain.

Yes; and every day and every night desires grow up many and formidable, and their demands are many.

They are indeed, he said.

His revenues, if he has any, are soon spent.

True.

Then comes debt and the cutting down of his property.

Of course.

When he has nothing left, must not his desires, crowding in the nest
574 like young ravens, be crying aloud for food; and he, goaded on by them, and especially by love himself, who is in a manner the captain of them, is in a frenzy, and would fain discover whom he can defraud or despoil of his property, in order that he may gratify them?

Yes, that is sure to be the case.

He must have money, no matter how, if he is to escape horrid pains and pangs.

He must.

And as in himself there was a succession of pleasures, and the new got the better of the old and took away their rights, so he being younger will claim to have more than his father and his mother, and if he has spent his own share of the property, he will take a slice of theirs.

No doubt he will.

And if his parents will not give way, then he will try first of all to cheat and deceive them.

Very true.

And if he fails, then he will use force and plunder them.

Yes, probably.

And if the old man and woman fight for their own, what then, my friend? Will the creature feel any compunction at tyrannizing over them?

Nay, he said, I should not feel at all comfortable about his parents.

But, O heavens! Adeimantus, on account of some new-fangled love of a harlot, who is anything but a necessary connection, can you believe that he would strike the mother who is his ancient friend and necessary to his very existence, and would place her under the authority of the other, when she is brought under the same roof with her; or that, under like circumstances, he would do the same to his withered old father, first and most indispensable of friends, for the sake of some newly-found blooming youth who is the reverse of indispensable?

Yes, indeed, he said; I believe that he would.

Truly, then, I said, a tyrannical son is a blessing to his father and mother.

He is indeed, he replied.

He first takes their property, and when that fails, and pleasures are
beginning to swarm in the hive of his soul, then he breaks into a house,
or steals the garments of some nightly wayfarer; next he proceeds to clear
a temple. Meanwhile the old opinions which he had when a child, and
which gave judgment about good and evil, are overthrown by those others
which have just been emancipated, and are now the body-guard of love
and share his empire. These in his democratic days, when he was still
subject to the laws and to his father, were only let loose in the dreams
of sleep. But now that he is under the dominion of Love, he becomes
always and in waking reality what he was then very rarely and in a dream
only; he will commit the foulest murder, or eat forbidden food, or be
guilty of any other horrid act. Love is his tyrant, and lives lordly in him 575
and lawlessly, and being himself a king, leads him on, as a tyrant leads
a State, to the performance of any reckless deed by which he can maintain
himself and the rabble of his associates, whether those whom evil com-
munications have brought in from without, or those whom he himself
has allowed to break loose within him by reason of a similar evil nature
in himself. Have we not here a picture of his way of life?

Yes, indeed, he said.

And if there are only a few of them in the State, and the rest of the people are well disposed, they go away and become the bodyguard or mercenary soldiers of some other tyrant who may probably want them for a war; and if there is no war, they stay at home and do many little pieces of mischief in the city.

What sort of mischief?

For example, they are the thieves, burglars, cut-purses, footpads, robbers of temples, man-stealers of the community; or if they are able to speak they turn informers, and bear false witness, and take bribes.

A small catalogue of evils, even if the perpetrators of them are few in number.

Yes, I said; but small and great are comparative terms, and all these things, in the misery and evil which they inflict upon a State, do not come within a thousand miles of the tyrant; when this noxious class and their followers grow numerous and become conscious of their strength, assisted by the infatuation of the people, they choose from among themselves the one who has most of the tyrant in his own soul, and him they create their tyrant.

Yes, he said, and he will be the most fit to be a tyrant.

If the people yield, well and good; but if they resist him, as he began by beating his own father and mother, so now, if he has the power, he beats them, and will keep his dear old fatherland or motherland, as the Cretans say, in subjection to his young retainers whom he has introduced to be their rulers and masters. This is the end of his passions and desires.

Exactly.

When such men are only private individuals and before they get power, this is their character; they associate entirely with their own flatterers or ready tools; or if they want anything from anybody, they in their turn are equally ready to bow down before them: they
576 profess every sort of affection for them; but when they have gained their
point they know them no more.

Yes, truly.

They are always either the masters or servants and never the friends of anybody; the tyrant never tastes of true freedom or friendship.

Certainly not.

And may we not rightly call such men treacherous?

No question.

Also they are utterly unjust, if we were right in our notion of justice?

Yes, he said, and we were perfectly right.

Let us then sum up in a word, I said, the character of the worst man: he is the waking reality of what we dreamed.

Most true.

And this is he who being by nature most of a tyrant bears rule, and the longer he lives the more of a tyrant he becomes.

That is certain, said Glaucon, taking his turn to answer.

And will not he who has been shown to be the wickedest, be also the most miserable? and he who has tyrannized longest and most, most continually and truly miserable; although this may not be the opinion of men in general?

Yes, he said, inevitably.

And must not the tyrannical man be like the tyrannical State, and the democratical man like the democratical State; and the same of the others?

Certainly.

And as State is to State in virtue and happiness, so is man in relation to man?

To be sure.

Then comparing our original city, which was under a king, and the city which is under a tyrant, how do they stand as to virtue?

They are the opposite extremes, he said, for one is the very best and the other is the very worst.

There can be no mistake, I said, as to which is which, and therefore I will at once enquire whether you would arrive at a similar decision about their relative happiness and misery. And here we must not allow ourselves to be panic-stricken at the apparition of the tyrant, who is only a unit and may perhaps have a few retainers about him; but let us go as we ought into every corner of the city and look all about, and then we will give our opinion.

A fair invitation, he replied; and I see, as every one must, that a tyranny is the wretchedest form of government, and the rule of a king the happiest.

And in estimating the men too, may I not fairly make a like request,
that I should have a judge whose mind can enter into and see through 577
human nature? he must not be like a child who looks at the outside and is dazzled at the pompous aspect which the tyrannical nature assumes to the beholder, but let him be one who has a clear insight. May I suppose that the judgment is given in the hearing of us all by one who is able to judge, and has dwelt in the same place with him, and been present at his

daily life and known him in his family relations, where he may be seen stripped of his tragedy attire, and again in the hour of public danger -- he shall tell us about the happiness and misery of the tyrant when compared with other men?

That again, he said, is a very fair proposal.

Shall I assume that we ourselves are able and experienced judges and have before now met with such a person? We shall then have some one who will answer our enquiries.

By all means.

Let me ask you not to forget the parallel of the individual and the State; bearing this in mind, and glancing in turn from one to the other of them, will you tell me their respective conditions?

What do you mean? he asked.

Beginning with the State, I replied, would you say that a city which is governed by a tyrant is free or enslaved?

No city, he said, can be more completely enslaved.

And yet, as you see, there are freemen as well as masters in such a State?

Yes, he said, I see that there are -- a few; but the people, speaking generally, and the best of them are miserably degraded and enslaved.

Then if the man is like the State, I said, must not the same rule prevail? his soul is full of meanness and vulgarity -- the best elements in him are enslaved; and there is a small ruling part, which is also the worst and maddest.

Inevitably.

And would you say that the soul of such an one is the soul of a freeman, or of a slave?

He has the soul of a slave, in my opinion.

And the State which is enslaved under a tyrant is utterly incapable of acting voluntarily?

Utterly incapable.

And also the soul which is under a tyrant (I am speaking of the soul taken as a whole) is least capable of doing what she desires; there is a gadfly which goads her, and she is full of trouble and remorse?

Certainly.

And is the city which is under a tyrant rich or poor?

Poor.

And the tyrannical soul must be always poor and insatiable? 578

True.

And must not such a State and such a man be always full of fear?

Yes, indeed.

Is there any State in which you will find more of lamentation and sorrow and groaning and pain?

Certainly not.

And is there any man in whom you will find more of this sort of misery than in the tyrannical man, who is in a fury of passions and desires?

Impossible.

Reflecting upon these and similar evils, you held the tyrannical State to be the most miserable of States?

And I was right, he said.

Certainly, I said. And when you see the same evils in the tyrannical man, what do you say of him?

I say that he is by far the most miserable of all men.

There, I said, I think that you are beginning to go wrong.

What do you mean?

I do not think that he has as yet reached the utmost extreme of misery.

Then who is more miserable?

One of whom I am about to speak.

Who is that?

He who is of a tyrannical nature, and instead of leading a private life has been cursed with the further misfortune of being a public tyrant.

From what has been said, I gather that you are right.

Yes, I replied, but in this high argument you should be a little more certain, and should not conjecture only; for of all questions, this respecting good and evil is the greatest.

Very true, he said.

Let me then offer you an illustration, which may, I think, throw a light upon this subject.

What is your illustration?

The case of rich individuals in cities who possess many slaves from them you may form an idea of the tyrant's condition, for they both have slaves; the only difference is that he has more slaves.

Yes, that is the difference.

You know that they live securely and have nothing to apprehend from their servants?

What should they fear?

Nothing. But do you observe the reason of this?

Yes; the reason is, that the whole city is leagued together for the protection of each individual.

Very true, I said. But imagine one of these owners, the master say of some fifty slaves, together with his family and property and slaves, carried off by a god into the wilderness, where there are no freemen to help him -- will he not be in an agony of fear lest he and his wife and children should be put to death by his slaves?

579 Yes, he said, he will be in the utmost fear.

The time has arrived when he will be compelled to flatter divers of his slaves, and make many promises to them of freedom and other things, much against his will -- he will have to cajole his own servants.

Yes, he said, that will be the only way of saving himself.

And suppose the same god, who carried him away, to surround him with neighbours who will not suffer one man to be the master of another, and who, if they could catch the offender, would take his life?

His case will be still worse, if you suppose him to be everywhere surrounded and watched by enemies.

And is not this the sort of prison in which the tyrant will be bound -- he who being by nature such as we have described, is full of all sorts of fears and lusts? His soul is dainty and greedy, and yet alone, of all men in the city, he is never allowed to go on a journey, or to see the things which other freemen desire to see, but he lives in his hole like a woman hidden in the house, and is jealous of any other citizen who goes into foreign parts and sees anything of interest.

Very true, he said.

And amid evils such as these will not he who is ill-governed in his own person -- the tyrannical man, I mean -- whom you just now decided to be the most miserable of all -- will not he be yet more miserable when, instead of leading a private life, he is constrained by fortune to be a public tyrant? He has to be master of others when he is not master of himself: he is like a diseased or paralytic man who is compelled to pass his life, not in retirement, but fighting and combating with other men.

Yes, he said, the similitude is most exact.

Is not his case utterly miserable? and does not the actual tyrant lead a worse life than he whose life you determined to be the worst?

Certainly.

He who is the real tyrant, whatever men may think, is the real slave, and is obliged to practise the greatest adulation and servility, and to be the flatterer of the vilest of mankind. He has desires which he is utterly unable to satisfy, and has more wants than any one, and is truly poor, if you know how to inspect the whole soul of him: all his life long he is beset with fear and is full of convulsions, and distractions, even as the State which he resembles: and surely the resemblance holds?

Very true, he said.

Moreover, as we were saying before, he grows worse from having 580
power: he becomes and is of necessity more jealous, more faithless, more unjust, more friendless, more impious, than he was at first; he is the purveyor and cherisher of every sort of vice, and the consequence is that he is supremely miserable, and that he makes everybody else as miserable as himself.

No man of any sense will dispute your words.

Come then, I said, and as the general umpire in theatrical contests proclaims the result, do you also decide who in your opinion is first in the scale of happiness, and who second, and in what order the others follow: there are five of them in all -- they are the royal, timocratical, oligarchical, democratical, tyrannical.

The decision will be easily given, he replied; they shall be choruses coming on the stage, and I must judge them in the order in which they enter, by the criterion of virtue and vice, happiness and misery.

Need we hire a herald, or shall I announce, that the son of Ariston [the best] has decided that the best and justest is also the happiest, and that this is he who is the most royal man and king over himself; and that the worst and most unjust man is also the most miserable, and that this is he who being the greatest tyrant of himself is also the greatest tyrant of his State?

Make the proclamation yourself, he said.

And shall I add, 'whether seen or unseen by gods and men'?

Let the words be added.

Then this, I said, will be our first proof; and there is another, which may also have some weight.

What is that?

The second proof is derived from the nature of the soul: seeing that the individual soul, like the State, has been divided by us into three principles, the division may, I think, furnish a new demonstration.

Of what nature?

It seems to me that to these three principles three pleasures correspond; also three desires and governing powers.

How do you mean? he said.

There is one principle with which, as we were saying, a man learns, another with which he is angry; the third, having many forms, has no special name, but is denoted by the general term appetitive, from the extraordinary strength and vehemence of the desires of eating and drinking and the other sensual appetites which are the main elements of it; also
581 money-loving, because such desires are generally satisfied by the help of money.

That is true, he said.

If we were to say that the loves and pleasures of this third part were concerned with gain, we should then be able to fall back on a single notion; and might truly and intelligibly describe this part of the soul as loving gain or money.

I agree with you.

Again, is not the passionate element wholly set on ruling and conquering and getting fame?

True.

Suppose we call it the contentious or ambitious -- would the term be suitable?

Extremely suitable.

On the other hand, every one sees that the principle of knowledge is wholly directed to the truth, and cares less than either of the others for gain or fame.

Far less.

'Lover of wisdom,'; of lover of knowledge,' are titles which we may fitly apply to that part of the soul?

Certainly.

One principle prevails in the souls of one class of men, another in others, as may happen?

Yes.

Then we may begin by assuming that there are three classes of men -- lovers of wisdom, lovers of honour, lovers of gain?

Exactly.

And there are three kinds of pleasure, which are their several objects?

Very true.

Now, if you examine the three classes of men, and ask of them in turn which of their lives is pleasantest, each will be found praising his own and depreciating that of others: the money-maker will contrast the vanity of honour or of learning if they bring no money with the solid advantages of gold and silver?

True, he said.

And the lover of honour -- what will be his opinion? Will he not think that the pleasure of riches is vulgar, while the pleasure of learning, if it brings no distinction, is all smoke and nonsense to him?

Very true.

And are we to suppose, I said, that the philosopher sets any value on other pleasures in comparison with the pleasure of knowing the truth, and in that pursuit abiding, ever learning, not so far indeed from the heaven of pleasure? Does he not call the other pleasures necessary, under the idea that if there were no necessity for them, he would rather not have them?

There can be no doubt of that, he replied.

Since, then, the pleasures of each class and the life of each are in dispute, and the question is not which life is more or less honourable,
or better or worse, but which is the more pleasant or painless -- how shall 582
we know who speaks truly?

I cannot myself tell, he said.

Well, but what ought to be the criterion? Is any better than experience and wisdom and reason?

There cannot be a better, he said.

Then, I said, reflect. Of the three individuals, which has the greatest experience of all the pleasures which we enumerated? Has the lover of gain, in learning the nature of essential truth, greater experience of the pleasure of knowledge than the philosopher has of the pleasure of gain?

The philosopher, he replied, has greatly the advantage; for he has of necessity always known the taste of the other pleasures from his childhood upwards: but the lover of gain in all his experience has not of necessity tasted -- or, I should rather say, even had he desired, could hardly have tasted -- the sweetness of learning and knowing truth.

Then the lover of wisdom has a great advantage over the lover of gain, for he has a double experience?

Yes, very great.

Again, has he greater experience of the pleasures of honour, or the lover of honour of the pleasures of wisdom?

Nay, he said, all three are honoured in proportion as they attain their object; for the rich man and the brave man and the wise man alike have their crowd of admirers, and as they all receive honour they all have experience of the pleasures of honour; but the delight which is to be found in the knowledge of true being is known to the philosopher only.

His experience, then, will enable him to judge better than any one?

Far better.

And he is the only one who has wisdom as well as experience?

Certainly.

Further, the very faculty which is the instrument of judgment is not possessed by the covetous or ambitious man, but only by the philosopher?

What faculty?

Reason, with whom, as we were saying, the decision ought to rest.

Yes.

And reasoning is peculiarly his instrument?

Certainly.

If wealth and gain were the criterion, then the praise or blame of the lover of gain would surely be the most trustworthy?

Assuredly.

Or if honour or victory or courage, in that case the judgment of the ambitious or pugnacious would be the truest?

Clearly.

But since experience and wisdom and reason are the judges --

The only inference possible, he replied, is that pleasures which are approved by the lover of wisdom and reason are the truest.

And so we arrive at the result, that the pleasure of the intelligent 583
part of the soul is the pleasantest of the three, and that he of us in whom this is the ruling principle has the pleasantest life.

Unquestionably, he said, the wise man speaks with authority when he approves of his own life.

And what does the judge affirm to be the life which is next, and the pleasure which is next?

Clearly that of the soldier and lover of honour; who is nearer to himself than the money-maker.

Last comes the lover of gain?

Very true, he said.

Twice in succession, then, has the just man overthrown the unjust in this conflict; and now comes the third trial, which is dedicated to Olympian Zeus the saviour: a sage whispers in my ear that no pleasure except that of the wise is quite true and pure -- all others are a shadow only; and surely this will prove the greatest and most decisive of falls?

Yes, the greatest; but will you explain yourself?

I will work out the subject and you shall answer my questions.

Proceed.

Say, then, is not pleasure opposed to pain?

True.

And there is a neutral state which is neither pleasure nor pain?

There is.

A state which is intermediate, and a sort of repose of the soul about either -- that is what you mean?

Yes.

You remember what people say when they are sick?

What do they say?

That after all nothing is pleasanter than health. But then they never knew this to be the greatest of pleasures until they were ill.

Yes, I know, he said.

And when persons are suffering from acute pain, you must have heard them say that there is nothing pleasanter than to get rid of their pain?

I have.

And there are many other cases of suffering in which the mere rest and cessation of pain, and not any positive enjoyment, is extolled by them as the greatest pleasure?

Yes, he said; at the time they are pleased and well content to be at rest.

Again, when pleasure ceases, that sort of rest or cessation will be painful?

Doubtless, he said.

Then the intermediate state of rest will be pleasure and will also be pain?

So it would seem.

But can that which is neither become both?

I should say not.

And both pleasure and pain are motions of the soul, are they not?

Yes.

584 But that which is neither was just now shown to be rest and not motion, and in a mean between them?

Yes.

How, then, can we be right in supposing that the absense of pain is pleasure, or that the absence of pleasure is pain?

Impossible.

This then is an appearance only and not a reality; that is to say, the rest is pleasure at the moment and in comparison of what is painful, and painful in comparison of what is pleasant; but all these representations, when tried by the test of true pleasure, are not real but a sort of imposition?

That is the inference.

Look at the other class of pleasures which have no antecedent pains and you will no longer suppose, as you perhaps may at present, that pleasure is only the cessation of pain, or pain of pleasure.

What are they, he said, and where shall I find them?

There are many of them: take as an example the pleasures of smell, which are very great and have no antecedent pains; they come in a moment, and when they depart leave no pain behind them.

Most true, he said.

Let us not, then, be induced to believe that pure pleasure is the cessation of pain, or pain of pleasure.

No.

Still, the more numerous and violent pleasures which reach the soul through the body are generally of this sort -- they are reliefs of pain.

That is true.

And the anticipations of future pleasures and pains are of a like nature?

Yes.

Shall I give you an illustration of them?

Let me hear.

You would allow, I said, that there is in nature an upper and lower and middle region?

I should.

And if a person were to go from the lower to the middle region, would he not imagine that he is going up; and he who is standing in the middle and sees whence he has come, would imagine that he is already in the upper region, if he has never seen the true upper world?

To be sure, he said; how can he think otherwise?

But if he were taken back again he would imagine, and truly imagine, that he was descending?

No doubt.

All that would arise out of his ignorance of the true upper and middle and lower regions?

Yes.

Then can you wonder that persons who are inexperienced in the truth, as they have wrong ideas about many other things, should also have wrong ideas about pleasure and pain and the intermediate state; so
that when they are only being drawn towards the painful they feel pain 585
and think the pain which they experience to be real, and in like manner, when drawn away from pain to the neutral or intermediate state, they firmly believe that they have reached the goal of satiety and pleasure;

they, not knowing pleasure, err in contrasting pain with the absence of pain, which is like contrasting black with grey instead of white -- can you wonder, I say, at this?

No, indeed; I should be much more disposed to wonder at the opposite.

Look at the matter thus: -- Hunger, thirst, and the like, are inanitions of the bodily state?

Yes.

And ignorance and folly are inanitions of the soul?

True.

And food and wisdom are the corresponding satisfactions of either?

Certainly.

And is the satisfaction derived from that which has less or from that which has more existence the truer?

Clearly, from that which has more.

What classes of things have a greater share of pure existence in your judgment -- those of which food and drink and condiments and all kinds of sustenance are examples, or the class which contains true opinion and knowledge and mind and all the different kinds of virtue? Put the question in this way: -- Which has a more pure being -- that which is concerned with the invariable, the immortal, and the true, and is of such a nature, and is found in such natures; or that which is concerned with and found in the variable and mortal, and is itself variable and mortal?

Far purer, he replied, is the being of that which is concerned with the invariable.

And does the essence of the invariable partake of knowledge in the same degree as of essence?

Yes, of knowledge in the same degree.

And of truth in the same degree?

Yes.

And, conversely, that which has less of truth will also have less of essence?

Necessarily.

Then, in general, those kinds of things which are in the service of the body have less of truth and essence than those which are in the service of the soul?

Far less.

And has not the body itself less of truth and essence than the soul?

Yes.

What is filled with more real existence, and actually has a more real existence, is more really filled than that which is filled with less real existence and is less real?

Of course.

And if there be a pleasure in being filled with that which is according to nature, that which is more really filled with more real being will more really and truly enjoy true pleasure; whereas that which participates in less real being will be less truly and surely satisfied, and will participate in an illusory and less real pleasure?

Unquestionably.

Those then who know not wisdom and virtue, and are always busy 586
with gluttony and sensuality, go down and up again as far as the mean; and in this region they move at random throughout life, but they never pass into the true upper world; thither they neither look, nor do they ever find their way, neither are they truly filled with true being, nor do they taste of pure and abiding pleasure. Like cattle, with their eyes always looking down and their heads stooping to the earth, that is, to the dining-table, they fatten and feed and breed, and, in their excessive love of these delights, they kick and butt at one another with horns and hoofs which are made of iron; and they kill one another by reason of their insatiable lust. For they fill themselves with that which is not substantial, and the part of themselves which they fill is also unsubstantial and incontinent.

Verily, Socrates, said Glaucon, you describe the life of the many like any oracle.

Their pleasures are mixed with pains -- how can they be otherwise? For they are mere shadows and pictures of the true, and are coloured by contrast, which exaggerates both light and shade, and so they implant in the minds of fools insane desires of themselves; and they are fought about as Stesichorus says that the Greeks fought about the shadow of Helen at Troy in ignorance of the truth.

Something of that sort must inevitably happen.

And must not the like happen with the spirited or passionate element of the soul? Will not the passionate man who carries his passion into action, be in the like case, whether he is envious and ambitious, or violent and contentious, or angry and discontented, if he be seeking to attain honour and victory and the satifaction of his anger without reason or sense?

Yes, he said, the same will happen with the spirited element also.

Then may we not confidently assert that the lovers of money and honour, when they seek their pleasures under the guidance and in the company of reason and knowledge, and pursue after and win the pleasures which wisdom shows them, will also have the truest pleasures in the highest degree which is attainable to them, inasmuch as they follow truth; and they will have the pleasures which are natural to them, if that which is best for eachone is also most natural to him?

Yes, certainly; the best is the most natural.

And when the whole soul follows the philosophical principle, and there is no division, the several parts are just, and do each of them their
587 own business, and enjoy severally the best and truest pleasures of which they are capable?

Exactly.

But when either of the two other principles prevails, it fails in attaining its own pleasure, and compels the rest to pursue after a pleasure which is a shadow only and which is not their own?

True.

And the greater the interval which separates them from philosophy and reason, the more strange and illusive will be the pleasure?

Yes.

And is not that farthest from reason which is at the greatest distance from law and order?

Clearly.

And the lustful and tyrannical desires are, as we saw, at the greatest distance?

Yes.

And the royal and orderly desires are nearest?

Yes.

Then the tyrant will live at the greatest distance from true or natural pleasure, and the king at the least?

Certainly.

But if so, the tyrant will live most unpleasantly, and the king most pleasantly?

Inevitably.

Would you know the measure of the interval which separates them?

Will you tell me?

There appear to be three pleasures, one genuine and two spurious: now the transgression of the tyrant reaches a point beyond the spurious; he has run away from the region of law and reason, and taken up his abode with certain slave pleasures which are his satellites, and the measure of his inferiority can only be expressed in a figure.

How do you mean?

I assume, I said, that the tyrant is in the third place from the oligarch; the democrat in the middle?

Yes.

And if there is truth in what has preceded, he will be wedded to an image of pleasure which is thrice removed as to truth from the pleasure of the oligarch?

He will.

And the oligarch is third from the royal; since we count as one royal and aristocratical?

Yes, he is third.

Then the tyrant is removed from true pleasure by the space of a number which is three times three?

Manifestly.

The shadow then of tyrannical pleasure determined by the number of length will be a plane figure.

Certainly.

And if you raise the power and make the plane a solid, there is no 588
difficulty in seeing how vast is the interval by which the tyrant is parted from the king.

Yes; the arithmetician will easily do the sum.

Or if some person begins at the other end and measures the interval by which the king is parted from the tyrant in truth of pleasure, he will find him, when the multiplication is complete, living 729 times more pleasantly, and the tyrant more painfully by this same interval.

What a wonderful calculation! And how enormous is the distance
which separates the just from the unjust in regard to pleasure and pain! 589

Yet a true calculation, I said, and a number which nearly concerns human life, if human beings are concerned with days and nights and months and years [729 nearly equals the number of days and nights in the year.]

Yes, he said, human life is certainly concerned with them.

Then if the good and just man be thus superior in pleasure to the evil and unjust, his superiority will be infinitely greater in propriety of life and in beauty and virtue?

Immeasurably greater.

Well, I said, and now having arrived at this stage of the argument, we may revert to the words which brought us hither: Was not some one saying that injustice was a gain to the perfectly unjust who was reputed to be just?

Yes, that was said.

Now then, having determined the power and quality of justice and injustice, let us have a little conversation with him.

What shall we say to him?

Let us make an image of the soul, that he may have his own words presented before his eyes.

Of what sort?

An ideal image of the soul, like the composite creations of ancient mythology, such as the Chimera or Scylla or Cerberus, and there are many others in which two or more different natures are said to grow into one.

There are said to have been such unions.

Then do you now model the form of a multitudinous, many-headed monster, having a ring of heads of all manner of beasts, tame and wild, which he is able to generate and metamorphose at will.

You suppose marvellous powers in the artist; but, as language is more pliable than wax or any similar substance, let there be such a model as you propose.

Suppose now that you make a second form as of a lion, and a third of a man, the second smaller than the first, and the third smaller than the second.

That, he said, is an easier task; and I have made them as you say.

And now join them, and let the three grow into one.

That has been accomplished.

Next fashion the outside of them into a single image, as of a man, so that he who is not able to look within, and sees only the outer hull, may believe the beast to be a single human creature.

I have done so, he said.

And now, to him who maintains that it is profitable for the human creature to be unjust, and unprofitable to be just, let us reply that, if he be right, it is profitable for this creature to feast the multitudinous monster and strengthen the lion and the lion-like qualities, but to starve and weaken the man, who is consequently liable to be dragged about at the mercy of either of the other two; and he is not to attempt to familiarize or harmonize them with one another -- he ought rather to suffer them to fight and bite and devour one another.

Certainly, he said; that is what the approver of injustice says.

To him the supporter of justice makes answer that he should ever so speak and act as to give the man within him in some way or other the most complete mastery over the entire human creature. He should watch over the many-headed monster like a good husbandman, fostering and cultivating the gentle qualities, and preventing the wild ones from growing; he should be making the lionheart his ally, and in common care of them all should be uniting the several parts with one another and with himself.

Yes, he said, that is quite what the maintainer of justice will say.

And so from every point of view, whether of pleasure, honour, or advantage, the approver of justice is right and speaks the truth, and the disapprover is wrong and false and ignorant?

Yes, from every point of view.

Come, now, and let us gently reason with the unjust, who is not intentionally in error. 'Sweet Sir,' we will say to him, 'what think you of things esteemed noble and ignoble? Is not the noble that which subjects the beast to the man, or rather to the god in man; and the ignoble that which subjects the man to the beast?' He can hardly avoid saying Yes -- can he now?

Not if he has any regard for my opinion.

But, if he agree so far, we may ask him to answer another question: 'Then how would a man profit if he received gold and silver on the condition that he was to enslave the noblest part of him to the worst? Who can imagine that a man who sold his son or daughter into slavery

for money, especially if he sold them into the hands of fierce and evil men, would be the gainer, however large might be the sum which he
590 received? And will any one say that he is not a miserable caitiff who remorselessly sells his own divine being to that which is most godless and detestable? Eriphyle took the necklace as the price of her husband's life, but he is taking a bribe in order to compass a worse ruin.'

Yes, said Glaucon, far worse -- I will answer for him.

Has not the intemperate been censured of old, because in him the huge multiform monster is allowed to be too much at large?

Clearly.

And men are blamed for pride and bad temper when the lion and serpent element in them disporportionately grows and gains strength?

Yes.

And luxury and softness are blamed, because they relax and weaken this same creature, and make a coward of him?

Very true.

And is not a man reproached for flattery and meanness who subordinates the spirited animal to the unruly monster, and, for the sake of money, of which he can never have enough, habituates him in the days of his youth to be trampled in the mire, and from being a lion to become a monkey?

True, he said.

And why are mean employments and manual arts a reproach? Only because they imply a natural weakness of the higher principle; the individual is unable to control the creatures within him, but has to court them, and his great study is how to flatter them.

Such appears to be the reason.

And therefore, being desirous of placing him under a rule like that of the best, we say that he ought to be the servant of the best, in whom the Divine rules; not, as Thrasymachus supposed, to the injury of the servant, but because every one had better be ruled by divine wisdom dwelling within him; or, if this be impossible, then by an external authority, in order that we may be all, as far as possible, under the same government, friends and equals.

True, he said.

And this is clearly seen to be the intention of the law, which is the ally of the whole city; and is seen also in the authority which we exercise

over children, and the refusal to let them be free until we have established in them a principle analogous to the constitution of a state, and by cultivation of this higher element have set up in their hearts a guardian and 591
ruler like our own, and when this is done they may go their ways.

Yes, he said, the purpose of the law is manifest.

From what point of view, then, and on what ground can we say that a man is profited by injustice or intemperance or other baseness, which will make him a worse man, even though he acquire money or power by his wickedness?

From no point of view at all.

What shall he profit, if his injustice be undetected and unpunished? He who is undetected only gets worse, whereas he who is detected and punished has the brutal part of his nature silenced and humanized; the gentler element in him is liberated, and his whole soul is perfected and ennobled by the acquirement of justice and temperance and wisdom, more than the body ever is by receiving gifts of beauty, strength and health, in proportion as the soul is more honourable than the body.

Certainly, he said.

To this nobler purpose the man of understanding will devote the energies of his life. And in the first place, he will honour studies which impress these qualities on his soul, and will disregard others?

Clearly, he said.

In the next place, he will regulate his bodily habit and training, and so far will he be from yielding to brutal and irrational pleasures, that he will regard even health as quite a secondary matter; his first object will be not that he may be fair or strong or well, unless he is likely thereby to gain temperance, but he will always desire so to attemper the body as to preserve the harmony of the soul?

Certainly he will, if he has true music in him.

And in the acquisition of wealth there is a principle of order and harmony which he will also observe; he will not allow himself to be dazzled by the foolish applause of the world, and heap up riches to his own infinite harm?

Certainly not, he said.

He will look at the city which is within him, and take heed that no disorder occur in it, such as might arise either from superfluity or from want; and upon this principle he will regulate his property and gain or spend according to his means.

Very true.

592 And, for the same reason, he will gladly accept and enjoy such honours as he deems likely to make him a better man; but those, whether private or public, which are likely to disorder his life, he will avoid?

Then, if that is his motive, he will not be a statesman.

By the dog of Egypt, he will! in the city which is his own he certainly will, though in the land of his birth perhaps not, unless he have a divine call.

I understand; you mean that he will be a ruler in the city of which we are the founders, and which exists in idea only; for I do not believe that there is such an one anywhere on earth?

In heaven, I replied, there is laid up a pattern of it, me thinks, which he who desires may behold, and beholding, may set his own house in order [Or, 'take up his abode there.']. But whether such an one exists, or ever will exist in fact, is no matter; for he will live after the manner of that city, having nothing to do with any other.

I think so, he said.

3

Aquinas

On Natural Law

The Summa Theologica

[First Part of the Second Part]

Question 90

Of the Essence of Law

(in Four Articles)

We have now to consider the extrinsic principles of acts. Now the extrinsic principle inclining to evil is the devil, of whose temptations we have spoken in the first Part (Q. 114). But the extrinsic principle moving to good is God, Who both instructs us by means of His law and assists us by His grace; wherefore in the first place we must speak of law; in the second place, of grace.

Concerning law, we must consider (1) law itself in general, (2) its parts. Concerning law in general three points offer themselves for our consideration: (1) its essence; (2) the different kinds of law; (3) the effects of law.

Under the first head there are four points of inquiry: (1) whether law is something pertaining to reason? (2) concerning the end of law; (3) its cause; (4) the promulgation of law.

First Article

WHETHER LAW IS SOMETHING PERTAINING TO REASON?

We proceed thus to the First Article:

Objection 1. It would seem that law is not something pertaining to reason. For the Apostle says: "I see another law in my members," etc. (Rom. vii,23). But nothing pertaining to reason is in the members, since the reason does not make use of a bodily organ. Therefore law is not something pertaining to reason.

Obj. 2. Further, in the reason there is nothing else but power, habit, and act. But law is not the power itself of reason. In like manner, neither is it a habit of reason, because the habits of reason are the intellectual virtues of which we have spoken above (S.I-II,Q.57). Nor again is it an act of reason, because then law would cease when the act of reason ceases, for instance, while we are asleep. Therefore law is nothing pertaining to reason.

Obj. 3. Further, the law moves those who are subject to it to act aright. But it belongs properly to the will to move to act, as is evident from what has been said above (*Ibid*., Q.9,A1). Therefore law pertains not to the reason, but to the will, according to the words of the Jurist: "Whatever pleases the sovereign, has the force of law" (*Digest,* i ff.I).

On the contrary, It belongs to the law to command and to forbid. But it belongs to reason to command, as stated above (S. I-II Q.17,A1). Therefore law is something pertaining to reason.

I answer that, Law is a rule and measure of acts whereby man is induced to act or is restrained from acting; for *lex* (law) is derived from *ligare* (to bind), because it binds one to act. Now the rule and measure of human acts is the reason, which is the first principle of human acts, as is evident from what has been stated above (*Ibid.,* Q.1,A.1, *ad* 3), since it belongs to the reason to direct to the end, which is the first principle in all matters of action (*Phys.* ii), according to the Philosopher. Now that which is the principle in any genus is the rule and measure of that genus: for instance, unity in the genus of numbers, and the first movement in the genus of movements. Consequently it follows that law is something pertaining to reason.

Reply Obj. 1. Since law is a kind of rule and measure, it may be in something in two ways. First, as in that which measures and rules; and since this is proper to reason, it follows that, in this way, law is in the reason alone. -- Secondly, as in that which is measured and ruled. In this way law is in all those things that are inclined to something by reason of some law, so that any inclination arising from a law may be called a law, not essentially but by participation as it were. And thus the inclination of the members to concupiscence is called "the law of the members."

Reply Obj. 2. Just as, in external action, we may consider the work and the work done -- for instance, the work of building and the house built, so in the acts of reason we may consider the act itself of reason, i.e., to understand and to reason, and something produced by this act. With regard to the speculative reason, this is first of all the definition; secondly, the proposition; thirdly, the syllogism or argument. And since also the practical reason makes use of a syllogism in respect of the work to be done, as stated above (S.I-II Q.13,A.3; Q.76.A.1) and as the Philosopher teaches (*Eth.* vii 3), hence we find in the practical reason something that holds the same position in regard to operations as, in the speculative intellect, the proposition holds in regard to conclusions. Suchlike universal propositions of the practical intellect that are directed to actions have the nature of law. And these propositions are sometimes under our actual consideration, while sometimes they are retained in the reason by means of a habit.

Reply Obj. 3. Reason has its power of moving from the will, as stated above (S.I-II,Q.17,A1), for it is due to the fact that one wills the end that the reason issues its commands as regards things ordained to the end. But in order that the volition of what is commanded may have the nature of law, it needs to be in accord with some rule of reason. And in this sense is to be understood the saying that the will of the sovereign has the force of law; otherwise the sovereign's will would savor of lawlessness rather than of law.

Second Article

WHETHER THE LAW IS ALWAYS DIRECTED TO THE COMMON GOOD?

We proceed thus to the Second Article:

Objection 1. It would seem that the law is not always directed to the common good as to its end. For it belongs to law to command and to forbid. But commands are directed to certain individual goods. Therefore the end of the law is not always the common good.

Obj. 2. Further, the law directs man in his actions. But human actions are concerned with particular matters. Therefore the law is directed to some particular good.

Obj. 3. Further, Isidore says: "If the law is based on reason, whatever is based on reason will be a law" (Etym. v.3). But reason is the foundation not only of what is ordained to the common good, but also of that which is directed to private good. Therefore the law is not only directed to the good of all, but also to the private good of an individual.

On the contrary, Isidore says that "laws are enacted for no private profit, but for the common benefit of the citizens" (*Ibid*., 21).

I answer that, As stated above (A. 1), the law belongs to that which is a principle of human acts, because it is their rule and measure. Now as reason is a principle of human acts, so in reason itself there is something which is the principle in respect of all the rest; wherefore to this principle chiefly and mainly law must needs be referred. -- Now the first principle in practical matters, which are the object of the practical reason, is the last end; and the last end of human life is bliss or happiness, as stated above (S.I-II, Q.2,A7; Q.3,A1). Consequently the law must needs regard principally the relationship to happiness. Moreover, since every part is ordained to the whole, as imperfect to perfect; and since one man is a part of the perfect community, the law must needs regard properly the relationship to universal happiness. Wherefore the Philosopher, in the above definition of legal matters, mentions both happiness and the body politic, for he says that we call those legal matters *just*, "which are adapted to produce and preserve happiness and its parts for the body politic" (*Eth*., v.,I), since the state is a perfect community, as he says in *Politics* i. I.

Now, in every genus, that which belongs to it chiefly is the principle of the others, and the others belong to that genus in subordination to that thing: thus fire, which is chief among hot things, is the cause of heat in mixed bodies, and these are said to be hot in so far as they have a share of fire. Consequently, since the law is chiefly ordained to the common good, any other precept in regard to some individual work must needs be devoid of the nature of a law, save in so far as it regards the common good. Therefore every law is ordained to the common good.

Reply Obj. 1. A command denotes an application of a law to matters regulated by the law. Now the order to the common good, at which the law aims, is applicable to particular ends. And in this way commands are given even concerning particular matters.

Reply Obj. 2. Actions are indeed concerned with particular matters, but those particular matters are referable to the common good, not as to a common genus or species, but as to a common final cause, according as the common good is said to be the common end.

Reply Obj. 3. Just as nothing stands firm with regard to the speculative reason except that which is traced back to the first indemonstrable principles, so nothing stands firm with regard to the practical reason unless it be directed to the last end which is the common good; and whatever stands to reason in this sense has the nature of a law.

Third Article

WHETHER THE REASON OF ANY MAN IS COMPETENT TO MAKE LAWS?

We proceed thus to the Third Article:

Objection 1. It would seem that the reason of any man is competent to make laws. For the Apostle says that "when the Gentiles, who have not the law, do by nature those things that are of the law . . . they are a law to themselves" (Rom. ii 14). Now he says this of all in general. Therefore anyone can make a law for himself.

Obj. 2. Further, as the Philosopher says, "The intention of the law giver is to lead men to virtue" (*Eth.*, ii 1). But every man can lead another to virtue. Therefore the reason of any man is competent to make laws.

Obj. 3. Further, just as the sovereign of a state governs the state, so every father of a family governs his household. But the sovereign of a state can make laws for the state. Therefore every father of a family can make laws for his household.

On the contrary, Isidore says: "A law is an ordinance of the people, whereby something is sanctioned by the Elders together with the Commonality" (*Etym.*, v. 10).

I answer that, A law, properly speaking, regards first and foremost the order to the common good. Now to order anything to the common good belongs either to the whole people or to someone who is the vicegerent of the whole people. And therefore the making of a law belongs either to the whole people or to a public personage who has care of the whole people, since in all other matters the directing of anything to the end concerns him to whom the end belongs.

Reply Obj. 1. As stated above (A. 1 *ad* 1), a law is in a person not only as in one that rules, but also by participation as in one that is ruled. In that latter way each one is a law to himself, in so far as he shares the direction that he receives from one who rules him. Hence the same text goes on, "who show the work of the law written in their hearts."

Reply Obj. 2. A private person cannot lead another to virtue efficaciously, for he can only advise, and if his advice be not taken, it has no coercive power, such as the law should have in order to prove an efficacious inducement to virtue, as the Philosopher says (*Eth*. x, 9). But this coercive power is vested in the whole people or in some public personage to whom it belongs to inflict penalties, as we shall state further on (Q.92,A.2 *ad* 3; II-II,Q.64,A.3). Where fore the framing of laws belongs to him alone.

Reply Obj. 3. As one man is a part of the household, so a household is a part of the state; and the state is a perfect community, according to *Politics* i. I. And therefore, as the good of one man is not the last end, but is ordained to the common good, so, too, the good of one household is ordained to the good of a single state, which is a perfect community. Consequently he that governs a family can indeed make certain commands or ordinances, but not such as to have properly the force of law.

Fourth Article

WHETHER PROMULGATION IS ESSENTIAL TO A LAW?

We proceed thus to the Fourth Article:

Objection 1. It would seem that promulgation is not essential to a law. For the natural law above all has the character of law. But the natural law needs no promulgation. Therefore it is not essential to a law that it be promulgated.

Obj. 2. Further, it belongs properly to a law to bind one to do or not to do something. But the obligation of fulfilling a law touches not only those in whose presence it is promulgated, but also others. Therefore promulgation is not essential to a law.

Obj. 3. Further, the binding force of a law extends even to the future, since "laws are binding in matters of the future," as the jurists say (*Codex X,* i.7). But promulgation concerns those who are present. Therefore it is not essential to a law.

On the contrary, It is laid down in the *Decretals,* dist. 4, that "laws are established when they are promulgated."

I answer that, As stated above (A.1), a law is imposed on others by way of a rule and measure. Now a rule or measure is imposed by being applied to those who are to be ruled and measured by it. Wherefore, in order that a law obtain the binding force which is proper to a law, it must needs be applied to the men who have to be ruled by it. Such application is made by its being notified to them by promulgation. Wherefore promulgation is necessary for the law to obtain its force.

Thus from the four preceding articles the defintion of law may be gathered; and it is nothing else than an ordinance of reason for the common good, made by him who has care of the community, and promulgated.

Reply Obj. 1. The natural law is promulgated by the very fact that God instilled it into man's mind so as to be known by him naturally.

Reply Obj. 2. Those who are not present when a law is promulgated are bound to observe the law, in so far as it is notified or can be notified to them by others, after it has been promulgated.

Reply Obj. 3. The promulgation that takes place now extends to future time by reason of the durability of written characters, by which means it is continually promulgated. Hence Isidore says that "*lex* (law) is derived from *legere* (to read) because it is written" (*Etym.,* V.35 ii.10)

Question 91

Of the Various Kinds of Law

(In Six Articles)

We must now consider the various kinds of law, under which head there are six points of inquiry: (1) Whether there is an eternal law? (2) Whether there is a natural law? (3) Whether there is a human law? (4) Whether there is a divine law? (5) Whether there is one divine law or several? (6) Whether there is a law of sin?

First Article

WHETHER THERE IS AN ETERNAL LAW?

We proceed thus to the First Article:

Objection 1. It would seem that there is no eternal law. Because every law is imposed on someone. But there was not someone from eternity on whom a law could be imposed, since God alone was from eternity. Therefore no law is eternal.

Obj. 2. Further, promulgation is essential to law. But promulgation could not be from eternity, because there was no one to whom it could be promulgated from eternity. Therefore no law can be eternal.

Obj. 3. Further, a law implies order to an end. But nothing ordained to an end is eternal, for the last end alone is eternal. Therefore no law is eternal.

On the contrary, Augustine says: "That Law which is the Supreme Reason cannot be understood to be otherwise than unchangeable and eternal" (*De lib.* arb. i,6).

I answer that, As stated above (Q.90,A.1 *ad* 2; Aa.3,4), a law is nothing else but a dictate of practical reason emanating from the ruler who governs a perfect community. Now it is evident, granted that the world is ruled by divine providence, as was stated in the First Part (S.I,Q.22,AaI,2), that the whole community of the universe is governed by divine reason. Wherefore the very Idea of the government of things in God the Ruler of the universe has the nature of a law. And since the divine reason's conception of things is not subject to time but is eternal, according to Proverbs viii. 23, therefore it is that this kind of law must be called eternal.

Reply Obj. 1. Those things that are not in themselves exist with God, inasmuch as they are foreknown and preordained by Him, according to Romans iv.17, "Who calls those things that are not, as those that are." Accordingly the eternal concept of the divine law bears the character of an eternal law in so far as it is ordained by God to the government of things foreknown by Him.

Reply Obj. 2. Promulgation is made by word of mouth or in writing; and in both ways the eternal law is promulgated, because both the divine word and the writing of the Book of Life are eternal. But the promulgation cannot be from eternity on the part of the creature that hears or reads.

Reply Obj. 3. The law implies order to the end actively, in so far as it directs certain things to the end, but not passively -- that is to say, the law itself is not ordained to the end -- except accidentally, in a governor whose end is extrinsic to him, and to which end his law must needs be ordained. But the end of the divine government is God Himself, and His law is not distinct from Himself. Wherefore the eternal law is not ordained to another end.

Second Article

WHETHER THERE IS IN US A NATURAL LAW?

We proceed thus to the Second Article:

Objection 1. It would seem that there is no natural law in us. Because man is governed sufficiently by the eternal law; for Augustine says that "the eternal law is that by which it is right that all things should be most orderly" (*De lib.* arb. i). But nature does not abound in superfluities, as neither does she fail in necessaries. Therefore no law is natural to man.

Obj. 2. Further, by the law man is directed in his acts to the end, as stated above (Q.90,A.2). But the directing of human acts to their end is not a function of nature, as is the case in irrational creatures, which act for an end solely by their natural appetite; whereas man acts for an end by his reason and will. Therefore no law is natural to man.

Obj. 3. Further, the more a man is free, the less is he under the law. But man is freer than all the animals, on account of his free will, with which he is endowed above all other animals. Since therefore other animals are not subject to a natural law, neither is man subject to a natural law.

On the contrary, A gloss of Romans ii.14: "When the Gentiles, who have not the law, do by nature those things that are of the law," comments as follows: "Although they have no written law, yet they have the natural law, whereby each one knows, and is conscious of, what is good and what is evil."

I answer that, As stated above (Q.90,A.1 *ad* 1), law, being a rule and measure, can be in a person in two ways: in one way, as in him that rules and measures; in another way, as in that which is ruled and measured, since a thing is ruled and measured in so far as it partakes of the rule or measure. Wherefore, since all things subject to divine providence are ruled and measured by the eternal law, as was stated above (A.1), it is evident that all things partake somewhat of the eternal law, in so far as, namely, from its being imprinted on them, they derive their respective inclinations to their proper acts and ends. Now among all others the rational creature is subject to divine providence in the most excellent way, in so far as it partakes of a share of providence, by being provident both for itself and for others. Wherefore it has a share of the eternal reason, whereby it has a natural inclination to its proper act and end: and this participation of the eternal law in the rational creature is called the natural law. Hence the Psalmist after saying: "Offer up the sacrifice of justice," as though someone asked what the works of justice are, adds: "Many say, Who showeth us good things?" in answer to which question he says: "The light of Thy countenance, O Lord, is signed upon us" (Ps IV,6); thus implying that the light of natural reason, whereby we discern what is good and what is evil, which is the function of the natural law, is nothing else than an imprint on us of the divine light. It is therefore evident that the natural law is nothing else than the rational creature's participation of the eternal law.

Reply Obj. 1. This argument would hold if the natural law were something different from the eternal law, whereas it is nothing but a participation thereof, as stated above.

Reply Obj. 2. Every act of reason and will in us is based on that which is according to nature, as stated above (S.I-II,Q.10,A1); for every act of reasoning is based on principles that are known naturally, and every act of appetite in respect of the means is derived from the natural appetite in respect of the last end. Accordingly the first direction of our acts to their end must needs be in virtue of the natural law.

Reply Obj. 3. Even irrational animals partake in their own way of the eternal reason, just as the rational creature does. But because the rational creature partakes thereof in an intellectual and rational manner, therefore the participation of the eternal law in the rational creature is properly called a law, since a law is something pertaining to reason, as stated above (Q.90,A.1). Irrational creatures, however, do not partake thereof in a rational manner, wherefore there is no participation of the eternal law in them, except by way of similitude.

• • • •

Question 92

Of the Effects of Law

(In Two Articles)

We must now consider the effects of law; under which head there are two points of inquiry: (1) Whether an effect of law is to make men good? (2) Whether the effects of law are to command, to forbid, to permit, and to punish, as the Jurist states?

First Article

WHETHER AN EFFECT OF LAW IS TO MAKE MEN GOOD?

We proceed thus to the First Article:

Objection 1. It seems that it is not an effect of law to make men good. For men are good through virtue, since virtue, as stated in *Ethics* ii. 6, is "that which makes its subject good." But virtue is in man from God alone, because He it is Who "works it in us without us," as we stated above (S.I-II,Q.55,A4) in giving the definition of virtue. Therefore the law does not make men good.

Obj. 2. Further, law does not profit a man unless he obeys it. But the very fact that a man obeys a law is due to his being good. Therefore in man goodness is presupposed to the law. Therefore the law does not make men good.

Obj. 3. Further, law is ordained to the common good, as stated above (Q.90,A.2). But some behave well in things regarding the community, who behave ill in things regarding themselves. Therefore it is not the business of the law to make men good.

Obj. 4. Further, some laws are tyrannical, as the Philosopher says (*Pol*. iii,6). But a tyrant does not intend the good of his subjects, but considers only his own profit. Therefore law does not make men good.

On the contrary, The Philosopher says that the "intention of every lawgiver is to make good citizens." (*Eth*. ii.I).

I answer that, As stated above (Q.90,A.1 *ad 2; AA.3,4)*, a law is nothing else than a dictate of reason in the ruler by whom his subjects are governed. Now the virtue of any subordinate thing consists in its being well subordinated to that by which it is regulated; thus we see that the virtue of the irascible and concupiscible faculties consists in their being obedient to reason; and accordingly "the virtue of every subject consists in his being well subjected to his ruler," as the Philosopher says (*Pol.* i). But every law aims at being obeyed by those who are subject to it. Consequently it is evident that the proper effect of law is to lead its subjects to their proper virtue; and since virtue is "that which makes its subject good," it follows that the proper effect of law is to make those to whom it is given good, either simply or in some particular respect. For if the intention of the lawgiver is fixed on true good, which is the common good regulated according to divine justice, it follows that the effect of the law is to make men good simply. If, however, the intention of the lawgiver is fixed on that which is not simply good, but useful or pleasurable to himself, or in opposition to divine justice, then the law does not make men good simply, but in respect to that particular government. In this way good is found even in things that are bad of themselves: thus a man is called a good robber because he works in a way that is adapted to his end.

Reply Obj. 1. Virtue is twofold, as explained above (S.I-II,Q.63,A2), viz., acquired and infused. Now the fact of being accustomed to an action contributes to both, but in different ways; for it causes the acquired virtue, while it disposes to infused virtue, and preserves and fosters it when it already exists. And since law is given for the purpose of directing human acts as far as human acts conduce to virtue, so far does law make men good. Wherefore the Philosopher says in the second book of the *Politics* that "lawgivers make men good by habituating them to good works."

Reply Obj. 2. It is not always through perfect goodness of virtue that one obeys the law, but sometimes it is through fear of punishment, and sometimes from the mere dictate of reason, which is beginning of virtue, as stated above (*Ibid.,* A.1).

Reply Obj. 3. The goodness of any part is considered in comparison with the whole; hence Augustine says that "unseemly is the part that harmonizes not with the whole." (*Conf.* iii). Since then every man is a part of the state, it is impossible that a man be good unless he be well proportionate to the common good; nor can the whole be well consistent unless its parts be proportionate to it. Consequently the common good of the state cannot flourish unless the citizens be virtuous, at least those whose business it is to govern. But it is enough for the good of the community that the other citizens be so far virtuous that they obey the commands of their rulers. Hence the Philosopher says that "the virtue of a sovereign is the same as that of a good man, but the virtue of any common citizen is not the same as that of a good man.'' (*Pol.* iii,2).

Reply Obj. 4. A tyrannical law, through not being according to reason, is not a law, absolutely speaking, but rather a perversion of law; and yet in so far as it is something in the nature of a law, it aims at the citizens being good. For all it has in the nature of a law consists in its being an ordinance made by a superior to his subjects, and aims at being obeyed by them, which is to make them good, not simply, but with respect to that particular government.

• • • •

Question 94

Of the Natural Law

(In Six Articles)

We must now consider the natural law, concerning which there are six points of inquiry: (1) What is the natural law? (2) What are the precepts of the natural law? (3) Whether all acts of virtue are prescribed by the natural law? (4) Whether the natural law is the same in all? (5) Whether it is changeable? (6) Whether it can be abolished from the heart of man?

First Article

WHETHER THE NATURAL LAW IS A HABIT?

We proceed thus to the First Article:

Objection 1. It would seem that the natural law is a habit. Because, as the Philosopher says, ''there are three things in the soul: power, habit, and passion.'' (*Eth.* ii,5). But the natural law is not one of the soul's powers, nor is it one of the passions, as we may see by going through them one by one. Therefore the natural law is a habit.

Obj. 2. Further, Basil says that conscience or "*synderesis* is the law of our mind" (*De fide orthod*. iv 22), which can only apply to the natural law. But the *synderesis* is a habit, as was shown in the First Part (S.I,Q.79,A.12). Therefore the natural law is a habit.

Obj. 3. Further, the natural law abides in man always, as will be shown further on (A.6). But man's reason, which the law regards does not always think about the natural law. Therefore the natural law is not an act, but a habit.

On the contrary, Augustine says that "a habit is that whereby something is done when necessary." (*De bono. conjug*. XXI). But such is not the natural law, since it is in infants and in the damned who cannot act by it. Therefore the natural law is not a habit.

I answer that, A thing may be called a habit in two ways. First, properly and essentially: and thus the natural law is not a habit. For it has been stated above (Q.90,A.1 *ad* 2) that the natural law is something appointed by reason, just as a proposition is a work of reason. Now that which a man does is not the same as that whereby he does it, for he makes a becoming speech by the habit of grammar. Since, then, a habit is that by which we act, a law cannot be a habit, properly and essentially.

Secondly, the term "habit" may be applied to that which we hold by a habit: thus faith may mean that which we hold by faith. And accordingly, since the precepts of the natural law are sometimes considered by reason actually, while sometimes they are in the reason only habitually, in this way the natural law may be called a habit. Thus, in speculative matters, the indemonstrable principles are not the habit itself whereby we hold those principles, but are the principles the habit of which we possess.

Reply Obj. 1. The Philosopher proposes there to discover the genus of virtue; and since it is evident that virtue is a principle of action, he mentions only those things which are principles of human acts, viz., powers, habits and passions. But there are other things in the soul besides these three: there are acts; thus to will is in the one that wills; again, things known are in the knower; moreover its own natural properties are in the soul, such as immortality and the like.

Reply Obj. 2. *Synderesis* is said to be the law of our mind, because it is a habit containing the precepts of the natural law, which are the first principles of human actions.

Reply Obj. 3. This argument proves that the natural law is held habitually; and this is granted.

To the argument advanced in the contrary sense we reply that sometimes a man is unable to make use of that which is in him habitually, on account of some impediment: thus, on account of sleep, a man is unable to use the habit of science. In like manner, through the deficiency of his age, a child cannot use the habit of understanding of principles, or the natural law, which is in him habitually.

Second Article

WHETHER THE NATURAL LAW CONTAINS SEVERAL PRECEPTS, OR ONE ONLY?

We proceed thus to the Second Article:

Objection 1. It would seem that the natural law contains, not several precepts, but one only. For law is a kind of precept, as stated above (Q.92,A.2). If therefore there were many precepts of the natural law, it would follow that there are also many natural laws.

Obj. 2. Further, the natural law is consequent to human nature. But human nature, as a whole, is one, though, as to its parts, it is manifold. Therefore, either there is but one precept of the law of nature, on account of the unity of nature as a whole, or there are many, by reason of the number of parts of human nature. The result would be that even things relating to the inclination of the concupiscible faculty belong to the natural law.

Obj. 3. Further, law is something pertaining to reason, as stated above (Q.90,A.1). Now reason is but one in man. Therefore there is only one precept of the natural law.

On the contrary, The precepts of the natural law in man stand in relation to practical matters, as the first principles to matters of demonstration. But there are several first indemonstrable principles. Therefore there are also several precepts of the natural law.

I answer that, As stated above (Q.91,A.3), the precepts of the natural law are to the practical reason what the first principles of demonstrations are to the speculative reason, because both are self-evident principles. Now a thing is said to be self-evident in two ways: first, in itself; secondly, in relation to us. Any proposition is said to be self-evident in itself if its predicate is contained in the notion of subject, although to one who knows not the definition of the subject it happens that such a proposition is not self-evident. For instance, this proposition, "Man is a rational being," is, in its very nature, self-evident, since who says "man" says "a rational being;" and yet to one who knows not what a man is, this proposition is not self-evident. Hence it is that, as Boethius says, certain axioms or propositions are universally self-evident to all (*De Hebdom.*); and such are those propositions whose terms are known to all, as, "Every whole is greater than its part," and, "Things equal to one and the same are equal to one another." But some propositions are self-evident only to the wise who understand the meaning of the terms of such propositions; thus to one who understands that an angel is not a body, it is self-evident that an angel is not circumspectively in a place; but this is not evident to the unlearned, for they cannot grasp it.

Now a certain order is to be found in those things that are apprehended universally. For that which, before aught else, falls under apprehension, is "being," the notion of which is included in all things whatsoever a man apprehends. Wherefore the first indemonstrable principle is that *the same thing cannot be affirmed and denied at the same time,* which is based on the notion of "being" and "not-being"; and on this principle all others are based, as it is stated in *Metaphysics* iv. text. 9. Now as "being" is the first thing that falls under the apprehension simply, so "good" is the first thing that falls under the apprehension of the practical reason, which is directed to action, since every agent acts for an end under the aspect of good. Consequently the first principle in the practical reason is one founded on the notion of good, viz., that *good is that which all things seek after.* Hence this is the first precept of law, that *good is to be done and ensued, and evil is to be avoided.* All other precepts of the natural law are based upon this, so that whatever the practical reason naturally apprehends as man's good (or evil) belongs to the precepts of the natural law as something to be done or avoided.

Since, however, good has the nature of an end, and evil the nature of a contrary, hence it is that all those things to which man has a natural inclination are naturally apprehended by reason as being good and, consequently, as objects of pursuit, and their contraries as evil and objects of avoidance. Wherefore the order of the precepts of the natural law is according to the order of natural inclinations. Because in man there is first of all an inclination to good in accordance with the nature which he has in common with all substances, inasmuch as every substance seeks the preservation of its own being, according to its nature; and by reason of this inclination, whatever is a means of preserving human life and of warding off its obstacles belongs to the natural law. Secondly, there is in man an inclination to things that pertain to him more specially, according to that nature which he has in common with other animals; and in virtue of this inclination, those things are said to belong to the natural law "which nature has taught to all animals," such as sexual intercourse, education of offspring, and so forth. Thirdly, there is in man an inclination to good, according to the nature of his reason, which nature is proper to him: thus man has a natural inclination to know the truth about God and to live in society; and in this respect, whatever pertains to this inclination belongs to the natural law, for instance, to shun ignorance, to avoid offending those among whom one has to live, and other such things regarding the above inclination.

Reply Obj. 1. All these precepts of the law of nature have the character of one natural law, inasmuch as they flow from one first precept.

Reply Obj. 2. All the inclinations of any parts whatsoever of human nature, e.g., of the concupiscible and irascible parts, in so far as they are ruled by reason, belong to the natural law and are reduced to one first precept, as stated above, so that the precepts of the natural law are many in themselves, but are based on one common foundation.

Reply Obj. 3. Although reason is one in itself, yet it directs all things regarding man, so that whatever can be ruled by reason is contained under the law of reason.

Third Article

WHETHER ALL ACTS OF VIRTURE ARE PRESCRIBED BY THE NATURAL LAW?

We proceed thus to the Third Article:

Objection 1. It would seem that not all acts of virtue are prescribed by the natural law. Because, as stated above (Q.90,A.2), it is essential to a law that it be ordained to the common good. But some acts of virtue are ordained to the private good of the individual, as is evident especially in regard to acts of temperance. Therefore not all acts of virtue are the subject of natural law.

Obj. 2. Further, every sin is opposed to some virtuous act. If therefore all acts of virtue are prescribed by the natural law, it seems to follow that all sins are against nature, whereas this applies to certain special sins.

Obj. 3. Further, those things which are according to nature are common to all. But acts of virtue are not common to all, since a thing is virtuous in one, and vicious in another. Therefore not all acts of virtue are prescribed by the natural law.

On the contrary, Damascene says that "virtues are natural" (*De fide orthod*. iii,4). Therefore virtuous acts also are a subject of the natural law.

I answer that, We may speak of virtuous acts in two ways: first, under the aspect of virtuous; secondly, as such and such acts considered in their proper species. If then we speak of acts of virtue considered as virtuous, thus all virtuous acts belong to the natural law. For it has been stated (A.2) that to the natural law belongs everything to which a man is inclined according to his nature. Now each thing is inclined naturally to an operation that is suitable to it according to its form: thus fire is inclined to give heat. Wherefore, since the rational soul is the proper form of man, there is in every man a natural inclination to act according to reason; and this is to act according to virtue. Consequently, considered thus, all acts of virtue are prescribed by the natural law, since each one's reason naturally dictates to him to act virtuously. But if we speak of virtuous acts considered in themselves, i.e., in their proper species, thus not all virtuous acts are prescribed by the natural law, the many things are done virtuously to which nature does not incline at first, but which, through the inquiry of reason, have been found by men to be conducive to well-living.

Reply Obj. 1. Temperance is about the natural concupiscences of food, drink, and sexual matters, which are indeed ordained to the natural common good, just as other matters of law are ordained to the moral common good.

Reply Obj. 2. By human nature we may mean either that which is proper to man -- and in this sense all sins, as being against reason, are also against nature, as Damascene states (*Ibid.*, ii,30) -- or we may mean that nature which is common to man and other animals; and in this sense, certain special sins are said to be against nature: thus contrary to sexual intercourse, which is natural to all animals, is unisexual lust, which has received the special name of the unnatural crime.

Reply Obj. 3. This argument considers acts in themselves. For it is owing to the various conditions of men that certain acts are virtuous for some, as being proportionate and becoming to them, while they are vicious for others, as being out of proportion to them.

Fourth Article

WHETHER THE NATURAL LAW IS THE SAME IN ALL MEN?

We proceed thus to the Fourth Article:

Objection 1. It would seem that the natural law is not the same in all. For it is stated in the *Decretals* that "the natural law is that which is contained in the Law and the Gospel." (Dist. I). But this is not common to all men because, as it is written, "all do not obey the gospel." (Rom. X,16). Therefore the natural law is not the same in all men.

Obj. 2. Further, "Things which are according to the law are said to be just," as stated in *Ethics* v. But it is stated in the same book that nothing is so universally just as not to be subject to change in regard to some men. Therefore, even the natural law is not the same in all men.

Obj. 3. Further, as stated above (AA.2,3), to the natural law belongs everything to which a man is inclined according to his nature. Now different men are naturally inclined to different things, some to the desire of pleasures, others to the desire of honors, and other men to other things. Therefore, there is not one natural law for all.

On the contrary, Isidore says: "The natural law is common to all nations." (*Etym.* v, 4).

I answer that, As stated above (AA.2,3), to the natural law belong those things to which a man is inclined naturally; and among these it is proper to man to be inclined to act according to reason. Now the process of reason is from the common to the proper, as stated in *Phys.* i. The speculative reason, however, is differently situated in this matter, from the practical reason. For, since the speculative reason is busied chiefly with necessary things, which cannot be otherwise than they are, its proper conclusions, like the universal principles, contain the truth without fail. The practical reason, on the other hand, is busied with contingent matters, about which human actions are concerned; and consequently, although there is necessity in the general principles, the more we descend to matters of detail, the more frequently we encounter defects. Accordingly then in speculative matters truth is the same in all men, both as to principles and as to conclusions, although the truth is not known to all as regards the conclusions, but only as regards the principles which are called common notions. But in matters of action, truth or practical rectitude is not the same for all, as to matters of detail but only as to the general principles; and where there is the same rectitude in matters of detail, it is not equally known to all.

It is therefore evident that, as regards the general principles whether of speculative or of practical reason, truth or rectitude is the same for all, and is equally known by all. As to the proper conclusions of the speculative reason, the truth is the same for all, but is not equally known to all: thus it is true for all that the three angles of a triangle are together equal to two right angles, although it is not known to all. But as to the proper conclusions of the practical reason, neither is the truth or rectitude the same for all, nor, where it is the same, is it equally known by all. Thus it is right and true for all to act according to reason: and from this principle it follows as a proper conclusion, that goods entrusted to another should be restored to their owner. Now this is true for the majority of cases: but it may happen in a particular case that it would be injurious, and therefore unreasonable, to restore goods held in trust; for instance if they are claimed for the purpose of fighting against one's country. And this principle will be found to fail the more, according as we descend further into detail, e.g., if one were to say that goods held in trust should be restored with such and such a guarantee, or in such and such a way; because the greater the number of conditions added, the greater the number of ways in which the principle may fail, so that it be not right to restore or not to restore.

Consequently we must say that the natural law, as to general principles, is the same for all, both as to rectitude and as to knowledge. But as to certain matters of detail, which are conclusions, as it were, of those general principles, it is the same for all in the majority of cases, both as to rectitude and as to knowledge; and yet in some few cases it may fail, both as to rectitude, by reason of certain obstacles (just as natures subject to generation and corruption fail in some few cases on account of some obstacle), and as to knowledge, since in some the reason is perverted by passion, or evil habit, or an evil disposition of nature; thus formerly theft, although it is expressly contrary to the natural law, was not considered wrong among the Germans, as Julius Caesar relates. (*De bello Gall. vi;*)

Reply Obj. 1. The meaning of the sentence quoted is not that whatever is contained in the Law and the Gospel belongs to the natural law, since they contain many things that are above nature, but that whatever belongs to the natural law is fully contained in them. Wherefore Gratian, after saying that "the natural law is what is contained in the Law and the Gospel," adds at once, by way of example, "by which everyone is commanded to do to others as he would be done by."

Reply Obj. 2. The saying of the Philosopher is to be understood of things that are naturally just, not as general principles, but as conclusions drawn from them, having rectitude in the majority of cases, but failing in a few.

Reply Obj. 3. As, in man, reason rules and commands the other powers, so all the natural inclinations belonging to the other powers must needs be directed according to reason. Wherefore it is universally right for all men that all their inclinations should be directed according to reason.

Fifth Article

WHETHER THE NATURAL LAW CAN BE CHANGED?

We proceed thus to the Fifth Article:

Objection 1. It would seem that the natural law can be changed. Because on Ecclesiasticus xvii. 9, "He gave them instructions, and the law of life," the gloss says: "He wished the law of the letter to be written, in order to correct the law of nature." But that which is corrected is changed. Therefore the natural law can be changed.

Obj. 2. Further, the slaying of the innocent, adultery, and theft are against the natural law. But we find these things changed by God: as when God commanded Abraham to slay his innocent son (Gen. xxii,2); and when He ordered the Jews to borrow and purloin the vessels of the Egyptians (Exod. xii, 35); and when He commanded Osee to take to himself "a wife of fornications" (Osee i,2). Therefore the natural law can be changed.

Obj. 3. Further, Isidore says that "the possession of all things in common and universal freedom are matters of natural law." (*Etym*. v,4). But these things are seen to be changed by human laws. Therefore it seems that the natural law is subject to change.

On the contrary, It is said in the *Decretals:* "The natural law dates from the creation of the rational creature. It does not vary according to time, but remains unchangeable." (Dist. 5).

I answer that, A change in the natural law may be understood in two ways. First, by way of addition. In this sense nothing hinders the natural law from being changed, since many things, for the benefit of human life, have been added over and above the natural law, both by the divine law and by human laws.

Secondly, a change in the natural law may be understood by way of subtraction, so that what previously was according to the natural law ceases to be so. In this sense the natural law is altogether unchangeable in its first principles, but in its secondary principles, which, as we have said (A.4), are certain detailed proximate conclusions drawn from the first principles, the natural law is not changed so that what it prescribes be not right in most cases. But it may be changed in some particular cases of rare occurrence, through some special causes hindering the observance of such precepts, as stated above (A.4).

Reply Obj. 1. The written law is said to be given for the correction of the natural law, either because it supplies what was wanting to the natural law or because the natural law was perverted in the hearts of some men, as to certain matters, so that they esteemed those things good which are naturally evil; which perversion stood in need of correction.

Reply Obj. 2. All men alike, both guilty and innocent, die the death of nature; which death of nature is inflicted by the power of God on account of original sin, according to I Kings ii.6: "The Lord killeth and maketh alive." Consequently, by the command of God, death can be inflicted on any man, guilty or innocent, without any injustice whatever. -- In like manner adultery is intercourse with another's wife, who is allotted to him by the law emanating from God. Consequently intercourse with any woman, by the command of God, is neither adultery nor fornication. -- The same applies to theft, which is the taking of another's property. For whatever is taken by the command of God, to Whom all things belong, is not taken against the will of its owner, whereas it is in this that theft consists. Nor is it only in human things that whatever is commanded by God is right, but also in natural things -- whatever is done by God is, in some way, natural, as stated in the First Part (S.I,Q.105,A.6 *ad* I)

Reply Obj. 3. A thing is said to belong to the natural law in two ways. First, because nature inclines thereto: e.g., that one should not do harm to another. Secondly, because nature did not bring in the contrary: thus we might say that for man to be naked is of the natural law because nature did not give him clothes, but art invented them. In this sense, "the possession of all things in common and universal freedom" are said to be of the natural law because, to wit, the distinction of possessions and slavery were not brought in by nature, but devised by human reason for the benefit of human life. Accordingly the law of nature was not changed in this respect, except by addition.

Sixth Article

WHETHER THE LAW OF NATURE CAN BE ABOLISHED FROM THE HEART OF MAN?

We proceed thus to the Sixth Article:

Objection 1. It would seem that the natural law can be abolished from the heart of man. Because on Romans ii. 14, "When the Gentiles who have not the law," etc., a gloss says that "the law of righteousness, which sin had blotted out, is graven on the heart of man when he is restored by grace." But the law of righteousness is the law of nature. Therefore the law of nature can be blotted out.

Obj. 2. Further, the law of grace is more efficacious than the law of nature. But the law of grace is blotted out by sin. Much more therefore can the law of nature be blotted out.

Obj. 3. Further, that which is established by law is made just. But many things are enacted by men which are contrary to the law of nature. Therefore the law of nature can be abolished from the heart of man.

On the contrary, Augustine says: "Thy law is written in the hearts of men, which iniquity itself effaces not." (*Conf.* ii). But the law which is written in men's hearts is the natural law. Therefore the natural law cannot be blotted out.

I answer that, As stated above (AA.4,5), there belong to the natural law, first, certain most general precepts, that are known to all; and secondly, certain secondary and more detailed precepts, which are, as it were, conclusions following closely from first principles. As to those general principles, the natural law, in the abstract, can nowise be blotted out from men's hearts. But it is blotted out in the case of a particular action, in so far as reason is hindered from applying the general principle to a particular point of practice, on account of concupiscence or some other passion, as stated above (S.I-II, Q.77,A2). But as to the other, i.e., the secondary precepts, the natural law can be blotted out from the human heart either by evil persuasions, just as in speculative matters errors occur in respect of necessary conclusions, or by vicious customs and corrupt habits, as among some men theft and even unnatural vices, as the Apostle states, were not esteemed sinful (Rom. i).

Reply Obj. 1. Sin blots out the law of nature in particular cases, not universally, except perchance in regard to the secondary precepts of the natural law, in the way stated above.

Reply Obj. 2. Although grace is more efficacious than nature, yet nature is more essential to man and therefore more enduring.

Reply Obj. 3. The argument is true of the secondary precepts of the natural law, against which some legislators have framed certain enactments which are unjust.

Question 95

Of Human Law

(In Four Articles)

We must now consider human law, and (1) this law considered in itself, (2) its power, (3) its mutability. Under the first head there are four points of inquiry: (1) its utility; (2) its origin; (3) its quality; (4) its division.

First Article

WHETHER IT WAS USEFUL FOR LAWS TO BE FRAMED BY MEN?

We proceed thus to the First Article:

Objection 1. It would seem that it was not useful for laws to be framed by men. Because the purpose of every law is that man be made good thereby, as stated above (Q.92,A.1). But men are more to be induced to be good willingly, by means of admonitions, than against their will, by means of laws. Therefore there was no need to frame laws.

Obj. 2. Further, as the Philosopher says, " men have recourse to a judge as to animate justice." (*Eth.*, v,4). But animate justice is better than inanimate justice, which is contained in laws. Therefore it would have been better for the execution of justice to be entrusted to the decision of judges than to frame laws in addition.

Obj. 3. Further, every law is framed for the direction of human actions, as is evident from what has been stated above (Q.90,AA.1,2). But since human actions are about singulars, which are infinite in number, matters pertaining to the direction of human actions cannot be taken into sufficient consideration except by a wise man, who looks into each one of them. Therefore it would have been better for human acts to be directed by the judgment of wise men than by the framing of laws. Therefore there was no need of human laws.

On the contrary, Isidore says: "Laws were made that in fear thereof human audacity might be held in check, that innocence might be safeguarded in the midst of wickedness, and that the dread of punishment might prevent the wicked from doing harm." (*Etym*. v.20). But these things are most necessary to mankind. Therefore it was necessary that human laws should be made.

I answer that, As stated above (Q.63,A.1; Q.94,A.3), man has a natural aptitude for virtue, but the perfection of virtue must be acquired by man by means of some kind of training. Thus we observe that man is helped by industry in his necessities, for instance, in food and clothing. Certain beginnings of these he has from nature, viz., his reason and his hands, but he has not the full complement, as other animals have to whom nature has given sufficiency of clothing and food. Now it is difficult to see how man could suffice for himself in the matter of this training, since the perfection of virtue consists chiefly in withdrawing man from undue pleasures, to which above all man is inclined, and especially the young, who are more capable of being trained. Consequently a man needs to receive this training from another, whereby to arrive at the perfection of virtue. And as to those young people who are inclined to acts of virtue, by their good natural disposition, or by custom, or rather by the gift of God, paternal training suffices, which is by admonitions. But since some are found to be depraved and prone to vice, and not easily amenable to words, it was necessary for such to be restrained from evil by force and fear, in order that, at least, they might desist from evil-doing and leave others in peace, and that they themselves, by being habituated in this way, might be brought to do willingly what hitherto they did from fear, and thus become virtuous. Now this kind of training which compels through fear of punishment is the discipline of laws. Therefore, in order that man might have peace and virtue, it was necessary for laws to be framed, for, as the Philosopher says, "as man is the most noble of animals if he be perfect in virtue, so is he the lowest of all if he be severed from law and righteousness" (*Pol.* i.2); because man can use his reason to devise means of satisfying his lusts and evil passions, which other animals are unable to do.

Reply Obj. 1. Men who are well disposed are led willingly to virtue by being admonished better than by coercion, but men who are evilly disposed are not led to virtue unless they are compelled.

Reply Obj. 2. As the Philosopher says, "It is better that all things be regulated by law than left to be decided by judges" (*Rhet.* i.I); and this for three reasons. First, because it is easier to find a few wise men competent to frame right laws than to find the many who would be necessary to judge aright of each single case. Secondly, because those who make laws consider long beforehand what laws to make, whereas judgment on each single case has to be pronounced as soon as it arises; and it is easier for man to see what is right by taking many instances into consideration than by considering one solitary fact. Thirdly, because lawgivers judge in the abstract and of future events, whereas those who sit in judgment judge of things present, toward which they are affected by love, hatred, or some kind of cupidity; wherefore their judgment is perverted.

Since then the animated justice of the judge is not found in every man, and since it can be deflected, therefore it was necessary, whenever possible, for the law to determine how to judge, and for very few matters to be left to the decision of men.

Reply Obj. 3. Certain individual facts which cannot be covered by the law "have necessarily to be committed to judges," as the Philosopher says in the same passage; for instance, "concerning something that has happened or not happened," and the like.

Second Article

WHETHER EVERY HUMAN LAW IS DERIVED FROM THE NATURAL LAW?

We proceed thus to the Second Article:

Objection 1. It would seem that not every human law is derived from the natural law. For the Philosopher says that "the legal just is that which originally was a matter of indifference." (*Eth.* v.7). But those things which arise from the natural law are not matters of indifference. Therefore the enactments of human laws are not all derived from the natural law.

Obj. 2. Further, positive law is contrasted with natural law, as stated by Isidore (*Etym.* v.4) and the Philosopher (*Eth.* v.7). But those things which flow as conclusions from the general principles of the natural law belong to the natural law, as stated above (Q.94,A.4). Therefore that which is established by human law does not belong to the natural law.

Obj. 3. Further, the law of nature is the same for all, since the Philosopher says that "the natural just is that which is equally valid everywhere." (*Ibid.*). *If, therefore, human laws were derived from the natural law, it would follow that they too are the same for all, which is clearly false.*

Obj. 4. Further, it is possible to give a reason for things which are derived from the natural law. But "it is not possible to give the reason for all the legal enactments of the lawgivers,'' as the Jurist says (*Digest* i.3.5). Therefore not all human laws are derived from the natural law.

On the contrary, Cicero says: ''Things which emanated from nature and were approved by custom were sanctioned by fear and reverence for the laws.'' (*Rhetor.* ii).

I answer that, As Augustine says, ''that which is not just seems to be no law at all'' (*De lib. arb* i.5); wherefore the force of a law depends on the extent of its justice. Now in human affairs a thing is said to be just from being right according to the rule of reason. But the first rule of reason is the law of nature, as is clear from what has been stated above (Q.91,A.2 *ad* 2). Consequently, every human law has just so much of the nature of law as it is derived from the law of nature. But if in any point it deflects from the law of nature, it is no longer a law but a perversion of law.

But it must be noted that something may be derived from the natural law in two ways: first, as a conclusion from premises; secondly, by way of determination of certain generalities. The first way is like to that by which, in the sciences, demonstrated conclusions are drawn from the principles, while the second mode is likened to that whereby, in the arts, general forms are particularized as to details: thus the craftsman needs to determine the general form of a house to some particular shape. Some things are therefore derived from the general principles of the natural law by way of conclusions, e.g., that ''one must not kill'' may be derived as a conclusion from the principle that ''one should do harm to no man''; while some are derived therefrom by way of determination, e.g., the law of nature has it that the evildoer should be punished; but that he be punished in this or that way is not directly by natural law but is a derived determination of it.

Accordingly, both modes of derivation are found in the human law. But those things which are derived in the first way are contained in human law, not as emanating therefrom exclusively, but having some force from the natural law also. But those things which are derived in the second way have no other force than that of human law.

Reply Obj. 1. The Philosopher is speaking of those enactments which are by way of determination or specification of the precepts of the natural law.

Reply Obj. 2. This argument avails for those things that are derived from the natural law, by way of conclusions.

Reply Obj. 3. The general principles of the natural law cannot be applied to all men in the same way, on account of the great variety of human affairs, and hence arises the diversity of positive laws among various people.

Reply Obj. 4. These words of the Jurist are to be understood as referring to decisions of rulers in determining particular points of the natural law, on which determinations the judgment of expert and prudent men is based as on its principles, in so far, to wit, as they see at once what is the best thing to decide.

Hence the Philosopher says that in such matters "we ought to pay as much attention to the undemonstrated sayings and opinions of persons who surpass us in experience, age, and prudence as to their demonstrations." (*Eth.* vi.II).

• • • •

Question 96

Of the Power of Human Law

(In Six Articles)

We must now consider the power of human law. Under this head there are six points of inquiry: (1) Whether human law should be framed for the community? (2) Whether human law should repress all vices? (3) Whether human law is competent to direct all acts of virtue? (4) Whether it binds man in conscience? (5) Whether all men are subject to human law? (6) Whether those who are under the law may act beside the letter of the law?

First Article

WHETHER HUMAN LAW SHOULD BE FRAMED FOR THE COMMUNITY RATHER THAN FOR THE INDIVIDUAL?

We proceed thus to the First Article:

Objection 1. It would seem that human law should be framed, not for the community, but rather for the individual. For the Philosopher says that "the legal just . . . includes all particular acts of legislation . . . and all those matters which are the subject of decrees" (*Eth.* v.7), which are also individual matters, since decrees are framed about individual actions. Therefore law is framed not only for the community, but also for the individual.

Obj. 2. Further, law is the director of human acts, as stated above (Q.90,AA.1,2). But human acts are about individual matters. Therefore human laws should be framed, not for the community, but rather for the individual.

Obj. 3. Further, law is a rule and measure of human acts, as stated above (Q.90,AA.1,2). But a measure should be most certain, as stated in *Metaphysics* x. Since therefore in human acts no general proposition can be so certain as not to fail in some individual cases, it seems that laws should be framed not in general but for individual cases.

On the contrary, The Jurist says that "laws should be made to suit the majority of instances; and they are not framed according to what may possibly happen in an individual case." (*Digest* i.3.2.)

I answer that, Whatever is for an end should be proportionate to that end. Now the end of law is the common good; because, as Isidore says, "law should be framed, not for any private benefit, but for the common good of all the citizens." (*Etym.* v.21). Hence human laws should be proportionate to the common good. Now the common good comprises many things. Wherefore law should take account of many things, as to persons, as to matters, and as to times; because the community of the state is composed of many persons and its good is procured by many actions; nor is it established to endure for only a short time, but to last for all time by the citizens succeeding one another, as Augustine says (*De civ. Dei.* ii 21; xxii,6).

Reply Obj. 1. The Philosopher divides the "legal just," i.e., positive law, into three parts. For some things are laid down simply in a general way: and these are the general laws. Of these he says that "the legal is that which originally was a matter of indifference, but which, when enacted, is so no longer," as the fixing of the ransom of a captive. -- Some things affect the community in one respect and individuals in another. These are called "privileges," i.e., "private laws," as it were, because they regard private persons, although their power extends to many matters; and in regard to these, he adds, " and further all particular acts of legislation." -- Other matters are legal, not through being laws, but through being applications of general laws to particular cases, such are decrees which have the force of law; and in regard to these, he adds "all matters subject to decrees." (*Eth.* v.7).

Reply Obj. 2. A principle of direction should be applicable to many, wherefore the Philosopher says that all things belonging to one genus are measured by one which is the principle in that genus (*Metaph.* x.*text* 4). For if there were as many rules or measures as there are things measured or ruled, they would cease to be of use, since their use consists in being applicable to many things. Hence law would be of no use if it did not extend further than to one single act. Because the decrees of prudent men are made for the purpose of directing individual actions, whereas law is a general precept, as stated above (Q.92,A.2,Obj.2).

Reply Obj. 3. "We must not seek the same degree of certainty in all things." (*Eth.* i 3). Consequently in contingent matters, such as natural and human things, it is enough for a thing to be certain, as being true in the greater number of instances, though at times and less frequently it fail.

Second Article

WHETHER IT BELONGS TO HUMAN LAW TO REPRESS ALL VICES?

We proceed thus to the Second Article:

Objection 1. It would seem that it belongs to human law to repress all vices. For Isidore says that "laws were made in order that, in fear thereof, man's audacity might be held in check." (*Etym.* v.20). But it would not be held in check sufficently unless all evils were repressed by law. Therefore human law should repress all evils.

Obj. 2. Further, the intention of the lawgiver is to make the citizens virtuous. But a man cannot be virtuous unless he forbear from all kinds of vice. Therefore it belongs to human law to repress all vices.

Obj. 3. Further, human law is derived from the natural law, as stated above (Q.95,A.2). But all vices are contrary to the law of nature. Therefore human law should repress all vices.

On the contrary, We read in *De libero arbitrio* i.5: "It seems to me that the law which is written for the governing of the people rightly permits these things, and that divine providence punishes them." But divine providence punishes nothing but vices. Therefore human law rightly allows some vices, by not repressing them.

I answer that, As stated above (Q.90,AA.1,2), law is framed as a rule or measure of human acts. Now a measure should be homogeneous with that which it measures, as stated in *Metaphysics* x. text. 3,4, since different things are measured by different measures. Wherefore laws imposed on men should also be in keepingwith their condition, for, as Isidore says (*Ibid.*, 21), law should be "possible both according to nature, and according to the customs of the country." Now possibility or faculty of action is due to an interior habit or disposition, since the same thing is not possible to one who has not a virtuous habit as is possible to one who has. Thus the same is not possible to a child as to a full-grown man; for which reason the law for children is not the same as for adults, since many things are permitted to children which in an adult are punished by law or at any rate are open to blame. In like manner many things are permissible to men not perfect in virtue which would be intolerable in a virtuous man.

Now human law is framed for a number of human beings, the majority of whom are not perfect in virtue. Wherefore human laws do not forbid all vices from which the virtuous abstain, but only the more grievous vices from which it is possible for the majority to abstain; and chiefly those that are to the hurt of others, without the prohibition of which human society could not be maintained: thus human law prohibits murder, theft, and such like.

Reply Obj. 1. Audacity seems to refer to the assailing of others. Consequently it belongs to those sins chiefly whereby one's neighbor is injured; and these sins are forbidden by human law, as stated.

Reply Obj. 2. The purpose of human law is to lead men to virtue, not suddenly, but gradually. Wherefore it does not lay upon the multitude of imperfect men the burdens of those who are already virtuous, viz., that they should abstain from all evil. Otherwise these imperfect ones, being unable to bear such precepts, would break out into yet greater evils; thus it is written: "He that violently bloweth his nose, bringeth out blood" (Prov. xxx.33); and that if "new wine," i.e., precepts of a perfect life, is "put into old bottles," i.e., into imperfect men, "the bottles break, and the wine runneth out," i.e., the precepts are despised and those men, from contempt, break out into evils worse still (Matth. ix.17).

Reply Obj. 3. The natural law is a participation in us of the eternal law, while human law falls short of the eternal law. Now Augustine says: "The law which is framed for the government of states allows and leaves unpunished many things that are punished by divine providence. Nor, if this law does not attempt to do everything, is this a reason why it should be blamed for what it does" (*De lib. arb.* i.5). Wherefore, too, human law does not prohibit everything that is forbidden by the natural law.

Third Article

WHETHER HUMAN LAW PRESCRIBES ACTS OF ALL THE VIRTUES?

We proceed thus to the Third Article:

Objection 1. It would seem that human law does not prescribe acts of all the virtues. For vicious acts are contrary to acts of virtue. But human law does not prohibit all vices, as stated above (A.2). Therefore neither does it prescribe all acts of virtue.

Obj. 2. Further, a virtuous act proceeds from a virtue. But virtue is the end of law, so that whatever is from a virtue cannot come under a precept of law. Therefore human law does not prescribe all acts of virtue.

Obj. 3. Further, law is ordained to the common good, as stated above (Q.90,A.2). But some acts of virtue are ordained, not to the common good, but to private good. Therefore the law does not prescribe all acts of virtue.

On the contrary, The Philosopher says that the law "prescribes the performance of the acts of a brave man . . . and the acts of the temperate man . . . and the acts of the meek man; and in like manner as regards the other virtues and vices, prescribing the former, forbidding the latter." (*Eth*. v.1).

I answer that, The species of virtues are distinguished by their objects, as explained above (S.I-II,Q.54,A.2; Q.60,A.1; Q.62,A.2). Now all the objects of virtues can be referred either to the private good of an individual or to the common good of the multitude: thus matters of fortitude may be achieved either for the safety of the state or for upholding the rights of a friend, and in like manner with the other virtues. But law, as stated above (Q.90,A.2), is ordained to the common good. Wherefore there is no virtue whose acts cannot be prescribed by the law. Nevertheless human law does not prescribe concerning all the acts of every virtue, but only in regard to those that are ordainable to the common good -- either immediately, as when certain things are done directly for the common good, or mediately, as when a lawgiver prescribes certain things pertaining to good order whereby the citizens are directed in the upholding of the common good of justice and peace.

Reply Obj. 1. Human law does not forbid all vicious acts by the obligation of a precept, as neither does it prescribe all acts of virtue. But it forbids certain acts of each vice, just as it prescribes some acts of each virtue.

Reply Obj. 2. An act is said to be an act of virtue in two ways. First, from the fact that a man does something virtuous; thus the act of justice is to do what is right, and an act of fortitude is to do brave things -- and in this way law prescribes certain acts of virtue. Secondly, an act of virtue is when a man does a virtuous thing in a way in which a virtuous man does it. Such an act always proceeds from virtue, and it does not come under a precept of law, but is the end at which every lawgiver aims.

Reply Obj. 3. There is no virtue whose act is not ordainable to the common good, as stated above, either mediately or immediately.

• • • •

Question 97

Of Change in Laws

(In Four Articles)

We must now consider change in laws, under which head there are four points of inquiry: (1) Whether human law is changeable? (2) Whether it should always be changed whenever something better occurs? (3) Whether it is abolished by custom, and whether custom obtains the force of law? (4) Whether the application of human law should be changed by dispensation of those in authority?

First Article

WHETHER HUMAN LAW SHOULD BE CHANGED IN ANY WAY?

We proceed thus to the First Article:

Objection 1. It would seem that human law should not be changed in any way at all. Because human law is derived from the natural law, as stated above (Q.95,A.2). But the natural law endures unchangeably. Therefore human law should also remain without any change.

Obj. 2. Further, as the Philosopher says, a measure should be absolutely stable (*Eth*., v.5). But human law is the measure of human acts, as stated above (Q.90,AA.1,2). Therefore it should remain without change.

Obj. 3. Further, it is of the essence of law to be just and right, as stated above (Q.95,A.2). But that which is right once is right always. Therefore that which is law once should be always law.

On the contrary, Augustine says: ''A temporal law, however just, may be justly changed in course of time.'' (*De lib. arb*. i.6).

I answer that, As stated above (Q.92,A.3), human law is a dictate of reason whereby human acts are directed. Thus there may be two causes for the just change of human law: one of the part of reason, the other on the part of man whose acts are regulated by law. The cause on the part of reason is that it seems natural to human reason to advance gradually from the imperfect to the perfect. Hence, in speculative sciences, we see that the teaching of the early philosophers was imperfect, and that it was afterward perfected by those who succeeded them. So also in practical matters; for those who first endeavored to discover something useful for the human community, not being able by themselves to take everything into consideration, set up certain institutions which were deficient in many ways, and these were changed by subsequent lawgivers who made institutions that might prove less frequently deficient in respect of the common weal.

On the part of man whose acts are regulated by law the law can be rightly changed on account of the changed condition of man, to whom different things are expedient according to the difference of his condition. An example is proposed by Augustine: ''If the people have a sense of moderation and responsibility and are most careful guardians of the common weal, it is right to enact a law allowing such a people to choose their own magistrates for the government of the commonwealth. But if, as time goes on, the same people become so corrupt as to sell their votes and entrust the government to scoundrels and criminals, then the right of appointing their public officials is rightly forfeit to such a people, and the choice devolves to a few good men.'' (*Ibid*.).

Reply Obj. 1. The natural law is a participation of the eternal law, as stated above (Q.91,A.2), and therefore endures without change, owing to the unchangeableness and perfection of the divine reason, the Author of nature. But the reason of man is changeable and imperfect, wherefore his law is subject to change. -- Moreover the natural law contains certain universal precepts which are everlasting, whereas human law contains certain particular precepts, according to various emergencies.

Reply Obj. 2. A measure should be as enduring as possible. But nothing can be absolutely unchangeable in things that are subject to change. And therefore human law cannot be altogether unchangeable.

Reply Obj. 3. In corporal things, right is predicated absolutely and therefore, as far as itself is concerned, always remains right. But right is predicated of law with reference to the common weal, to which one and the same thing is not always adapted, as stated above; wherefore rectitude of this kind is subject to change.

Second Article

WHETHER HUMAN LAW SHOULD ALWAYS BE CHANGED WHENEVER SOMETHING BETTER OCCURS?

We proceed thus to the Second Article:

Objection 1. It would seem that human law should be changed whenever something better occurs. Because human laws are devised by human reason, like other arts. But in the other arts, the tenets of former times give place to others if something better occurs. Therefore the same should apply to human laws.

Obj. 2. Further, by taking note of the past we can provide for the future. Now unless human laws had been changed when it was found possible to improve them, considerable inconvenience would have ensued because the laws of old were crude in many points. Therefore it seems that laws should be changed whenever anything better occurs to be enacted.

Obj. 3. Further, human laws are enacted about single acts of man. But we cannot acquire perfect knowledge in singular matters except by experience, which "requires time," as stated in *Ethics* ii. Therefore it seems that as time goes on it is possible for something better to occur for legislation.

On the contrary, It is stated in the *Decretals:* "It is absurd and a detestable shame that we should suffer those traditions to be changed which we have received from the fathers of old." (*Dist.* 12.5).

I answer that, As stated above (A.1), human law is rightly changed in so far as such change is conducive to the common weal. But, to a certain extent, the mere change of law is of itself prejudicial to the common good because custom avails much for the observance of laws, seeing that what is done contrary to general custom, even in slight matters, is looked upon as grave. Consequently, when a law is changed, the binding power of the law is diminished in so far as custom is abolished. Wherefore human law should never be changed unless, in some way or other, the common weal be compensated according to the extent of the harm done in this respect. Such compensation may arise either from some very great and very evident benefit conferred by the new enactment or from the extreme urgency of the case, due to the fact that either the existing law is clearly unjust or its observance extremely harmful. Wherefore the Jurist says that "in establishing new laws, there should be evidence of the benefit to be derived, before departing from a law which has long been considered just." (*Digest* i.4).

Reply Obj. 1. Rules of art derive their force from reason alone, and therefore, whenever something better occurs, the rule followed hitherto should be changed. But "laws derive very great force from custom," as the Philosopher states (*Pol.* ii.5); consequently they should not be quickly changed.

Reply Obj. 2. This argument proves that laws ought to be changed, not in view of any improvement, but for the sake of a great benefit or in a case of great urgency, as stated above. This answer applies also to the *Third Objection.*

• • • •

4

Hobbes
On Man and the State

Leviathan

[Part I] Of Man

Chapter VI

OF THE INTERIOR BEGINNINGS OF VOLUNTARY MOTIONS; COMMONLY CALLED THE PASSIONS; AND THE SPEECHES BY WHICH THEY ARE EXPRESSED

There be in animals, two sorts of *motions* peculiar to them: one called *vital;* begun in generation, and continued without interruption through their whole life; such as are the *course* of the *blood,* the *pulse,* the *breathing,* the *concoction, nutrition, excretion,* &c. to which motions there needs no help of imagination: the other is *animal motion,* otherwise called *voluntary motion;* as to *go,* to *speak,* to *move* any of our limbs, in such manner as is first fancied in our minds. That sense is motion in the organs and interior parts of man's body, caused by the action of the things we see, hear, &c.; and that fancy is but the relics of the same motion, remaining after sense, has been already said in the first and second chapters. And because *going, speaking,* and the like voluntary motions, depend always upon a precedent thought of *whither, which way,* and *what;* it is evident, that the imagination is the first internal beginning of all voluntary motion. And although unstudied men do not conceive any motion at all to be there, where the thing moved is invisible; or the space it is moved in is, for the shortness of it, insensible; yet that doth not hinder, but that such motions are. For let a space be never so little, that which is moved over a greater space, whereof that little one is part, must first be moved over that. These small beginnings of motion, within the body of man, before they appear in walking, speaking, striking, and other visible actions, are commonly called ENDEAVOUR.

This endeavour, when it is toward something which causes it, is called APPETITE, or DESIRE; the latter, being the general name; and the other oftentimes restrained to signify the desire of food, namely *hunger* and *thirst*. And when the endeavour is fromward something, it is generally called AVERSION. These words, *appetite* and *aversion,* we have from the Latins; and they both of them signify the motions, one of approaching, the other of retiring. So also do the Greek words for the same. For nature itself does often press upon men those truths, which afterwards, when they look for somewhat beyond nature, they stumble at. For the Schools find in mere appetite to go, or move, no actual motion at all: but because some motion they must acknowledge, they call it metaphorical motion; which is but an absurd speech: for though words may be called metaphorical; bodies and motions can not.

That which men desire, they are also said to LOVE: and to HATE those things for which they have aversion. So that desire and love are the same thing; save that by desire, we always signify the absence of the object; by love, most commonly the presence of the same. So also by aversion, we signify the absence; and by hate, the presence of the object.

Of appetites and aversions, some are born with men; as appetite of food, appetite of excretion, and exoneration, which may also and more properly be called aversions, from somewhat they feel in their bodies; and some other appetites, not many. The rest, which are appetites of particular things, proceed from experience, and trial of their effects upon themselves or other men. For of things we know not at all, or believe not to be, we can have no further desire, than to taste and try. But aversion we have for things, not only which we know have hurt us, but also that we do not know whether they will hurt us, or not.

Those things which we neither desire, nor hate, we are said to *contemn;* CONTEMPT being nothing else but an immobility, or contumacy of the heart, in resisting the action of certain things; and proceeding from that the heart is already moved otherwise, by other more potent objects; or from want of experience of them.

And because the constitution of a man's body is in continual mutation, it is impossible that all the same things should always cause in him the same appetites, and aversions: much less can all men consent, in the desire of almost any one and the same object.

But whatsoever is the object of any man's appetite or desire, that is it which he for his part calleth *good:* and the object of his hate and aversion, *evil;* and of his contempt, *vile* and *inconsiderable*. For these words of good, evil, and contemptible, are ever used with relation to the person that useth them: there being nothing simply and absolutely so; nor any common rule of good and evil, to be taken from the nature of the objects themselves; but from the person of the man, where there is no commonwealth; or, in a commonwealth, from the person that representeth it; or from an arbitrator or judge, whom men disagreeing shall by consent set up, and make his sentence the rule thereof.

The Latin tongue has two words, whose significations approach to those of good and evil; but are not precisely the same; and those are *pulchrum* and *turpe*. Whereof the former signifies that, which by some apparent signs promiseth good; and the latter, that which promiseth evil. But in our tongue we have not so general names to express them by. But for *pulchrum* we say in some things, *fair;* in others, *beautiful,* or *handsome,* or *gallant,* or *honourable,* or *comely,* or *amiable;* and for *turpe, foul, deformed, ugly, base, nauseous,* and the like, as the subject shall require; all which words, in their proper places, signify nothing else but the *mien,* or countenance, that promiseth good and evil. So that of good there be three kinds; good in the promise, that is *pulchrum;* good in effect, as the end desired, which is called *jucundum, delightful;* and good as the means, which is called *utile, profitable;* and as many of evil: for *evil* in promise, is that they call *turpe;* evil in effect, and end, is *molestum, unpleasant, troublesome;* and evil in the means, *inutile, unprofitable, hurtful*.

As, in sense, that which is really within us, is, as I have said before, only motion, caused by the action of external objects, but in apparence; to the sight, light and colour; to the ear, sound; to the nostril, odour, &c.: so, when the action of the same object is continued from the eyes, ears, and other organs to the heart, the real effect there is nothing but motion, or endeavour; which consisteth in appetite, or aversion, to or from the object moving. But the apparence, or sense of that motion, is that we either call *delight,* or *trouble of mind*.

This motion, which is called appetite, and for the apparence of it *delight,* and *pleasure,* seemeth to be a corroboration of vital motion, and a help thereunto; and therefore such things as caused delight, were not improperly called *jucunda, à juvando,* from helping or fortifying; and the contrary, *molesta, offensive,* from hindering, and troubling the motion vital.

Pleasure therefore, or *delight,* is the apparence, or sense of good; and *molestation,* or *displeasure,* the apparence, or sense of evil. And consequently all appetite, desire, and love, is accompanied with some delight more or less; and all hatred and aversion, with more or less displeasure and offence.

Of pleasures or delights, some arise from the sense of an object present; and those may be called *pleasure of sense;* the word *sensual,* as it is used by those only that condemn them, having no place till there be laws. Of this kind are all onerations and exonerations of the body; as also all that is pleasant, in the *sight, hearing, smell, taste,* or *touch.* Others arise from the expectation, that proceeds from foresight of the end, or consequence of things; whether those things in the sense please or displease. And these are *pleasures of the mind* of him that draweth those consequences, and are generally called JOY. In the like manner, displeasures are some in the sense, and called PAIN; others in the expectation of consequences, and are called GRIEF.

These simple passions called *appetite, desire, love, aversion, hate, joy,* and *grief,* have their names for divers considerations diversified. As first, when they one succeed another, they are diversely called from the opinion men have of the likelihood of attaining what they desire. Secondly, from the object loved or hated. Thirdly, from the consideration of many of them together. Fourthly, from the alteration or succession itself.

For *appetite,* with an opinion of attaining, is called HOPE.

The same, without such opinion, DESPAIR.

Aversion, with opinion of HURT from the object, FEAR.

The same, with hope of avoiding that hurt by resistance, COURAGE.

Sudden *courage,* ANGER.

Constant *hope,* CONFIDENCE of ourselves.

Constant *despair,* DIFFIDENCE of ourselves.

Anger for great hurt done to another, when we conceive the same to be done by injury, INDIGNATION.

Desire of good to another, BENEVOLENCE, GOOD WILL, CHARITY. If to man generally, GOOD NATURE.

Desire of riches, COVETOUSNESS; a name used always in signification of blame; because men contending for them are displeased with one another attaining them; though the desire in itself, be to be blamed, or allowed, according to the means by which these riches are sought.

Desire of office, or precedence, AMBITION: a name used also in the worse sense, for the reason before mentioned.

Desire of things that conduce but a little to our ends, and fear of things that are but of little hindrance, PUSILLANIMITY.

Contempt of little helps and hindrances, MAGNANIMITY.

Magnanimity, in danger of death or wounds, VALOUR, FORTITUDE.

Magnanimity in the use of riches, LIBERALITY.

Pusillanimity in the same, WRETCHEDNESS, MISERABLENESS, or PARSIMONY; as it is liked or disliked.

Love of persons for society, KINDNESS.

Love of persons for pleasing the sense only, NATURAL LUST.

Love of the same, acquired from rumination, that is, imagination of pleasure past, LUXURY.

Love of one singularly, with desire to be singularly beloved, THE PASSION OF LOVE. The same, with fear that the love is not mutual, JEALOUSY.

Desire, by doing hurt to another, to make him condemn some fact of his own, REVENGEFULNESS.

Desire to know why, and how, CURIOSITY; such as is in no living creature but *man:* so that man is distinguished, not only by his reason, but also by this singular passion from other *animals;* in whom the appetite of food, and other pleasures of sense, by predominance, take away the care of knowing causes; which is a lust of the mind, that by a perseverance of delight in the continual and indefatigable generation of knowledge, exceedeth the short vehemence of any carnal pleasure.

Fear of power invisible, feigned by the mind, or imagined from tales publicly allowed, RELIGION; not allowed, SUPERSTITION. And when the power imagined, is truly such as we imagine, TRUE RELIGION.

Fear, without the apprehension of why, or what, PANIC TERROR, called so from the fables, that make Pan the author of them; whereas, in truth, there is always in him that so feareth, first, some apprehension of the cause, though the rest run away by example, every one supposing his fellow to know why. And therefore this passion happens to none but in a throng, or multitude of people.

Joy, from apprehension of novelty, ADMIRATION; proper to man, because it excites the appetite of knowing the cause.

Joy, arising from imagination of a man's own power and ability, is that exultation of the mind which is called GLORYING: which if grounded upon the experience of his own former actions, is the same with *confidence;* but if grounded on the flattery of others; or only supposed by himself, for delight in the consequences of it, is called *VAINGLORY:* which name is properly given; because a well grounded *confidence* begetteth attempt; whereas the supposing of power does not, and is therefore rightly called *vain*.

Grief, from opinion of want of power, is called DEJECTION of mind.

The *vain-glory* which consisteth in the feigning or supposing of abilities in ourselves, which we know are not, is most incident to young men, and nourished by the histories, or fictions of gallant persons; and is corrected oftentimes by age, and employment.

Sudden glory, is the passion which maketh those *grimaces* called LAUGHTER; and is caused either by some sudden act of their own, that pleaseth them; or by the apprehension of some deformed thing in another, by comparison whereof they suddenly applaud themselves. And it is incident most to them, that are conscious of the fewest abilities in themselves; who are forced to keepthemselves in their own favour, by observing the imperfections of other men. And therefore much laughter at the defects of others, is a sign of pusillanimity. For of great minds, one of the proper works is, to help and free others from scorn; and compare themselves only with the most able.

On the contrary, *sudden dejection,* is the passion that causeth WEEPING; and is caused by such accidents, as suddenly take away some vehement hope, or some prop of their power: and they are most subject to it, that rely principally on helps external, such as are women, and children. Therefore some weep for the loss of friends; others for their unkindness; others for the sudden stop made to their thoughts of revenge, by reconciliation. But in all cases, both laughter, and weeping, are sudden motions; custom taking them both away. For no man laughs at old jests; or weeps for an old calamity.

Grief, for the discovery of some defect of ability, is SHAME, or the passion that discovereth itself in BLUSHING; and consisteth in the apprehension of some thing dishonourable; and in young men, is a sign of the love of good reputation, and commendable: in old men it is a sign of the same; but because it comes too late, not commendable.

The *contempt* of good reputation is called IMPUDENCE. *Grief,* for the calamity of another, is PITY; and ariseth from the imagination that the like calamity may befall himself; and therefore is called also COMPASSION, and in phrase of this present time a FELLOW-FEELING: and therefore for calamity arriving from great wickedness, the best men have the least pity; and for the same calamity, those hate pity, that think themselves least obnoxious to the same.

Contempt, or little sense of the calamity of others, is that which men call CRUELTY; proceeding from security of their own fortune. For, that any man should take pleasure in other men's great harms; without other end of his own, I do not conceive it possible.

Grief, for the success of a competitor in wealth, honour, or other good, if it be joined with endeavour to enforce our own abilities to equal or exceed him, is called EMULATION: but joined with endeavour to supplant, or hinder a competitor, ENVY.

When in the mind of man, appetites, and aversions, hopes, and fears, concerning one and the same thing, arise alternately; and divers good and evil consequences of the doing, or omitting the thing propounded, come successively into our thoughts; so that sometimes we have an appetite to it; sometimes an aversion from it; sometimes hope to be able to do it; sometimes despair, or fear to attempt it; the whole sum of desires, aversions, hopes and fears continued till the thing be either done, or thought impossible, is that we call DELIBERATION.

Therefore of things past, there is no *deliberation;* because manifestly impossible to be changed: nor of things known to be impossible, or thought so; because men know, or think such deliberation vain. But of things impossible, which we think possible, we may deliberate; not knowing it is in vain. And it is called *deliberation;* because it is a putting an end to the *liberty* we had of doing, or omitting, according to our own appetite, or aversion.

This alternate succession of appetites, aversions, hopes and fears, is no less in other living creatures than in man: and therefore beasts also deliberate.

Every *deliberation* is then said to *end,* when that whereof they deliberate, is either done, or thought impossible; because till then we retain the liberty of doing, or omitting; according to our appetite, or aversion.

In *deliberation,* the last appetite, or aversion, immediately adhering to the action, or to the omission thereof, is that we call the WILL; the act, not the faculty, of *willing*. And beasts that have *deliberation,* must necessarily also have *will*. The definition of *will,* given commonly by the Schools, that it is a *rational appetite,* is not good. For if it were, then could there be no voluntary act against reason. For a *voluntary act* is that, which proceedeth from the *will,* and no other. But if instead of a rational appetite, we shall say an appetite resulting from a precedent deliberation, then the definition is the same that I have given here. *Will therefore is the last appetite in deliberating*. And though we say in common discourse, a man had a will once to do a thing, that nevertheless he forbore to do; yet that is properly but an inclination, which makes no action voluntary; because the action depends not of it, but of the last inclination, or appetite. For if the intervenient appetites, make any action voluntary; then by the same reason all intervenient aversions, should make the same action involuntary; and so one and the same action, should be both voluntary and involuntary.

• • • • • •

Chapter VIII

OF THE VIRTUES COMMONLY CALLED INTELLECTUAL; AND THEIR CONTRARY DEFECTS

Virture generally, in all sorts of subjects, is somewhat that is valued for eminence; and consisteth in comparison. For if all things were equal in all men, nothing would be prized. Any by *virtues intellectual,* are always understood such abilities of the mind, as men praise, value, and desire should be in themselves; and go commonly under the name of a *good wit;* though the same word *wit,* be used also, to distinguish one certain ability from the rest.

These *virtues* are of two sorts; *natural,* and *acquired.* By natural, I mean not, that which a man hath from his birth: for that is nothing else but sense; wherein men differ so little one from another, and from brute beasts, as it is not to be reckoned amongst virtues. But I mean, that *wit,* which is gotten by use only, and experience; without method, culture, or instruction. This NATURAL WIT, consisteth principally in two things; *celerity of imagining,* that is, swift succession of one thought to another; and *steady direction* to some approved end. On the contrary a slow imagination maketh that defect, or fault of the mind, which is commonly called DULLNESS, *stupidity,* and sometimes by other names that signify slowness of motion, or difficulty to be moved.

And this difference of quickness, is caused by the difference of men's passions; that love and dislike, some one thing, some another: and therefore some men's thoughts run one way, some another; and are held to, and observe differently the things that pass through their imagination.

• • • • • •

The passions that most of all cause the difference of wit, are principally, the more or less desire of power, of riches, of knowledge, and of honour. All which may be reduced to the first, that is, desire of power. For riches, knowledge, and honour, are but several sorts of power.

And therefore, a man who has no great passion for any of these things; but is, as men term it, indifferent; though he may be so far a good man, as to be free from giving offence; yet he cannot possibly have either a great fancy, or much judgment. For the thoughts are to the desires, as scouts, and spies, to range abroad, and find the way to the things desired: all steadiness of the mind's motion, and all quickness of the same, proceeding from thence: for as to have no desire, is to be dear: so to have weak passions, is dullness; and to have passions indifferently for everything, GIDDINESS, and *distraction;* and to have stronger and more vehement passions for anything, than is ordinarily seen in others, is that which men call MADNESS.

• • • • • •

Chapter XI

OF THE DIFFERENCE OF MANNERS

By manners, I mean not here, decency of behaviour; as how one should salute another, or how a man should wash his mouth or pick his teeth before company, and such other points of the *small morals;* but those qualities of mankind, that concern their living together in peace, and unity. To which end we are to consider, that the felicity of this life, consisteth not in the repose of a mind satisfied. For there is no such *finis ultimus,* utmost aim, nor *summum bonum,* greatest good, as is spoken of in the books of the old moral philosophers. Nor can a man any more live, whose desires are at an end, than he, whose senses and imaginations are at a stand. Felicity is a continual progress of the desire, from one object to another; the attaining of the former, being still but the way to the latter. The cause whereof is, that the object of man's desire, is not to enjoy once only, and for one instant of time; but to assure for ever, the way of his future desire. And therefore the voluntary actions, and inclinations of all men, tend, not only to the procuring, but also to the assuring of a contented life; and differ only in the way: which ariseth partly from the diversity of passions, in divers men; and partly from the difference of the knowledge, or opinion each one has of the causes, which produce the effect desired.

So that in the first place, I put for a general inclination of all mankind, a perpetual and restless desire of power after power, that ceaseth only in death. And the cause of this, is not always that a man hopes for a more intensive delight, than he has already attained to; or that he canot be content with a moderate power: but because he cannot assure the power and means to live well, which he hath present, without the acquisition of more.

• • • • • • •

Chapter XIII

OF THE NATURAL CONDITION OF MANKIND AS CONCERNING THEIR FELICITY, AND MISERY

Nature hath made men so equal, in the faculties of the body, and mind; as that though there be found one man sometimes manifestly stronger in body, or of quicker mind than another; yet when all is reckoned together, the difference between man, and man, is not so considerable, as that one man can thereupon claim to himself any benefit, to which another may not pretend, as well as he. For as to the strength of body, the weakest has strength enough to kill the strongest, either by secret machination, or by confederacy with others, that are in the same danger with himself.

And as to the faculties of the mind, setting aside the arts grounded upon words, and especially that skill of proceeding upon general, and infallible rules, called science; which very few have, and but in few things; as being not a native faculty, born with us; nor attained, as prudence, while we look after somewhat else, I find yet a greater equality amongst men, than that of strength. For prudence, is but experience; which equal time, equally bestows on all men, in those things they equally apply themselves unto. That which may perhaps make such equality incredible, is but a vain conceit of one's own wisdom, which almost all men think they have in a greater degree, than the vulgar; that is, than all men but themselves, and a few others, whom by fame, or for concurring with themselves, they approve. For such is the nature of men, that howsoever they may acknowledge many others to be more witty, or more eloquent, or more learned; yet they will hardly believe there be many so wise as themselves; for they see their own wit at hand, and other men's at a distance. But this proveth rather that men are in that point equal, than unequal. For there is not ordinarily a greater sign of the equal distribution of any thing, than that every man is contented with his share.

From this equality of ability, ariseth equality of hope in the attaining of our ends. And therefore if any two men desire the same thing, which nevertheless they cannot both enjoy, they become enemies; and in the way to their end, which is principally their own conservation, and sometimes their delectation only, endeavour to destroy, or subdue one another. And from hence it comes to pass, that where an invader hath no more to fear, than another man's single power; if one plant, sow, build, or possess a convenient seat, others may probably be expected to come prepared with forces united, to dispossess, and deprive him, not only of the fruit of his labour, but also of his life, or liberty. And the invader again is in the like danger of another.

And from this difference of one another, there is no way for any man to secure himself, so reasonable, as anticipation; that is, by force, or wiles, to master the persons of all men he can, so long, till he see no other power great enough to endanger him: and this is no more than his own conservation requireth, and is generally allowed. Also because there be some, that taking pleasure in contemplating their own power in the acts of conquest, which they pursue farther than their security requires; if others, that otherwise would be glad to be at ease within modest bounds, should not by invasion increase their power, they would not be able, long time, by standing only on their defence, to subsist. And by consequence, such augmentation of dominion over men being necessary to a man's conservation, it ought to be allowed him.

Again, men have no pleasure, but on the contrary a great deal of grief, in keeping company, where there is no power able to over-awe them all. For every man looketh that his companion should value him, at the same rate he sets upon himself: and upon all signs of contempt, or undervaluing, naturally endeavours, as far as he dares, (which amongst them that have no common power to keep them in quiet, is far enough to make them destroy each other), to extort a greater value from his contemners, by damage; and from others, by the example.

So that in the nature of man, we find three principal causes of quarrel. First, competition; secondly, diffidence; thirdly, glory.

The first, maketh men invade for gain; the second, for safety; and the third, for reputation. The first use violence, to make themselves masters of other men's persons, wives, children, and cattle; the second, to defend them; the third, for trifles, as a word, a smile, a different opinion, and any other sign of undervalue, either direct in their persons, or by reflection in their kindred, their friends, their nation, their profession, or their name.

Hereby it is manifest, that during the time men live without a common power to keep them all in awe, they are in that condition which is called war; and such a war, as is of every man, against every man. For WAR, consisteth not in battle only, or the act of fighting; but a tract of time, wherein the will to contend by battle is sufficiently known: and therefore the notion of *time,* is to be considered in the nature of war; as it is in the nature of weather. For as the nature of foul weather, lieth not in a shower or two of rain; but in an inclination thereto of many days together: so the nature of war, consisteth not in actual fighting; but in the known disposition thereto, during all the time there is no assurance to the contrary. All other time is PEACE.

Whatsoever therefore is consequent to a time of war, where every man is enemy to every man; the same is consequent to the time, wherein men live without other security, than what their own strength, and their own invention shall furnish them withal. In such condition, there is no place for industry; because the fruit thereof is uncertain: and consequently no culture of the earth; no navigation, nor use of the commodities that may be imported by sea; no commodious building; no instruments of moving, and removing, such things as require much force; no knowledge of the face of the earth; no account of time; no arts; no letters; no society; and which is worst of all, continual fear, and danger of violent death; and the life of man, solitary, poor, nasty, brutish, and short.

It may seem strange to some man, that has not well weighed these things; that nature should thus dissociate, and render men apt to invade, and destroy one another: and he may therefore, not trusting to this inference, made from the passions, desire perhaps to have the same confirmed by experience. Let him therefore consider with himself, when taking a journey, he arms himself, and seeks to go well accompanied; when going to sleep, he locks his doors; when even in his house he locks his chests; and this when he knows there be laws, and public officers, armed, to revenge all injuries shall be done him; what opinion he has of his fellow-subjects, when he rides armed; of his fellow citizens, when he locks his doors; and of his children, and servants, when he locks his chests. Does he not there as much accuse mankind by his actions, as I do by my words? But neither of us accuse man's nature in it. The desires, and other passions of man, are in themselves no sin. No more are the actions, that proceed from those passions, till they know a law that forbids them: which till laws be made they cannot know: nor can any law be made, till they have agreed upon the person that shall make it.

It may peradventure be thought, there was never such a time, nor condition of war as this; and I believe it was never generally so, over all the world: but there are many places, where they live so now. For the savage people in many places of America, except the government of small families, the concord whereof dependeth on natural lust, have no government at all; and live at this day in that brutish manner, as I said before. Howsoever, it may be perceived what manner of life there would be, where there were no common power to fear, by the manner of life, which men that have formerly lived under a peaceful government, use to degenerate into, in a civil war.

But though there had never been any time, wherein particular men were in a condition of war one against another; yet in all times, kings, and persons of sovereign authority, because of their independency, are in continual jealousies, and in the state and posture of gladiators; having their weapons pointing, and their eyes fixed on one another; that is, their forts, garrisons, and guns upon the frontiers of their kingdoms; and continual spies upon their neighbours; which is a posture of war. But because they uphold thereby, the industry of their subjects; there does not follow from it, that misery, which accompanies the liberty of particular men.

To this war of every man, against every man this also is consequent; that nothing can be unjust. The notions of right and wrong, justice and injustice have there no place. Where there is no common power, there is no law: where no law, no injustice. Force, and fraud, are in war the two cardinal virtues. Justice, and injustice are none of the faculties neither of the body, nor mind. If they were, they might be in a man that were alone in the world, as well as his senses, and passions. They are qualities, that relate to men in society, not in solitude. It is consequent also to the same condition, that there be no propriety, no dominion, no *mine* and *thine* distinct; but only that to be every man's, that he can get; and for so long, as he can keep it. And thus much for the ill condition, which man by mere nature is actually placed in; though with a possibility to come out of it, consisting partly in passions, partly in his reason.

The passions that incline men to peace, are fear of death; desire of such things as are necessary to commodious living; and a hope by their industry to obtain them. And reason suggesteth convenient articles of peace, upon which men may be drawn to agreement. These articles, are they, which otherwise are called the Laws of Nature: whereof I shall speak more particularly, in the two following chapters.

Chapter XIV

OF THE FIRST AND SECOND NATURAL LAWS, AND OF CONTRACTS

THE RIGHT OF NATURE, which writers commonly call *jus naturale,* is the liberty each man hath, to use his own power, as he will himself, for the preservation of his own nature; that is to say, of his own life; and consequently, of doing any thing, which in his own judgment, and reason, he shall conceive to be the aptest means thereunto.

By LIBERTY, is understood, according to the proper signification of the word, the absence of external impediments: which impediments, may oft take away part of a man's power to do what he would; but cannot hinder him from using the power left him, according as his judgment, and reason shall dictate to him.

A LAW OF NATURE, *lex naturalis,* is a precept or general rule, found out by reason, by which a man is forbidden to do that, which is destructive of his life, or taketh away the means of preserving the same; and to omit that, by which he thinketh it may be best preserved. For though they that speak of this subject, use to confound *jus,* and *lex, right* and *law:* yet they ought to be distinguished; because RIGHT, consisteth in liberty to do, or to forbear; whereas LAW, determineth, and bindeth to one of them: so that law, and right, differ as much, as obligation, and liberty; which in one and the same matter are inconsistent.

And because the condition of man, as hath been declared in the precedent chapter, is a condition of war of every one against every one: in which case every one is governed by his own reason; and there is nothing he can make use of, that may not be a help unto him, in preserving his life against his enemies; it followeth, that in such a condition, every man has a right to every thing; even to one another's body. And therefore, as long as this natural right of every man to every thing endureth, there can be no security to any man, how strong or wise soever he be, of living out the time, which nature ordinarily alloweth men to live. And consequently it is a precept, or general rule of reason, *that every man, ought to endeavour peace, as far as he has hope of obtaining it; and when he cannot obtain it, that he may seek, and use, all helps, and advantages of war*. The first branch of which rule, containeth the first, and fundamental law of nature; which is, *to seek peace, and follow it*. The second, the sum of the right of nature; which is, *by all means we can, to defend ourselves*.

From this fundamental law of nature, by which men are commanded to endeavour peace, is derived this second law; *that a man be willing, when others are so too, as far-forth, as for peace, and defence of himself he shall think it necessary, to lay down this right to all things; and be contented with so much liberty against other men, as he would allow other men against himself.* For as long as every man holdeth this right, of doing any thing he liketh; so long are all men in the condition of war. But if other men will not lay down their right, as well as he; then there is no reason for any one, to divest himself of his: for that were to expose himself to prey, which no man is bound to, rather than to dispose himself to peace. This is that law of the Gospel; *whatsoever you require that others should do to you, that do ye to them*. And that law of all men, *quod tibi fieri non vis, alteri ne feceris*.

To *lay down* a man's *right* to any thing, is to *divest* himself of the *liberty*, of hindering another of the benefit of his own right to the same. For he that renounceth, or passeth away his right, giveth not to any other man a right which he had not before; because there is nothing to which every man had not right by nature; but only standeth out of his way, that he may enjoy his own original right, without hindrance from him; not without hindrance from another. So that the effect which redoundeth to one man, by another man's defect of right, is but so much diminution of impediments to the use of his own right original.

Right is laid aside, either by simply renouncing it; or by transferring it to another. By *simply* RENOUNCING; when he cares not to whom the benefit thereof redoundeth. By TRANSFERRING; when he intendeth the benefit thereof to some certain person, or persons. And when a man hath in either manner abandoned, or granted away his right; then is he said to be OBLIGED, or BOUND, not to hinder those, to whom such right is granted, or abandoned, from the benefit of it: and that he *ought,* and it is his DUTY, not to make void that voluntary act of his own: and that such hindrance is INJUSTICE, and INJURY, as being *sine jure;* the right being before renounced, or transferred. So that *injury,* or *injustice,* in the controversies of the world, is somewhat like to that, which in the disputations of scholars is called *absurdity*. For as it is there called an absurdity, to contradict what one maintained in the beginning: so in the world, it is called injustice, and injury, voluntarily to undo that, which from the beginning he had voluntarily done. The way by which a man either simply renounceth, or transferreth his right, is a declaration, or signification, by some voluntary and sufficient sign, or signs, that he doth so renounce, or transfer; or hath so renounced, or transferred the same, to him that accepteth it. And these signs are either words only, or actions only; or, as it happeneth most often, both words, and actions. And the same are the BONDS, by which men are bound, and obliged: bonds, that have their strength, not from their own nature, for nothing is more easily broken than a man's word, but from fear of some evil consequence upon the rupture.

Whensoever a man transferreth his right, or renounceth it; it is either in consideration of some right reciprocally transferred to himself; or for some other good he hopeth for thereby. For it is a voluntary act: and of the voluntary acts of every man, the object is some *good to himself*. And therefore there be some rights, which no man can be understood by any words, or other signs, to have abandoned, or transferred. As first a man cannot lay down the right of resisting them, that assault him by force, to take away his life; because he cannot be understood to aim thereby, at any good to himself. The same may be said of wounds, and chains, and imprisonment; both because there is no benefit consequent to such patience; as there is to the patience of suffering another to be wounded, or imprisoned: as also because a man cannot tell, when he seeth men proceed against him by violence, whether they intend his death or not. And lastly the motive, and end for which this renouncing, and transferring of right is introduced, is nothing else but the security of a man's person, in his life, and in the means of so preserving life, as not to be weary of it. And therefore if a man by words, or other signs, seem to despoil himself of the end, for which those signs were intended; he is not to be understood as if he meant it, or that it was his will; but that he was ignorant of how such words and actions were to be interpreted.

The mutual transferring of right, is that which men call CONTRACT.

• • • • • •

If a covenant be made, wherein neither of the parties perform presently, but trust one another; in the condition of mere nature, which is a condition of war of every man against every man, upon any reasonable suspicion, it is void: but if there be a common power set over them both, with right and force sufficient to compel performance, it is not void. For he that performeth first, has no assurance the other will perform after; because the bonds of words are too weak to bridle men's ambition, avarice, anger, and other passions, without the fear of some coercive power; which in the condition of mere nature, where all men are equal, and judges of the justness of their own fears, cannot possibly be supposed. And therefore he which performeth first, does but betray himself to his enemy; contrary to the right, he can never abandon, of defending his life, and means of living.

But in a civil estate, where there is a power set up to constrain those that would otherwise violate their faith, that fear is no more reasonable; and for that cause, he which by the covenant is to perform first, is obliged so to do.

• • • • • •

Covenants entered into by fear, in the condition of mere nature, are obligatory. For example, if I covenant to pay a ransom, or service for my life, to an enemy; I am bound by it: for it is a contract, wherein one receiveth the benefit of life; the other is to receive money, or service for it; and consequently, where no other law, as in the condition of mere nature, forbiddeth the performance, the covenant is valid. Therefore prisoners of war, if trusted with the payment of their ransom, are obliged to pay it: and if a weaker prince, make a disadvantageous peace with a stronger, for fear; he is bound to keep it; unelss, as hath been said before, there ariseth some new, and just cause of fear, to renew the war. And even in commonwealths, if I be forced to redeem myself from a thief by promising him money, I am bound to pay it, till the civil law discharge me. For whatsoever I may lawfully do without obligation, the same I may lawfully covenant to do through fear: and what I lawfully covenant, I cannot lawfully break.

A former covenant, makes void a later. For a man that hath passed away his right to one man to-day, hath it not to pass to-morrow to another: and therefore the later promise passeth no right, but is null.

A covenant not to defend myself from force, by force, is always void. For, as I have showed before, no man can transfer, or lay down his right to save himself from death, wounds, and imprisonment, the avoiding whereof is the only end of laying down any right; and therefore the promise of not resisting force, in no covenant transferreth any right; nor is obliging. For though a man may covenant thus, *unless I do so, or so, kill me;* he cannot covenant thus, *unless I do so, or so, I will not resist you, when you come to kill me*. For man by nature chooseth the lesser evil, which is danger of death in resisting; rather than the greater, which is certain and present death in not resisting. And this is granted to be true by all men, in that they lead criminals to execution, and prison, with armed men, notwithstanding that such criminals have consented to the law, by which they are condemned.

• • • • • •

Chapter XV

OF OTHER LAWS OF NATURE

From that law of nature, by which we are obliged to transfer to another, such rights, as being retained, hinder the peace of mankind, there followeth a third; which is this, *that men perform their covenants made:* without which, covenants are in vain, and but empty words; and the right of all men to all things remaining, we are still in the condition of war.

And in this law of nature, consisteth the fountain and original of JUSTICE. For where no covenant hath preceded, there hath no right been transferred, and every man has right to every thing; and consequently, no action can be unjust. But when a covenant is made, then to break it is *unjust:* and the definition of INJUSTICE, is no other than *the not performance of covenant*. And whatsoever is not unjust, is *just*.

But because covenants of mutual trust, where there is a fear of not performance on either part, as hath been said in the former chapter, are invalid; though the original of justice be the making of covenants; yet injustice actually there can be none, till the cause of such fear be taken away; which while men are in the natural condition of war, cannot be done. Therefore before the names of just, and unjust can have place, there must be some coercive power, to compel men equally to the performance of their covenants, by the terror of some punishment, greater than the benefit they expect by the breach of their covenant; and to make good that propriety, which by mutual contract men acquire, in recompense of the universal right they abandon: and such power there is none before the erection of a commonwealth. And this is also to be gathered out of the ordinary definition of justice in the Schools: for they say, that *justice is the constant will of giving to every man his own*. And therefore where there is no *own,* that is no propriety, there is no injustice; and where there is no coercive powr erected, that is, where there is no commonwealth, there is no propriety; all men having right to all things: therefore where there is no commonwealth, there nothing is unjust. So that the nature of justce, consisteth in keeping of valid covenants: but the validity of covenants begins not but with the constitution of a civil power, sufficient to compel men to keep them: and then it is also that propriety begins.

The fool hath said in his heart, there is no such thing as justice; and sometimes also with his tongue; seriously alleging, that every man's conservation, and contentment, being committed to his own care, there could be no reason, why every man might not do what he thought conduced thereunto: and therefore also to make, or not make; keep, or not keep covenants, was not against reason, when it conduced to one's benefit. He does not therein deny, that there be covenants; and that they are sometimes broken, sometimes kept; and that such breach of them may be called injustice, and the observance of them justice: but he questioneth, whether injustice, taking away the fear of God, for the same fool hath said in his heart there is no God, may not sometimes stand with that reason, which dictateth to every man his own good; and particularly then, when it conduceth to such a benefit, as shall put a man in a condition, to neglect not only the dispraise, and revilings, but also the power of other men. The kingdom of God is gotten by violence: but what if it could be gotten by unjust violence? were it against reason so to get it, when it is impossible to receive hurt by it? and if it be not against reason, it is not against justice; or else justice is not to be approved for good. From such reasoning as this, successful wickedness hath obtained the name of virtue: and some that in all other things have disallowed the violation of faith; yet have allowed it, when it is for the getting of a kingdom. And the heathen that believed, that Saturn was deposed by his son Jupiter, believed nevertheless the same Jupiter to be the avenger of injustice: somewhat like to a piece of law in Coke's *Commentaries on Littleton;* where he says, if the right heir of the crown be attainted of treason; yet the crown shall descend to him, and *eo instante* the attainder be void: from which instances a man will be very prone to infer; that when the heir apparent of a kingdom, shall kill him that is in possession, though his father; you may call it injustice, or by what other name you will; yet it can never be against reason, seeing all the voluntary actions of men tend to the benefit of themselves; and those actions are most reasonable, that conduce most to their ends. This specious reasoning is nevertheless false.

For the question is not of promises mutual, where there is no security of performance on either side, as when there is no civil power erected over the parties promising; for such promises are no covenants: but either where one of the parties has performed already; or where there is a power to make him perform; there is the question whether it be against reason, that is, against the benefit of the other to perform, or not. And I say it is not against reason. For the manifestation whereof, we are to consider; first, that when a man doth a thing, which notwithstanding any thing can be foreseen, and reckoned on, tendeth to his own destruction, howsoever some accident which he could not expect, arriving may turn it to his benefit; yet such events do not make it reasonably or wisely done. Secondly, that in a condition of war, wherein every man to every man, for want of a common power to keep them all in awe, is an enemy, there is no man can hope by his own strength, or wit, to defend himself from destruction, without the help of confederates; where every one expects the same defence by the confederation, that any one else does: and therefore he which declares he thinks it reason to deceive those that help him, can in reason expect no other means of safety, than what can be had from his own single power. He therefore that breaketh his covenant, and consequently declareth that he thinks he may with reason do so, cannot be received into any society, that unite themselves for peace and defence, but by the error of them that receive him; nor when he is received, be retained in it, without seeing the danger of their error; which errors a man cannot reasonably reckon upon as the means of his security: and therefore if he be left, or cast out of society, he perisheth; and if he live in society, it is by the errors of other men, which he could not foresee, nor reckon upon; and consequently against the reason of his preservation; and so, as all men that contribute not to his destruction, forbear him only out of ignorance of what is good for themselves.

As for the instance of gaining the secure and perpetual felicity of heaven, by any way; it is frivolous: there being but one way imaginable; and that is not breaking, but keeping of covenant.

And for the other instance of attaining sovereignty by rebellion; it is manifest, that though the event follow, yet because it cannot reasonably be expected, but rather the contrary; and because by gaining it so, others are taught to gain the same in like manner, the attempt thereof is against reason. Justice therefore, that is to say, keeping of covenant, is a rule of reason, by which we are forbidden to do any thing destructive to our life; and consequently a law of nature.

There be some that proceed further; and will not have the law of nature, to be those rules which conduce to the preservation of man's life on earth; but to the attaining of an eternal felicity after death; to which they think the breach of covenant may conduce; and consequently be just and reasonable; such are they that think it a work of merit to kill, or depose, or rebel against, the sovereign power constituted over them by their own consent. But because there is no natural knowledge of man's estate after death; much less of the reward that is then to be given to breach of faith; but only a belief grounded upon other men's saying, that they know it supernaturally, or that they know those, that knew them, that knew others, that knew it supernaturally; breach of faith cannot be called a precept of reason, or nature.

Others, that allow for a law of nature, the keeping of faith, do nevertheless make exception of certain persons; as heretics, and such as use not to perform their covenant to others: and this also is against reason. For if any fault of a man, be sufficient to discharge our covenant made; the same ought in reason to have been sufficient to have hindered the making of it.

• • • • • •

These dictates of reason, men used to call by the name of laws, but improperly: for they are but conclusions, or theorems concerning what conduceth to the conservation and defence of themselves; whereas law, properly, is the word of him, that by right hath command over others. But yet if we consider the same theorems, as delivered in the word of God, that by right commandeth all things; then are they properly called laws.

• • • • • •

[Part II] Of Commonwealth

Chapter XVII

OF THE CAUSES, GENERATION, AND DEFINITION OF A COMMONWEALTH

The final cause, end, or design of men, who naturally love liberty, and dominion over others, in the introduction of that restraint upon themselves, in which we see them live in commonwealths, is the foresight of their own preservation, and of a more contented life thereby; that is to say, of getting themselves out from that miserable condition of war, which is necessarily consequent, as hath been shown in chapter XIII, to the natural passions of men, when there is no visible power to keepthem in awe, and tie them by fear of punishment to the performance of their covenants, and observation of those laws of nature set down in the fourteenth and fifteenth chapters.

• • • • • •

The only way to erect such a common power, as may be able to defend them from the invasion of foreigners, and the injuries of one another, and thereby to secure them in such sort, as that by their own industry, and by the fruits of the earth, they may nourish themselves and live contentedly; is, to confer all their power and strength upon one man, or upon one assembly of men, that may reduce all their wills, by plurality of voices, unto one will: which is as much as to say, to appoint one man, or assembly of men, to bear their person; and every one to own, and acknowledge himself to be author of whatsoever he that so beareth their person, shall act, or cause to be acted, in those thing which concern the common peace and safety; and therein to submit their wills, every one to his will, and their judgments, to his judgment. This is more than consent, or concord; it is a real unity of them all, in one and the same person, made by covenant of every man with every man, in such manner, as if every man should say to every man, *I authorize and give up my right of governing myself, to this man, or to this assembly of men, on this condition, that thou give up thy right to him, and authorize all his actions in like manner*. This done, the multitude so united in one person, is called a COMMONWEALTH, in Latin CIVITAS. This is the generation of that great LEVIATHAN, or rather, to speak more reverently, of that *mortal god,* to which we owe under the *immortal God,* our peace and defence. For by this authority, given him by every particular man in the commonwealth, he hath the use of so much power and strength conferred on him, that by terror thereof, he is enabled to perform the wills of them all, to peace at home, and mutual aid against their enemies abroad. And in him consisteth the essence of the commonwealth; which, to define it, is *one person, of whose acts a great multitude, by mutual covenants one with another, have made themselves every one the author, to the end he may use the strength and means of them all, as he shall think expedient, for their peace and common defence*.

And he that carrieth this person, is called SOVEREIGN, and said to have *sovereign power;* and every one besides, his SUBJECT.

• • • • • •

Chapter XVIII

OF THE RIGHTS OF SOVEREIGNS BY INSTITUTION

• • • • • •

But a man may here object, that the condition of subjects is very miserable; as being obnoxious to the lusts, and other irregular passions of him, or them that have so unlimited a power in their hands. And commonly they that live under a monarch, think it the fault of monarchy; and they that live under the government of democracy, or other sovereign assembly, attribute all the inconvenience to that form of commonwealth; whereas the power in all forms, if they be perfect enough to protect them, is the same: not considering that the state of man can never be without some incommodity or other; and that the greatest, that in any form of government can possibly happen to the people in general, is scarce sensible, in respect of the miseries, and horrible calamities, that accomany a civil war, or that dissolute condition of masterless men, without subjection to laws, and a coercive power to tie their hands from rapine and revenge: nor considering that the greatest pressure of sovereign governors, proceedeth not from any delight, or profit they can expect in the damage or weakening of their subjects, in whose vigour, consisteth their own strength and glory; but in the restiveness of themselves, that unwillingly contributing to their own defence, make it necessary for their governors to draw from them what they can in time of peace, that they may have means on any emergent occasion, or sudden need, to resist, or take advantage of their enemies. For all men are by nature provided of notable multiplying glasses, that is their passions and self-love, through which, every little payment appeareth a great grievance; but are destitute of those prospective glasses, namely moral and civil science, to see afar off the miseries that hang over them, and cannot without such payments be avoided.

Chapter XXVI

OF CIVIL LAWS

• • • • • •

And first it is manifest, that law in general, is not counsel, but command; nor a command of any man to any man; but only of him, whose command is addressed to one formerly obliged to obey him. And as for civil law, it addeth only the name of the person commanding, which is *persona civitatis,* the person of the commonwealth.

Which considered, I define civil law in this manner. CIVIL LAW, *is to every subject, those rules, which the commonwealth hath commanded him, by word, writing, or other sufficient sign of the will, to make use of, for the distinction of right, and wrong; that is to say, of what is contrary, and what is not contrary to the rule.*

In which definition, there is nothing that is not at first sight evident. For every man seeth, that some laws are addressed to all the subjects in general; some to particular provinces; some to particular vocations; and some to particular men; and are therefore laws, to every of those to whom the command is directed, and to none else. And also, that laws are the rules of just, and unjust; nothing being reputed unjust, that is not contrary to some law. Likewise, that none can make laws but the commonwealth; because our subjection is to the commonwealth only: and that commands, are to be signified by sufficient signs; because a man knows not otherwise how to obey them. And therefore, whatsoever can from this definition by necessary consequence be deduced, ought to be acknowledged for truth. Now I deduce from it this that followeth.

1. The legislator in all commonwealths, is only the sovereign, be he one man, as in a monarchy, or one assembly of men, as in a democracy, or aristocracy. For the legislator is he that maketh the law. And the commonwealth only prescribes, and commandeth the observation of those rules, which we call law: therefore the commonwealth is the legislator. But the commonwealth is no person, nor has capacity to do anything, but by the representative, that is, the sovereign; and therfore the sovereign is the sole legislator. For the same reason, none can abrogate a law made, but the sovereign; because a law is not abrogated, but by another law, that forbiddeth it to be put in execution.

2. The sovereign of a commonwealth, be it an assembly, or one man, is not subjectt to the civil laws. For having power to make, and repeal laws, he may when he pleaseth, free himself from that subjection, by repealing those laws that trouble him, and making of new; and consequently he was free before. For he is free, that can be free when he will: nor is it possible for any person to be bound to himself; because he that can bind, can release; and therefore he that is bound to himself only, is not bound.

3. When long use obtaineth the authority of a law, it is not the length of time that maketh the authority, but the will of the sovereign signified by his silence, for silence is sometimes an argument of consent; and it is no longer law, than the sovereign shall be silent therein. And therefore if the sovereign shall have a question of right grounded, not

upon his present will, but upon the laws formerly made; the length of time shall bring no prejudice to his right; but the question shall be judged by equity. For many unjust actions, and unjust sentences, go uncontrolled a longer time than any man can remember. And our lawyers account no customs law, but such as are reasonable, and that evil customs are to be abolished. But the judgment of what is reasonable, and of what is to be abolished, belongeth to him that maketh the law, which is the sovereign assembly, or monarch.

4. The law of nature, and the civil law, contain each other, and are of equal extent. For the laws of nature, which consist in equity, justice, gratitude, and other moral virtues on these depending, in the condition of mere nature, as I have said before in the end of the fifteenth chapter, are not properly laws, but qualities that dispose men to peace and obedience. When a commonwealth is once settled, then are they actually laws, and not before; as being then the commands of the commonwealth; and therefore also civil laws: for it is the sovereign power that obliges men to obey them. For in the differences of private men, to declare, what is equity, what is justice, and what is moral virtue, and to make them binding, there is need of the ordinances of sovereign power, and punishments to be ordained for such as shall break them; which ordinances are therefore part of the civil law. The law of nature therefore is a part of the civil law in all commonwealths of the world. Reciprocally also, the civil law is a part of the dictates of nature. For justice, that is to say, performance of covenant, and giving to every man his own, is a dictate of the law of nature. But every subject in a commonwealth, hath covenanted to obey the civil law; either one with another, as when they assemble to make a common representative, or with the representative itself one by one, when subdued by the sword they promise obedience, that they may receive life; and therefore obedience to the civil law is part also of the law of nature. Civil, and natural law are not different kinds, but different parts of law; whereof one part being written, is called civil, the other unwritten, natural. But the right of nature, that is, the natural liberty of man, may by the civil law be abridged, and restrained: nay, the end of making laws, is no other, but such restraint; without the which there cannot possibly be any peace. And law was brought into the world for nothing else, but to limit the natural liberty of particular men, in such manner, as they might not hurt, but assist one another, and join together against a common enemy.

5. If the sovereign of one commonwealth, subdue a people that have lived under other written laws, and afterwards govern them by the same laws, by which they were governed before; yet those laws are the civil

laws of the victor, and not of the vanquished commonwealth. For the legislator is he, not by whose authority the laws were first made, but by whose authority they now continue to be laws. And therefore where there be divers provinces, within the dominion of a commonwealth, and in those provinces diversity of laws, which commonly are called the customs of each several province, we are not to understand that such customs have their force, only from length of time; but that they were anciently laws written, or otherwise made known, for the constitutions, and statutes of their sovereigns; and are now laws, not by virtue of the prescription of time, but by the constitutions of their present sovereigns. But if an unwritten law, in all the provinces of a dominion, shall be generally observed, and no iniquity appear in the use thereof; that law can be no other but a law of nature, equally obliging all mankind.

• • • • • •

8. From this, that the law is a command, and a command consisteth in declaration, or manifestation of the will of him that commandeth, by voice, writing, or some other sufficient argument of the same, we may understand, that the command of the commonwealth is law only to those, that have means to take notice of it. Over natural fools, children, or madmen, there is no law, no more than over brute beasts; nor are they capable of the title of just, or unjust; because they had never power to make any covenant, or to understand the consequences thereof; and consequently never took upon them to authorize the actions of any sovereign, as they must do that make to themselves a commonwealth. And as those from whom nature or accident hath taken away the notice of all laws in general; so also every man, from whom any accident, not proceeding from his own default, hath taken away the means to take notice of any particular law, is excused, if he observe it not: and to speak properly, that law is no law to him. It is therefore necessary, to consider in this place, what arguments, and signs be sufficient for the knowledge of what is the law; that is to say, what is the will of the sovereign, as well in monarchies, as in other forms of government.

And first, if it be a law that obliges all the subjects without exception, and is not written, nor otherwise published in such places as they may take notice thereof, it is a law of nature. For whatsoever men are to take knowledge of for law, not upon other men's words, but every one from his own reason, must be such as is agreeable to the reason of all men;

which no law can be, but the law of nature. The laws of nature therefore need not any publishing, nor proclamation; as being contained in this one sentence, approved by all the world, *Do not that to another, which thou thinkest unreasonable to be done by another to thyself.*

Secondly, if it be a law that obliges only some condition of men, or one particular man, and be not written, nor published by word, then also it is a law of nature; and known by the same arguments, and signs, that distinguish those in such a condition, from other subjects. For whatsoever law is not written, or some way published by him that makes it law, can be known no way, but by the reason of him that is to obey it; and is therefore also a law not only civil, but natural. For example, if the sovereign employ a public minister, without written instructions what to do; he is obliged to take for instructions the dictates of reason; as if he make a judge, the judge is to take notice, that his sentence ought to be according to the reason of his sovereign, which being always understood to be equity, he is bound to it by the law of nature: or if an ambassador, he is, in all things not contained in his written instructions, to take for instruction that which reason dictates to be most conducing to his sovereign's interest; and so of all other ministers of the sovereignty, public and private. All which instructions of natural reason may be comprehended under one name of *fidelity;* which is a branch of natural justice.

The law of nature excepted, it belongeth to the essence of all other laws, to be made known, to every man that shall be obliged to obey them, either by word, or writing, or some other act, known to proceed from the sovereign authority. For the will of another cannot be understood, but by his own word, or act, or by conjecture taken from his scope and purpose; which in the person of the commonwealth, is to be supposed always consonant to equity and reason. And in ancient time, before letters were in common use, the laws were many times put into verse; that the rude people taking pleasure in singing, or reciting them, might the more easily retain them in memory. And for the same reason Solomon (*Prov.* vii.3) adviseth a man, to bind the ten commandments upon his ten fingers. And for the law which Moses gave to the people of Israel at the renewing of the covenant (*Deut.* xi.19), he biddeth them to teach it their children, by discoursing of it both at home, and upon the way; at going to bed, and at rising from bed; and to write it upon the posts, and doors of their houses; and (*Deut.* xxxi.12) to assemble the people, man, woman, and child, to hear it read.

Nor is it enough the law be written, and published; but also that there be manifest signs, that it proceedeth from the will of the sovereign. For private men, when they have, or think they have force enough to secure their unjust designs, and convoy them safely to their ambitious ends, may publish for laws what they please, without, or against the legislative authority. There is therefore requisite, not only a declaration of the law, but also sufficient signs of the author and authority. The author, or legislator is supposed in every commonwealth to be evident, because he is the sovereign, who having been constituted by the consent of every one, is supposed by every one to be sufficiently known. And though the ignorance and security of men be such, for the most part, as that when the memory of the first constitution of their commonwealth is worn out, they do not consider, by whose power they used to be defended against their enemies, and to have their industry protected, and to be righted when injury is done them; yet because no man that considers, can make question of it, no excuse can be derived from the ignorance of where the sovereignty is placed. And it is a dictate of natural reason, and consequently an evident law of nature, that no man ought to weaken that power, the protection whereof he hath himself demanded, or wittingly received against others. Therefore of who is sovereign, no man, but by his own fault, (whatsoever evil men suggest,) can make any doubt. The difficult consisteth in the evidence of the authority derived from him; the removing whereof, dependeth on the knowledge of the public registers, public counsels, public ministers, and public seals; by which all laws are sufficiently verified; verified, I say, not authorized: for the verification, is but the testimony and record, not the authority of the law; which consisteth in the command of the sovereign only.

If therefore a man have a question of injury, depending on the law of nature; that is to say, on common equity; the sentence of the judge, that by commission hath authority to take cognizance of such causes, is a sufficient verification of the law of nature in that individual case. For though the advice of one that professeth the study of the law, be useful for the avoiding of contention; yet it is but advise: it is the judge must tell men what is law, upon the hearing of the controversy.

But when the question is of injury, or crime, upon a written law; every man by recourse to the registers, by himself or others, may, if he will, be sufficiently informed, before he do such injury, or commit the crime, whether it be an injury, or not: nay he ought to do so: for when a man doubts whether the act he goeth about, be just, or unjust; and nay inform himself, if he will; the doing is unlawful. In like manner, he that supposeth himself injured, in a case determined by the written law, which he may, by himself or others, see and consider; if he complain before he consults with the law, he does unjustly, and bewrayeth a disposition rather to vex other men, than to demand his own right.

If the question be of obedience to a public officer; to have seen his commission, with the public seal, and heard it read; or to have had the means to be informed of it, if a man would, is a sufficient verification of his authority. For every man is obliged to do his best endeavour, to inform himself of all written laws, that may concern his own future actions.

The legislator known; and the laws, either by writing, or by the light of nature, sufficiently published; there wanteth yet another very material circumstance to make them obligatory. For it is not the letter, by the intendment, or meaning, that is to say, the authentic interpretation of the law (which is the sense of the legislator), in which the nature of the law consisteth; and therefore the interpretation of all laws dependeth on the authority sovereign; and the interpreters can be none but those, which the sovereign, to whom only the subject oweth obedience, shall appoint. For else, by the craft of an interpreter, the law may be made to bear a sense, contrary to that of the sovereign: by which means the interpreter becomes the legislator.

All laws, written, and unwritten, have need of interpretation. The unwritten law of nature, though it be easy to such, as without partiality and passion, make use of their natural reason, and therefore leaves the violators thereof without excuse; yet considering there be very few, perhaps none, that in some cases are not blinded by self-love, or some other passion; it is now become of all laws the most obscure, and has consequently the greatest need of able interpreters. The written laws, if they be short, are easily misinterpreted, from the divers significations of a word, or two: if long, they be more obscure by the divers significations of many words: insomuch as no written law, delivered in few, or many words, can be well understood, without a perfect understanding of the final causes, for which the law was made; the knowledge of which final causes is in the legislator. To him therefore there cannot be any knot in the law, insoluble; either by finding out the ends, to undo it by; or else by making what ends he will, as Alexander did with his sword in the Gordian knot, but the legislative power; which no other interpreter can do.

The interpretation of the laws of nature, in a commonwealth, dependeth not on the books of moral philosophy. The authority of writers, without the authority of the commonwealth, maketh not their opinions law, be they never so true. That which I have written in this treatise, concerning the moral virtues, and of their necessity for the procuring, and maintaining peace, though it be evident truth, is not therefore presently law; but because in all commonwealths in the world, it is part of the civil law. For though it be naturally reasonable; yet it is by the sovereign power that it is law: otherwise, it were a great error, to call the laws of nature unwritten law; whereof we see so many volumes published, and in them so many contradictions of one another, and of themselves.

The interpretation of the law of nature, is the sentence of the judge constituted by the sovereign authority, to hear and determine such controversies, as depend thereon; and consisteth in the application of the law to the present case. For in the act of judicature, the judge doth no more but consider, whether the demand of the party, be consonant to natural reason, and equity; and the sentence he giveth, is therefore the interpretation of the law of nature; which interpretation is authentic; not because it is his private sentence; but because he giveth it by authority of the sovereign, whereby it becomes the sovereign's sentence; which is law for that time, to the parties pleading.

• • • • • •

5

Locke
On Natural Law and Natural Right

The Second Treatise of Government

Chapter II

OF THE STATE OF NATURE

4. To understand political power right and derive it from its original, we must consider what state all men are naturally in, and that is a state of perfect freedom to order their actions and dispose of their possessions and persons as they think fit, within the bounds of the law of nature, without asking leave or depending upon the will of any other man.

A state also of equality, wherein all the power and jurisdiction is reciprocal, no one having more than another; there being nothing more evident than that creatures of the same species and rank, promiscuously born to all the same advantages of nature and the use of the same faculties, should also be equal one amongst another without subordination or subjection; unless the lord and master of them all should, by any manifest declaration of his will, set one above another, and confer on him by an evident and clear appointment an undoubted right to dominion and sovereignty.

5. This equality of men by nature the judicious Hooker looks upon as so evident in itself and beyond all question that he makes it the foundation of that obligation to mutual love amongst men on which he

builds the duties we owe one another, and from whence he derives the great maxims of justice and charity. His words are:

> The like natural inducement hath brought men to know that it is no less their duty to love others than themselves; for seeing those things which are equal must needs all have one measure; if I cannot but wish to receive good, even as much at every man's hands as any man can wish unto his own soul, how should I look to have any part of my desire herein satisfied unless myself be careful to satisfy the like desire, which is undoubtedly in other men, being of one and the same nature? To have anything offered them repugnant to this desire must needs in all respects grieve them as much as me; so that, if I do harm, I must look to suffer, there being no reason that others should show greater measure of love to me than they have by me showed unto them; my desire therefore to be loved of my equals in nature, as much as possibly may be, imposeth upon me a natural duty of bearing to them-ward fully the like affection; from which relation of equality between ourselves and them that are as ourselves, what several rules and canons natural reason hath drawn, for direction of life, no man is ignorant. (*Eccl. Pol.* lib.i.).

6. But though this be a state of liberty, yet it is not a state of license; though man in that state have an uncontrollable liberty to dispose of his person or possessions, yet he has not liberty to destroy himself, or so much as any creature in his possession, but where some nobler use than its bare preservation calls for it. The state of nature has a law of nature to govern it, which obliges every one; and reason, which is that law, teaches all mankind who will but consult it that, being all equal and independent, no one ought to harm another in his life, health, liberty, or possessions; for men being all the workmanship of one omnipotent and infinitely wise Maker -- all the servants of one sovereign master, sent into the world by his order, and about his business -- they are his property whose workmanship they are, made to last during his, not one another's, pleasure; and being furnished with like faculties, sharing all in one community of nature, there cannot be supposed any such subordination among us that may authorize us to destroy another, as if we were made for one another's uses as the inferior ranks of creatures are for ours. Every one, as he is bound to preserve himself and not to quit his station wilfully, so by the like reason, when his own preservation comes not in competition, ought he, as much as he can, to preserve the rest of mankind, and may not, unless it be to do justice to an offender, take away or impair the life, or what tends to the preservation of the life, the liberty, health, limb, or goods of another.

7. And that all men may be restrained from invading others' rights and from doing hurt to one another, and the law of nature be observed,

which wills the peace and preservation of all mankind, the execution of the law of nature is, in that state, put into every man's hands, whereby everyone has a right to punish the transgressors of that law to such a degree as may hinder its violation; for the law of nature would, as all other laws that concern men in this world, be in vain if there were nobody that in that state of nature had a power to execute that law and thereby preserve the innocent and restrain offenders. And if anyone in the state of nature may punish another for any evil he has done, everyone may do so; for in that state of perfect equality, where naturally there is no superiority or jurisdiction of one over another, what any may do in prosecution of that law, everyone must needs have a right to do.

8. And thus in the state of nature one man comes by a power over another; but yet no absolute or arbitrary power to use a criminal, when he has got him in his hands, according to the passionate heats or boundless extravagance of his own will; but only to retribute to him, so far as calm reason and conscience dictate, what is proportionate to his transgression, which is so much as may serve for reparation and restraint; for these two are the only reasons why one man may lawfully do harm to another, which is that we call punishment. In transgressing the law of nature, the offender declares himself to live by another rule than that of reason and common equity, which is that measure God has set to the actions of men for their mutual security; and so he becomes dangerous to mankind, the tie which is to secure them from injury and violence being slighted and broken by him. Which being a trespass against the whole species and the peace and safety of it provided for by the law of nature, every man upon this score, by the right he has to preserve mankind in general, may restrain, or, where it is necessary, destroy things noxious to them, and so may bring such evil on any one who has transgressed that law, as may make him repent the doing of it and thereby deter him, and by his example others, from doing the like mischief. And in this case, and upon this ground, *every man has a right to punish the offender and be executioner of the law of nature*.

9. I doubt not but this will seem a very strange doctrine to some men; but before they condemn it, I desire them to resolve me by what right any prince or state can put to death or punish any alien for any crime he commits in their country. It is certain their laws, by virtue of any sanction they receive from the promulgated will of the legislative, reach not a stranger; they speak not to him, nor, if they did, is he bound to hearken to them. The legislative authority, by which they are in force over the subjects of that commonwealth, has no power over him. Those who have the supreme power of making laws in England, France, or

Holland, are to an Indian but like the rest of the world -- men without authority; and therefore, if by the law of nature every man has not a power to punish offenses against it as he soberly judges the case to require, I see not how the magistrates of any community can punish an alien of another country, since, in reference to him, they can have no more power than what every man naturally may have over another.

10. Besides the crime which consists in violating the law and varying from the right rule of reason, whereby a man so far becomes degenerate and declares himself to quit the principles of human nature and to be a noxious creature, there is commonly injury done to some person or other, and some other man receives damage by his transgression; in which case he who has received any damage has, besides the right of punishment common to him with other men, a particular right to seek reparation from him that has done it; and any other person, who finds it just, may also join with him that is injured and assist him in recovering from the offender so much as may make satisfaction for the harm he has suffered.

11. From these two distinct rights -- the one of punishing the crime for restraint and preventing the like offense, which right of punishing is in everybody; the other of taking reparation, which belongs only to the injured party -- comes it to pass that the magistrate, who by being magistrate has the common right of punishing put into his hands, can often, where the public good demands not the execution of the law, remit the punishment of criminal offenses by his own authority, but yet cannot remit the satifaction due to any private man for the damage he has received. That he who has suffered the damage has a right to demand in his own name, and he alone can remit; the damnified person has this power of appropriating to himself the goods or service of the offender by right of self-preservation, as every man has a power to punish the crime to prevent its being committed again, by the right he has of preserving all mankind and doing all reasonable things he can in order to that end; and thus it is that every man, in the state of nature, has a power to kill a murderer, both to deter others from doing the like injury, which no reparation can compensate, by the example of the punishment that attends it from everybody, and also to secure men from the attempts of a criminal who, having renounced reason -- the common rule and measure God has given to mankind -- has, by the unjust violence and slaughter he has committed upon one, declared war against all mankind, and therefore may be destroyed as a lion or a tiger, one of those wild savage beasts with whom men can have no society nor security. And upon this is grounded that great law of nature, "Whoso sheddeth man's blood, by man shall his blood be shed." And Cain was so fully convinced that

every one had a right to destroy such a criminal that, after the murder of his brother, he cries out, "Every one that findeth me, shall slay me"; so plain was it written in the hearts of mankind.

12. By the same reason may a man in the state of nature punish the lesser breaches of that law. It will perhaps be demanded: with death? I answer: Each transgression may be punished to that degree and with so much severity as will suffice to make it an ill bargain to the offender, give him cause to repent, and terrify others from doing the like. Every offense that can be committed in the state of nature may in the state of nature be also punished equally, and as far forth as it may in a commonwealth; for though it would be beside my present purpose to enter here into the particulars of the law of nature, or its measures of punishment, yet it is certain there is such a law, and that, too, as intelligible and plain to a rational creature and a studier of that law as the positive laws of commonwealths, nay, possibly plainer, as much as reason is easier to be understood than the fancies and intricate contrivances of men, following contrary and hidden interests put into words; for so truly are a great part of the municipal laws of countries, which are only so far right as they are founded on the law of nature, by which they are to be regulated and interpreted.

13. To this strange doctrine -- viz., that in the state of nature every one has the executive power of the law of nature -- I doubt not but it will be objected that it is unreasonable for men to be judges in their own cases, that self-love will make men partial to themselves and their friends, and, on the other side, that ill-nature, passion, and revenge will carry them too far in punishing others, and hence nothing but confusion and disorder will follow; and that therefore God has certainly appointed government to restrain the partiality and violence of men. I easily grant that civil government is the proper remedy for the inconveniences of the state of nature, which must certainly be great where men may be judges in their own case; since it is easy to be imagined that he who was so unjust as to do his brother an injury will scarce be so just as to condemn himself for it; but I shall desire those who make this objection to remember that absolute monarchs are but men, and if government is to be the remedy of those evils which necessarily follow from men's being judges in their own cases, and the state of nature is therefore not to be endured, I desire to know what kind of government that is, and how much better it is than the state of nature, where one man commanding a multitude has the liberty to be judge in his own case, and may do to all his subjects whatever he pleases, without the least liberty to any one to question or control those who execute his pleasure, and in whatsoever he does, whether led

by reason, mistake, or passion, must be submitted to? Much better it is in the state of nature, wherein men are not bound to submit to the unjust will of another; and if he that judges, judges amiss in his own or any other case, he is answerable for it to the rest of mankind.

14. It is often asked as a mighty objection, "Where are or ever were there any men in such a state of nature?" To which it may suffice as an answer at present that since all princes and rulers of independent governments all through the world are in a state of nature, it is plain the world never was, nor ever will be, without numbers of men in that state. I have named all governors of independent communities, whether they are, or are not, in league with others; for it is not every compact that puts an end to the state of nature between men, but only this one of agreeing together mutually to enter into one community and make one body politic; other promises and compacts men may make one with another and yet still be in the state of nature. The promises and bargains for truck, etc., between the two men in the desert island, mentioned by Garcilasso de la Vega, in his history of Peru, or between a Swiss and an Indian in the woods of America, are binding to them, though they are perfectly in a state of nature in reference to one another; for truth and keeping of faith belongs to men as men, and not as members of society.

15. To those that say there were never any men in the state of nature, I will not only oppose the authority of the judicious Hooker, *Eccl. Pol.*, lib.i.,sect.10, where he says,

> The laws which have been hitherto mentioned (i.e., the laws of nature) do bind men absolutely, even as they are men, although they have never any settled fellowship, never any solemn agreement amongst themselves what to do, or not to do; but forasmuch as we are not by ourselves sufficient to furnish ourselves with competent store of things needful for such a life as our nature doth desire, a life fit for the dignity of man; therefore to supply those defects and imperfections which are in us, as living singly and solely by ourselves, we are naturally induced to seek communion and fellowship with others. This was the cause of men's uniting themselves at first in politic societies.

But I, moreover, affirm that all men are naturally in that state and remain so till by their own consents they make themselves members of some politic society; and I doubt not in the sequel of this discourse to make it very clear.

Chapter III

OF THE STATE OF WAR

16. The state of war is a state of enmity and destruction; and, therefore, declaring by word or action, not a passionate and hasty but a sedate, settled design upon another man's life, puts him in a state of war with him against whom he has declared such an intention, and so has exposed his life to the other's power to be taken away by him or anyone that joins with him in his defense and espouses his quarrel; it being reasonable and just I should have a right to destroy that which threatens me with destruction; for, by the fundamental law of nature, man being to be preserved as much as possible when all cannot be preserved, the safety of the innocent is to be preferred; and one may destroy a man who makes war upon him, or has discovered an enmity to his being, for the same reason that he may kill a wolf or a lion, because such men are not under the ties of the common law of reason, have no other rule but that of force and violence, and so may be treated as beasts of prey, those dangerous and noxious creatures that will be sure to destroy him whenever he falls into their power.

17. And hence it is that he who attempts to get another man into his absolute power does thereby put himself into a state of war with him, it being to be understood as a declaration of a design upon his life; for I have reason to conclude that he who would get me into his power without my consent would use me as he pleased when he got me there, and destroy me, too, when he had a fancy to it; for nobody can desire to have me in his absolute power unless it be to compel me by force to that which is against the right of my freedom, i.e., make me a slave. To be free from such force is the only security of my preservation; and reason bids me look on him as an enemy to my preservation who would take away that freedom which is the fence to it; so that he who makes an attempt to enslave me thereby puts himself into a state of war with me. He that, in the state of nature, would take away the freedom that belongs to any one in that state must necessarily be supposed to have a design to take away everything else, that freedom being the foundation of all the rest; as he that, in the state of society, would take away the freedom belonging to those of that society or commonwealth must be supposed to design to take away from them everything else, and so be looked on as in a state of war.

18. This makes it lawful for a man to kill a thief who has not in the least hurt him, nor declared any design upon his life any farther than, by the use of force, so to get him in his power as to take away his money, or what he pleases, from him; because using force where he has no right to get me into his power, let his pretense be what it will, I have no reason to suppose that he who would take away my liberty would not, when he had me in his power, take away everything else. And therefore it is lawful for me to treat him as one who has put himself into a state of war with me, i.e., kill him if I can; for to that hazard does he justly expose himself whoever introduces a state of war and is aggressor in it.

19. And here we have the plain difference between the state of nature and the state of war which, however some men have confounded, are as far distant as a state of peace, good-will, mutual assistance, and preservation, and a state of enmity, malice, violence, and mutual destruction are one from another. Men living together according to reason, without a common superior on earth with authority to judge between them, is properly the state of nature. But force, or a declared design of force, upon the person of another, where there is no common superior on earth to appeal to for relief, is the state of war; and it is the want of such an appeal [that] gives a man the right of war even against an aggressor, though he be in society and a fellow subject. Thus a thief, whom I cannot harm but by appeal to the law for having stolen all that I am worth, I may kill when he sets on me to rob me but of my horse or coat; because the law, which was made for my preservation, where it cannot interpose to secure my life from present force, which, if lost, is capable of no reparation, permits me my own defense and the right of war, a liberty to kill the aggressor, because the aggressor allows not time to appeal to our common judge, nor the decision of the law, for remedy in a case where the mischief may be irreparable. Want of a common judge with authority puts all men in a state of nature; force without right upon a man's person makes a state of war both where there is and is not a common judge.

20. But when the actual force is over, the state of war ceases between those that are in society and are equally on both sides subjected to the fair determination of the law, because then there lies open the remedy of appeal for the past injury and to prevent future harm. But where no such appeal is, as in the state of nature, for want of positive laws and judges with authority to appeal to, the state of war once begun continues with a right to the innocent party to destroy the other whenever he can, until the aggressor offers peace and desires reconciliation on such terms as may repair any wrongs he has already done and secure the innocent

for the future; nay, where an appeal to the law and constituted judges lies open, but the remedy is denied by a manifest perverting of justice and a barefaced wresting of the laws to protect or indemnify the violence or injuries of some men, or party of men, there it is hard to imagine anything but a state of war; for wherever violence is used and injury done, though by hands appointed to administer justice, it is still violence and injury, however colored with the name, pretenses, or forms of law, the end whereof being to protect and redress the innocent by an unbiased application of it to all who are under it; wherever that is not bona fide done, war is made upon the sufferers, who having no appeal on earth to right them, they are left to the only remedy in such cases -- an appeal to heaven.

21. To avoid this state of war -- wherein there is no appeal but to heaven, and wherein every the least difference is apt to end, where there is no authority to decide between the contenders -- is one great reason of men's putting themselves into society and quitting the state of nature; for where there is an authority, a power on earth from which relief can be had by appeal, there the continuance of the state of war is excluded, and the controversy is decided by that power. Had there been any such court, any superior jurisdiction on earth, to determine the right between Jephthah and the Ammonites, they had never come to a state of war; but we see he was forced to appeal to heaven: "The Lord the Judge," says he, "be judge this day between the children of Israel and the children of Ammon" (Judges xi.27), and then prosecuting and relying on his appeal, he leads out his army to battle. And, therefore, in such controversies where the question is put, "Who shall be judge?" it cannot be meant, "who shall decide the controversy"; every one knows what Jephthah here tells us, that "the Lord the Judge" shall judge. Where there is no judge on earth, the appeal lies to God in heaven. That question then cannot mean: who shall judge whether another has put himself in a state of war with me, and whether I may, as Jephthah did, appeal to heaven in it? Of that I myself can only be judge in my own conscience, as I will answer it, at the great day, to the supreme Judge of all men.

Chapter IX

OF THE ENDS OF POLITICAL SOCIETY AND GOVERNMENT

123. If man in the state of nature be so free, as has been said, if he be absolute lord of his own person and possessions, equal to the greatest, and subject to nobody, why will he part with his freedom, why will he give up his empire and subject himself to the dominion and control of any other power? To which it is obvious to answer that though in the state of nature he has such a right, yet the enjoyment of it is very uncertain and constantly exposed to the invasion of others; for all being kings as much as he, every man his equal, and the greater part no strict observers of equity and justice, the enjoyment of the property he has in this state is very unsafe, very unsecure. This makes him willing to quit a condition which, however free, is full of fears and continual dangers; and it is not without reason that he seeks out and is willing to join in society with others who are already united, or have a mind to unite, for the mutual preservation of their lives, liberties, and estates, which I call by the general name 'property.'

124. The great and chief end, therefore, of men's uniting into commonwealths and putting themselves under government is the preservation of their property. To which in the state of nature there are many things wanting:

First, there wants an established, settled, known law, received and allowed by common consent to be the standard of right and wrong and the common measure to decide all controversies between them; for though the law of nature be plain and intelligible to all rational creatures, yet men, being biased by their interest as well as ignorant for want of studying it, are not apt to allow of it as a law binding to them in the application of it to their particular cases.

125. Secondly, in the state of nature there wants a known and indifferent judge with authority to determine all differences according to the established law; for every one in that state being both judge and executioner of the law of nature, men being partial to themselves, passion and revenge is very apt to carry them too far and with too much heat in their own cases, as well as negligence and unconcernedness to make them too remiss in other men's.

126. Thirdly, in the state of nature there often wants power to back and support the sentence when right, and to give it due execution. They who by any injustice offend will seldom fail, where they are able, by force, to make good their injustice; such resistance many times makes the punishment dangerous and frequently destructive to those who attempt it.

127. Thus mankind, notwithstanding all the privileges of the state of nature, being but in an ill condition while they remain in it, are quickly driven into society. Hence it comes to pass that we seldom find any number of men live any time together in this state. The inconveniences that they are therein exposed to by the irregular and uncertain exercise of the power every man has of punishing the transgressions of others make them take sanctuary under the established laws of government and therein seek the preservation of their property. It is this makes them so willingly give up every one his single power of punishing, to be exercised by such alone as shall be appointed to it amongst them; and by such rules as the community, or those authorized by them to that purpose, shall agree on. And in this we have the original right of both the legislative and executive power, as well as of the governments and societies themselves.

128. For in the state of nature, to omit the liberty he has of innocent delights, a man has two powers:

The first is to do whatsoever he thinks fit for the preservation of himself and others within the permission of the law of nature, by which law, common to them all, he and all the rest of mankind are one community, make up one society, distinct from all other creatures. And, were it not for the corruption and viciousness of degenerate men, there would be no need of any other, no necessity that men should separate from this great and natural community and by positive agreements combine into smaller and divided associations.

The other power a man has in the state of nature is the power to punish the crimes committed against that law. Both these he gives up when he joins in a private, if I may so call it, or particular politic society and incorporates into any commonwealth separate from the rest of mankind.

129. The first power, viz., of doing whatsoever he thought fit for the preservation of himself and the rest of mankind, he gives up to be regulated by laws made by the society, so far forth as the preservation of himself and the rest of that society shall require; which laws of the society in many things confine the liberty he had by the law of nature.

130. Secondly, the power of punishing he wholly gives up, and engages his natural force -- which he might before employ in the execution of the law of nature by his own single authority, as he thought fit -- to assist the executive power of the society, as the law thereof shall require; for being now in a new state, wherein he is to enjoy many conveniences from the labor, assistance, and society of others in the same community as well as protection from its whole strength, he is to part also with as much of his natural liberty, in providing for himself, as the good, prosperity, and safety of the society shall require, which is not only necessary, but just, since the other members of the society do the like.

131. But though men when they enter into society give up the equality, liberty, and executive power they had in the state of nature into the hands of the society, to be so far disposed of by the legislative as the good of the society shall require, yet it being only with an intention in every one the better to preserve himself, his liberty and property -- for no rational creature can be supposed to change his condition with an intention to be worse -- the power of the society, or legislative constituted by them, can never be supposed to extend farther than the common good, but is obliged to secure every one's property by providing against those three defects above-mentioned that made the state of nature so unsafe and uneasy. And so whoever has the legislative or supreme power of any commonwealth is bound to govern by established standing laws, promulgated and known to the people, and not by extemporary decrees; by indifferent and upright judges who are to decide controversies by those laws; and to employ the force of the community at home only in the execution of such laws, or abroad to prevent or redress foreign injuries, and secure the community from inroads and invasion. And all this to be directed to no other end but the peace, safety, and public good of the people.

Chapter XI

OF THE EXTENT OF THE LEGISLATIVE POWER

134. The great end of men's entering into society being the enjoyment of their properties in peace and safety, and the great instrument and means of that being the laws established in that society, the first and fundamental positive law of all commonwealths is the establishing of the legislative power; as the first and fundamental natural law which is to

govern even the legislative itself is the preservation of the society and, as far as will consist with the public good, of every person in it. This legislative is not only the supreme power of the commonwealth, but sacred and unalterable in the hands where the community have once placed it; nor can any edict of anybody else, in what form soever conceived or by what power soever backed, have the force and obligation of a law which has not its sanction from that legislative which the public has chosen and appointed; for without this the law could not have that which is absolutely necessary to its being a law: the consent of the society over whom nobody can have a power to make laws, but by their own consent and by authority received from them.[1] And therefore all the obedience, which by the most solemn ties any one can be obliged to pay, ultimately terminates in this supreme power and is directed by those laws which it enacts; nor can any oaths to any foreign power whatsoever, or any domestic subordinate power, discharge any member of the society from his obedience to the legislative acting pursuant to their trust, nor oblige him to any obedience contrary to the laws so enacted, or farther than they do allow; it being ridiculous to imagine one can be tied ultimately to obey any power in the society which is not supreme.

135. Though the legislative, whether placed in one or more, whether it be always in being, or only by intervals, though it be the supreme power in every commonwealth; yet:

First, it is not, nor can possibly be, absolutely arbitrary over the lives and fortunes of the people; for it being but the joint power of every member of the society given up to that person or assembly which is legislator, it can be no more than those persons had in a state of nature before they entered into society and gave up to the community; for nobody can transfer to another more power than he has in himself, and nobody has an absolute arbitrary power over himself or over any other, to destroy his own life or take away the life or property of another. A man, as has been proved, cannot subject himself to the arbitrary power of another; and having in the state of nature no arbitrary power over the life, liberty, or possession of another, but only so much as the law of nature gave him for the preservation of himself and the rest of mankind, this is all he does or can give up to the commonwealth, and by it to the legislative power, so that the legislative can have no more than this. Their power, in the utmost bounds of it, is limited to the public good of the society. It is a power that has no other end but preservation, and therefore can never have a right to destroy, enslave, or designedly to impoverish the subjects.[2] The obligations of the law of nature cease not in society but only in many cases are drawn closer and have by human laws known penalties annexed to them to enforce their observation. Thus the law of nature stands as an eternal rule to all men, legislators as well as others. The rules that they make for other men's actions must, as well as their own and other men's actions, be conformable to the law of nature -- i.e., to the will of God, of which that is a declaration -- and the fundamental law of nature being the preservation of mankind, no human sanction can be good or valid against it.

• • • • • •

Chapter XIX

OF THE DISSOLUTION OF GOVERNMENT

211. He that will with any clearness speak of the dissolution of government ought in the first place to distinguish between the dissolution of the society and the dissolution of the government. That which makes the community and brings men out of the loose state of nature into one politic society is the agreement which everybody has with the rest to incorporate and act as one body, and so be one distinct commonwealth. The usual and almost only way whereby this union is dissolved is the inroad of foreign force making a conquest upon them; for in that case, not being able to maintain and support themselves as one entire and independent body, the union belonging to that body which consisted therein must necessarily cease, and so every one return to the state he was in before, with a liberty to shift for himself and provide for his own safety, as he thinks fit, in some other society. Whenever the society is dissolved, it is certain the government of that society cannot remain. Thus conquerors' swords often cut up governments by the roots and mangle societies to pieces, separating the subdued or scattered multitude from the protection of and dependence on that society which ought to have preserved them from violence. The world is too well instructed in, and too forward to allow of, this way of dissolving of governments to need any more to be said of it; and there wants not much argument to prove that where the society is dissolved, the government cannot remain -- that being as impossible as for the frame of a house to subsist when the

materials of it are scattered and dissipated by a whirlwind, or jumbled into a confused heap by an earthquake.

212. Besides this overturning from without, governments are dissolved from within.

First, when the legislative is altered. Civil society being a state of peace amongst those who are of it, from whom the state of war is excluded by the umpirage which they have provided in their legislative for the ending all differences that may arise amongst any of them, it is in their legislative that the members of a commonwealth are united and combined together into one coherent living body. This is the soul that gives form, life, and unity to the commonwealth; from hence the several members have their mutual influence, sympathy, and connection; and, therefore, when the legislative is broken dissolved, dissolution and death follows; for the essence and union of the society consisting in having one will, the legislative, when once established by the majority, has the declaring and, as it were, keeping of that will. The constitution of the legislative is the first and fundamental act of society, whereby provision is made for the continuation of their union under the direction of persons and bonds of laws made by persons authorized thereunto by the consent and appointment of the people, without which no one man or number of men amongst them can have authority of making laws that shall be binding to the rest. When any one or more shall take upon them to make laws, whom the people have not appointed so to do, they make laws without authority, which the people are not therefore bound to obey; by which means they come again to be out of subjection and may constitute to themselves a new legislative as they think best, being in full liberty to resist the force of those who without authority would impose anything upon them. Everyone is at the disposure of his own will when those who had by the delegation of the society the declaring of the public will are excluded from it, and others usurp the place who have no such authority or delegation.

• • • • • •

219. There is one way more whereby such a government may be dissolved, and that is when he who has the supreme executive power neglects and abandons that charge, so that the laws already made can no longer be put in execution. This is demonstratively to reduce all to anarchy, and so effectually to dissolve the government; for laws not being

made for themselves, but to be by their execution the bonds of the society, to keep every part of the body politic in its due place and function, when that totally ceases, the government visibly ceases, and the people become a confused multitude, without order or connection. Where there is no longer the administration of justice for the securing of men's rights, nor any remaining power within the community to direct the force to provide for the necessities of the public, there certainly is no government left. Where the laws cannot be executed, it is all one as if there were no laws; and a government without laws is, I suppose, a mystery in politics, inconceivable to human capacity and inconsistent with human society.

220. In these and the like cases, when the government is dissolved, the people are at liberty to provide for themselves by erecting a new legislative, differing from the other by the change of persons or form, or both, as they shall find it most for their safety and good; for the society can never by the fault of another lose the native and original right it has to preserve itself, which can only be done by a settled legislative, and a fair and impartial execution of the laws made by it. But the state of mankind is not so miserable that they are not capable of using this remedy till it be too late to look for any. To tell people they may provide for themselves by erecting a new legislative, when by oppression, artifice, or being delivered over to a foreign power, their old one is gone, is only to tell them they may expect relief when it is too late and the evil is past cure. This is in effect no more than to bid them first be slaves, and then to take care of their liberty; and when their chains are on, tell them they may act like freemen. This, if barely so, is rather mockery than relief; and men can never be secure from tyranny if there be no means to escape it till they are perfectly under it; and therefore it is that they have not only a right to get out of it, but to prevent it.

221. There is, therefore, secondly, another way whereby governments are dissolved, and that is when the legislative or the prince, either of them, act contrary to their trust.

First, the legislative acts against the trust reposed in them when they endeavor to invade the property of the subject, and to make themselves or any part of the community masters or arbitrary disposers of the lives, liberties, or fortunes of the people.

222. The reason why men enter into society is the preservation of their property; and the end why they choose and authorize a legislative is that there may be laws made and rules set as guards and fences to the properties of all the members of the society to limit the power and moderate the dominion of every part and member of the society; for since it

can never be supposed to be the will of the society that the legislative should have a power to destroy that which every one designs to secure by entering into society, and for which the people submitted themselves to legislators of their own making. Whenever the legislators endeavor to take away and destroy the property of the people, or to reduce them to slavery under arbitrary power, they put themselves into a state of war with the people who are thereupon absolved from any further obedience, and are left to the common refuge which God has provided for all men against force and violence. Whensoever, therefore, the legislative shall transgress this fundamental rule of society, and either by ambition, fear, folly, or corruption, endeavor to grasp themselves, or put into the hands of any other, an absolute power over the lives, liberties, and estates of the people, by this breach of trust they forfeit the power the people had put into their hands for quite contrary ends, and it devolves to the people, who have a right to resume their original liberty and, by the establishment of a new legislative, such as they shall think fit, provide for their own safety and security, which is the end for which they are in society. What I have said here concerning the legislative in general holds true also concerning the supreme executor, who having a double trust put in him -- both to have a part in the legislative and the supreme execution of the law -- acts against both when he goes about to set up his own arbitrary will as the law of the society. He acts also contrary to his trust when he either employs the force, treasure, and offices of the society to corrupt the representatives and gain them to his purposes, or openly pre-engages the electors and prescribes to their choice such whom he has by solicitations, threats, promises, or otherwise won to his designs, and employs them to bring in such who have promised beforehand what to vote and what to enact. Thus to regulate candidates and electors, and new-model the ways of election, what is it but to cut up the government by the roots, and poison the very fountain of public security? For the people, having reserved to themselves the choice of their representatives, as the fence to their properties, could do it for no other end but that they might always be freely chosen, and, so chosen, freely act and advise as the necessity of the commonwealth and the public good should upon examination and mature debate be judged to require. This those who give their votes before they hear the debate and have weighed the reasons on all sides are not capable of doing. To prepare such an assembly as this, and endeavor to set up the declared abettors of his own will for the true representatives of the people and the lawmakers of the society, is certainly as great a breach of trust and as perfect a declaration of a design to subvert the government as is possible to be met with. To which if one shall add rewards and punishments visibly employed to the same end, and all the arts of perverted law made use of to take off and destroy all that stand in the way of such a design, and will not comply and consent to betray the liberties of their country, it will be past doubt what is doing. What power they ought to have in the society who thus employ it contrary to the trust that went along with it in its first institution is easy to determine; and one cannot but see that he who has once attempted any such thing as this cannot any longer be trusted.

223. To this perhaps it will be said that, the people being ignorant and always discontented, to lay the foundation of government in the unsteady opinion and uncertain humor of the people is to expose it to certain ruin; and no government will be able long to subsist if the people may set up a new legislative whenever they take offense at the old one. To this I answer: Quite the contrary. People are not so easily got out of their old forms as some are apt to suggest. They are hardly to be prevailed with to amend the acknowledged faults in the frame they have been accustomed to. And if there by any original defects, or adventitious ones introduced by time or corruption, it is not an easy thing to get them changed, even when all the world sees there is an opportunity for it. This slowness and aversion in the people to quit their old constitutions has in the many revolutions which have been seen in this kingdom, in this and former ages, still kept us to, or after some interval of fruitless attempts still brought us back again to, our old legislative of king, lords, and commons; and whatever provocations have made the crown be taken from some of our princes' heads, they never carried the people so far as to place it in another line.

224. But it will be said this hypothesis lays a ferment for frequent rebellion. To which I answer:

First, no more than any other hypothesis; for when the people are made miserable, and find themselves exposed to the ill-usage of arbitrary power, cry up their governors as much as you will for sons of Jupiter, let them be sacred or divine, descended or authorized from heaven, give them out for whom or what you please, the same will happen. The people generally ill-treated, and contrary to right, will be ready upon any occasion to ease themselves of a burden that sits heavy upon them. They will wish and seek for the opportunity, which in the change, weakness, and accidents of human affairs seldom delays long to offer itself. He must have lived but a little while in the world who has not seen examples of this in his time, and he must have read very little who cannot produce examples of it in all sorts of governments in the world.

225. Secondly, I answer, such revolutions happen not upon every little mismanagement in public affairs. Great mistakes in the ruling part, many wrong and inconvenient laws, and all the slips of human frailty will be born by the people without mutiny or murmur. But if a long train of abuses, prevarications, and artifices, all tending the same way, make the design visible to the people, and they cannot but feel what they lie under and see whither they are going, it is not to be wondered that they should then rouse themselves and endeavor to put the rule into such hands which may secure to them the ends for which government was at first erected, and without which ancient names and specious forms are so far from being better that they are much worse than the state of nature or pure anarchy -- the inconveniences being all as great and as near, but the remedy farther off and more difficult.

226. Thirdly, I answer that this doctrine of a power in the people of providing for their safety anew by a new legislative, when their legislators have acted contrary to their trust by invading their property, is the best fence against rebellion, and the probablest means to hinder it; for rebellion being an opposition, not to persons, but authority which is founded only in the constitutions and laws of the government, those, whoever they be, who by force break through, and by force justify their violation of them, are truly and properly rebels; for when men, by entering into society and civil government, have excluded force and introduced laws for the preservation of property, peace, and unity amongst themselves, those who set up force again in opposition to the laws do *rebellare* -- that is, bring back again the state of war -- and are properly rebels; which they who are in power, by the pretense they have to authority, the temptation of force they have in their hands, and the flattery of those about them, being likeliest to do, the properest way to prevent the evil is to show them the danger and injustice of it who are under the greatest temptation to run into it.

227. In both the forementioned cases, when either the legislative is changed or the legislators act contrary to the end for which they were constituted, those who are guilty are guilty of rebellion; for if any one by force takes away the established legislative of any society, and the laws of them made pursuant to their trust, he thereby takes away the umpirage which every one had consented to for a peaceable decision of all their controversies, and a bar to the state of war amongst them. They who remove or change the legislative take away this decisive power which nobody can have but by the appointment and consent of the people, and so destroying the authority which the people did, and nobody else can, set up, and introducing a power which the people has not authorized,

they actually introduce a state of war which is that of force without authority; and thus by removing the legislative established by the society -- in whose decisions the people acquiesced and united as to that of their own will -- they untie the knot and expose the people anew to the state of war. And if those who by force take away the legislative are rebels, the legislators themselves, as has been shown, can be no less esteemed so, when they who were set up for the protection and preservation of the people, their liberties and properties, shall by force invade and endeavor to take them away; and so they putting themselves into a state of war with those who made them the protectors and guardians of their peace, are properly, and with the greatest aggravation, *rebellantes,* rebels.

228. But if they who say "it lays a foundation for rebellion" mean that it may occasion civil wars or intestine broils, to tell the people they are absolved from obedience when illegal attempts are made upon their liberties or properties, and may oppose the unlawful violence of those who were their magistrates when they invade their properties contrary to the trust put in them, and that therefore this doctrine is not to be allowed, being so destructive to the peace of the world; they may as well say, upon the same ground, that honest men may not oppose robbers or pirates because this may occasion disorder or bloodshed. If any mischief come in such cases, it is not to be charged upon him who defends his own right, but on him that invades his neighbor's. If the innocent honest man must quietly quit all he has, for peace's sake, to him who will lay violent hands upon it, I desire it may be considered what a kind of peace there will be in the world, which consists only in violence and rapine, and which is to be maintained only for the benefit of robbers and oppressors. Who would not think it an admirable peace betwixt the mighty and the mean when the lamb without resistance yielded his throat to be torn by the imperious wolf. Polyphemus' den gives us a perfect pattern of such a peace and such a government, wherein Ulysses and his companions had nothing to do but quietly to suffer themselves to be devoured. And no doubt Ulysses, who was a prudent man, preached up passive obedience, and exhorted them to a quiet submission by representing to them of what concernment peace was to mankind, and by showing the inconveniences which might happen if they should offer to resist Polyphemus, who had now the power over them.

229. The end of government is the good of mankind. And which is best for mankind? That the people should be always exposed to the boundless will of tyranny, or that the rulers should be sometimes liable to be opposed when they grow exorbitant in the use of their power and

employ it for the destruction and not the preservation of the properties of their people?

230. Nor let any one say that mischief can arise from hence, as often as it shall please a busy head or turbulent spirit to desire the alteration of the government. It is true such men may stir whenever they please, but it will be only to their own just ruin and perdition; for till the mischief be grown general, and the ill designs of the rulers become visible, or their attempts sensible to the greater part, the people, who are more disposed to suffer than right themselves by resistance, are not apt to stir. The examples of particular injustice or oppression of here and there an unfortunate man moves them not. But if they universally have a persuasion grounded upon manifest evidence that designs are carrying on against their liberties, and the general course and tendency of things cannot but give them strong suspicions of the evil intention of their governors, who is to be blamed for it? Who can help it if they who might avoid it bring themselves into their suspicion? Are the people to be blamed if they have the sense of rational creatures and can think of things no otherwise than as they find and feel them? And is it not rather their fault who put things into such a posture that they would not have them thought to be as they are? I grant that the pride, ambition, and turbulence of private men have sometimes caused great disorders in commonwealths, and factions have been fatal to states and kingdoms. But whether the mischief has oftener begun in the people's wantonness and a desire to cast off the lawful authority of their rulers, or in the rulers' insolence and endeavors to get and exercise an arbitrary power over their people -- whether oppression or disobedience gave the first rise to the disorder, I leave it to impartial history to determine. This I am sure: whoever, either ruler or subject, by force goes about to invade the rights of either prince or people and lays the foundation for overturning the constitution and frame of any just government is highly guilty of the greatest crime I think a man is capable of -- being to answer for all those mischiefs of blood, rapine, and desolation, which the breaking to pieces of governments bring on a country. And he who does it is justly to be esteemed the common enemy and pest of mankind, and is to be treated accordingly.

• • • • • •

240. Here, it is like, the common question will be made: Who shall be judge whether the prince or legislative act contrary to their trust? This, perhaps, ill-affected and factious men may spread amongst the people,

when the prince only makes use of his due prerogative. To this I reply: The people shall be judge; for who shall be judge whether his trustee or deputy acts well and according to the trust reposed in him but he who deputes him and must, by having deputed him, have still a power to discard him when he fails in his trust? If this be reasonable in particular cases of private men, why should it be otherwise in that of the greatest moment where the welfare of millions is concerned, and also where the evil, if not prevented, is greater and the redress very difficult, dear, and dangerous?

241. But further, this question, Who shall be judge? cannot mean that there is no judge at all; for where there is no judicature on earth to decide controversies amongst men, God in heaven is Judge. He alone, it is true, is Judge of the right. But every man is judge for himself, as in all other cases, so in this, whether another has put himself into a state of war with him, and whether he should appeal to the Supreme Judge, as Jephthah did.

242. If a controversy arise betwixt a prince and some of the people in a matter where the law is silent or doubtful, and the thing be of great consequence, I should think the proper umpire in such a case should be the body of the people; for in cases where the prince has a trust reposed in him and is dispensed from the common ordinary rules of the law, there, if any men find themselves aggrieved and think the prince acts contrary to or beyond that trust, who so proper to judge as the body of the people (who, at first, lodged that trust in him) how far they meant it should extend? But if the prince, or whoever they be in the administration, decline that way of determination, the appeal then lies nowhere but to heaven; force between either persons who have no known superior on earth, or which permits no appeal to a judge on earth, being properly a state of war wherein the appeal lies only to heaven; and in that state the injured party must judge for himself when he will think fit to make use of that appeal and put himself upon it.

243. To conclude, the power that every individual gave the society when he entered into it can never revert to the individuals again as long as the society lasts, but will always remain in the community, because without this there can be no community, no commonwealth, which is contrary to the original agreement; so also when the society has placed the legislative in any assembly of men, to continue in them and their successors with direction and authority for providing such successors, the legislative can never revert to the people while that government lasts, because having provided a legislative with power to continue for ever, they have given up their political power to the legislative and cannot

resume it. But if they have set limits to the duration of their legislative and made this supreme power in any person or assembly only temporary, or else when by the miscarriages of those in authority it is forfeited, upon the forfeiture, or at the determination of the time set, it reverts to the society, and the people have a right to act as supreme and continue the legislative in themselves, or erect a new form, or under the old form place it in new hands, as they think good.

Notes

1 "The lawful power of making laws to command whole politic societies of men, belonging so properly unto the same entire societies, that for any prince or potentate of what kind soever upon earth to exercise the same of himself, and not by express commission immediately and personally received from God, or else by authority derived at the first from their consent, upon whose persons they impose laws, it is no better than mere tyranny. Laws they are not, therefore, which public approbation hath not made so" (Hooker's *Eccl. Pol.*lib. i. sect. 10).

"Of this point, therefore, we are to note, that such men naturally have no full and perfect power to command whole politic multitudes of men, therefore utterly without our consent we could in such sort be at no man's commandment living. And to be commanded we do consent, when that society whereof we be a part hath at any time before consented, without revoking the same by the like universal agreement. Laws therefore human, of what kind soever, are available by consent" (*Ibid.*).

2 "Two foundations there are which bear up public societies; the one a natural inclination whereby all men desire sociable life and fellowship; the other an order, expressly or secretly agreed upon, touching the manner of their union in living together. The latter is that which we call the law of a commonweal, the very soul of a politic body, the parts whereof are by law animated, held together, and set on work in such actions as the common good requireth. Laws politic, ordained for external order and regiment amongst men, are never framed as they should be, unless presuming the will of man to be inwardly obstinate, rebellious, and averse from all obedience to the sacred laws of his nature; in a word, unless presuming the will of man to be inwardly obstinate, rebellious, and averse from all obedience to the sacred laws of his nature; in a word, unless presuming man to be, in regard of his depraved mind, little better than a wild beast, they do accordingly provide, notwithstanding, so to drame his outward actions that they be no hindrance unto the common good, for which societies are instituted. Unless they do this, they are not perfect" (Hooker's *Eccl. Pol.* lib. i. sect. 10).

6

Austin
On Law and Utility

The Province of Jurisprudence Determined

LECTURE I

The matter of jurisprudence is positive law: law, simply and strictly so called: or law set by poltical superiors to political inferiors. But positive law (or law, simply and strictly so called) is often confounded with objects to which it is related by *resemblance,* and with objects to which it is related in the way of *analogy:* with objects which are *also* signified, *properly* and *improperly,* by the large and vague expression *law.* To obviate the difficulties springing from that confusion, I begin my projected Course with determining the province of jurisprudence from those various related objects: trying to define the subject of which I intend to treat, before I endeavour to analyze its numerous and complicated parts.

Taking it with the largest of its meanings which are not merely metaphorical, the term *law* embraces the following objects: Laws set by *God* to his human creatures, and laws set by *men* to men.

The whole or a portion of the laws set by God to men, is frequently styled the *law of nature,* or *natural law:* being, in truth, the only *natural law,* of which it is possible to speak without a metaphor, or without a blending of objects which ought to be distinguished broadly. But, rejecting the ambiguous expression *natural law,* I name those laws or rules, as considered collectively or in mass, the *Divine law,* or the *law of God.*

The laws or rules set by men to men, are of two leading or principal classes: classes which are often blended, although they differ extremely;

and which, for that reason, should be severed precisely, and opposed distinctly and conspicuously.

Of the laws or rules set by men to men, some are established by *political* superiors, sovereign and subject: by persons exercising supreme and subordinate *government,* in independent nations, or independent political societies. The aggregate of the rules thus established, or some aggregate forming a portion of that aggregate, is the appropriate matter of jurisprudence, general or particular. To the aggregate of the rules thus established, or to some aggregate forming a portion of that aggregate, the term *law,* as used simply and strictly, is exclusively applied. But, as contradistinguished to *natural* law, or to the law *of nature* (meaning, by those expressions, the law of God), the aggregate of the rules, established by political superiors, is frequently styled *positive* law, or law existing *by position.* As contradistinguished to the rules which I style *positive morality,* and on which I shall touch immediately, the aggregate of the rules, established by political superiors, may also be marked commodiously with the name of *positive law.* For the sake, then, of getting a name brief and distinctive at once, and agreeably to frequent usage, I style that aggregate of rules, or any portion of that aggregate, *positive law:* though rules, which are *not* established by political superiors, are also *positive,* or exist *by position,* if they be rules or laws, in the proper signification of the term.

Though *some* of the laws or rules, which are set by men to men, are established by political superiors, *others* are *not* established by political superiors, or are *not* established by political superiors, in that capacity or character.

Of human laws belonging to this second class, *some* are laws, properly so called. But *others* are styled *laws* by an improper application of the term, although that improper application rests upon a close analogy.

For such of the human laws belonging to this second class as are *properly* called *laws,* current or established language has no collective name.

But the aggregate of the human laws, which are *improperly* styled *laws,* is not unfrequently denoted by one of the following expressions: "*moral* rules," "the *moral* law," "the law set or prescribed by *general* or *public opinion.*" Certain parcels of the aggregate denoted by those expressions, are usually styled "the law or rules of *honour,*" and "the law set by *fashion.*"

As opposed to the laws which are set by God to men, and to the laws which are established by political superiors, the aggregate of the human laws, which are *improperly* styled *laws,* may be named commodiously *positive morality*. The name *morality* severs them from *positive law:* whilst the epithet *positive* disjoins them from the *law of God*. And to the end of obviating confusion, it is necessary or expedient that they *should* be disjoined from the latter by that distinguishing epithet. For the name *morality* (or *morals),* when standing unqualified or alone, denotes indifferently either of the following objects: namely, positive morality *as it is,* or without regard to its merits; and positive morality *as it would be,* if it conformed to the law of God, and were, therefore, deserving of *approbation*.

Laws set by God to men, laws established by political superiors, and laws set by men to men (though *not* by political superiors), are distinguished by numerous and important differences, but agree in this: -- that all of them are set by intelligent and rational beings to intelligent and rational beings. Every law of any of those kinds, is either a law (properly so called), or is related to a law (properly so called) by a close and striking analogy.

But in numerous cases wherein it is applied improperly, the applications of the term *law* rest upon a slender analogy, and are merely metaphorical or figurative. Such is the case when we talk of *laws observed by the lower animals; of laws* regulating the growth or decay of vegetables; of *laws* determining the movements of inanimate bodies or masses. For where *intelligence* is not, or where it is too bounded to take the name of *reason,* and, therefore, is too bounded to conceive the purpose of a law, there is not the *will* which law can work on, or which duty can incite or restrain. Yet through these misapplications of a *name,* flagrant as the metaphor is, has the field of jurisprudence and morals been deluged with muddy speculation.

• • • • • •

Every *law* or *rule* (taken with the largest signification which can be given to the term *properly)* is a *command*. Or, rather, laws or rules, properly so called, are a *species* of commands.

Now since the term *command* comprises the term *law,* the first is the simpler as well as the larger of the two. But simple as it is, it admits of explanation. And, since it is the *key* to the sciences of jurisprudence and morals, its meaning should be analyzed with precision.

• • • • • •

If you express or intimate a wish that I shall do or forbear from some act, and if you will visit me with an evil in case I comply not with your wish, the *expression* or *intimation* of your wish is a *command*. A command is distinguished from other significations of desire, not by the style in which the desire is signified, but by the power and the purpose of the party commanding to inflict an evil or pain in case the desire be disregarded. If you cannot or will not harm me in case I comply not with your wish, the expression of your wish is not a command, although you utter your wish in imperative phrase. If you are able and willing to harm me in case I comply not with your wish, the expression of your wish amounts to a command, although you are prompted by a spirit of courtesy to utter it in the shape of a request . . .

A command, then, is a signification of desire. But a command is distinguished from other significations of desire by this peculiarity; that the party to whom it is directed is liable to evil from the other, in case he comply not with the desire.

Being liable to evil from you if I comply not with a wish which you signify, I am *bound* or *obliged* by your command, or I lie under a *duty* to obey it. If, in spite of that evil in prospect, I comply not with the wish which you signify, I am said to disobey your command, or to violate the duty which it imposes.

Command and duty, are, therefore, correlative terms: the meaning denoted by each being implied or supposed by the other. Or (changing the expression) wherever a duty lies, a command has been signified; and whenever a command is signified, a duty is imposed.

Concisely expressed, the meaning of the correlative expressions is this. He who will inflict an evil in case his desire be disregarded, utters a command by expressing or intimating his desire: He who is liable to the evil in case he disregard the desire, is bound or obliged by the command.

The evil which will probably be incurred in case a command be disobeyed, or (to use an equivalent expression) in case a duty be broken, is frequently called a *sanction*, or an *enforcement of obedience*. Or (varying the phrase) the command or the duty is said to be *sanctioned* or *enforced* by the chance of incurring the evil.

Considered as thus abstracted from the command the duty which it enforces, the evil to be incurred by disobedience is frequently styled a *punishment*.

Again: If a law hold out a *reward* as an inducement to do some act, an eventual *right* is conferred, and not an *obligation* imposed, upon those who shall act accordingly: The *imperative* part of the law being addressed or directed to the party whom it requires to *render* the reward.

In short, I am determined or inclined to comply with the wish of another, by the fear of disadvantage or evil. I am also determined or inclined to comply with the wish of another, by the hope of advantage or good. But it is only by the chance of incurring *evil,* that I am *bound* or *obliged* to compliance. It is only by conditional *evil,* that duties are *sanctioned* or *enforced*. It is the power and the purpose of inflicting eventual *evil,* and *not* the power and the purpose of imparting eventual *good,* which gives to the expression of a wish the name of a *command*.

• • • • • •

It appears, then, from what has been premised, that the ideas or notions comprehended by the term *command* are the following. 1. A wish or desire conceived by a rational being, that another rational being shall do or forbear. 2. An evil to proceed from the former, and to be incurred by the latter, in case the latter comply not with the wish. 3. An expression or intimation of the wish by words or other signs.

It also appears from what has been premised, that *command, duty* and *sanction* are inseparably connected terms: that each embraces the same ideas as the others, though each denotes those ideas in a peculiar order or series.

• • • • • •

Commands are of two species. Some are *laws* or *rules*. The others have not acquired an appropriate name, nor does language afford an expression which will mark them briefly and precisely. I must, therefore, note them, as well as I can, by the ambiguous and inexpressive name of "*occasional* or *particular* commands."

The term *laws* or *rules* being not unfrequently applied to occasional or particular commands, it is hardly possible to describe a line of separation which shall consist in every respect with established forms of speech. But the distinction between laws and particular commands, may, I think, be stated in the following manner.

By every command, the party to whom it is directed is obliged to do or to forbear.

Now where it obliges *generally* to acts or forbearances of a *class,* a command is a law or rule. But where it obliges to a *specific* act or forbearance, or to acts or forbearances which it determines *specifically* or *individually,* a command is occasional or particular. In other words, a class or description of acts is determined by a law or rule, and acts of that class or description are enjoined or forbidden generally. But where a command is occasional or particular, the act or acts, which the command enjoins or forbids, are assigned or determined by their specific or individual natures, as well as by the class or description to which they belong.

The statement which I have now given in abstract expressions, I will endeavour to illustrate by apt examples.

If you command your servant to go on a given errand, or *not* to leave your house on a given evening, or to rise at such an hour on such a morning, or to rise at that hour during the next week or month, the command is occasional or particular. For the act or acts enjoined or forbidden, are specifically determined or assigned.

But if you command him *simply* to rise at that hour, or to rise at that hour *always,* or to rise at that hour *till further orders,* it may be said, with propriety, that you lay down a *rule* for the guidance of your servant's conduct. For no specific act is assigned by the command, but the command obliges him generally to acts of a determined class.

• • • • • •

Laws and other commands are said to proceed from *superiors,* and to bind or oblige *inferiors*. I will, therefore, analyze the meaning of those correlative expressions; and will try to strip them of a certain mystery, by which that simple meaning appears to be obscured.

Superiority is often synonymous with *precedence* or *excellence*. We talk of superiors in rank; of superiors in wealth; of superiors in virtue: comparing certain persons with certain other persons; and meaning that the former precede or excel the latter, in rank, in wealth, or in virtue.

But, taken with the meaning wherein I here understand it, the term *superiority* signifies *might:* the power of affecting others with evil or pain, and of forcing them, through fear of that evil, to fashion their conduct to one's wishes.

For example, God is emphatically the *superior* of Man. For his power of affecting us with pain, and of forcing us to comply with his will, is unbounded and resistless.

To a limited extent, the sovereign One or Number is the superior of the subject or citizen: the master, of the slave or servant: the father, of the child.

In short, whoever can *oblige* another to comply with his wishes, is the *superior* of that other, so far as the ability reaches: The party who is obnoxious to the impending evil, being, to that same extent, the *inferior*.

The might or superiority of God, is simple or absolute. But in all or most cases of human superiority, the relation of superior and inferior, and the relation of inferior and superior, are reciprocal. Or (changing the expression) the party who is the superior as viewed from one aspect, is the inferior as viewed from another.

For example, To an indefinite, though limited extent, the monarch is the superior of the governed: his power being commonly sufficient to enforce compliance with his will. But the governed, collectively or in mass, are also the superior of the monarch: who is checked in the abuse of his might by his fear of exciting their anger; and of rousing to active resistance, the might which slumbers in the multitude.

A member of a sovereign assembly is the superior of the judge: the judge being bound by the law which proceeds from that sovereign body. But, in his character of citizen or subject, he is the inferior of the judge: the judge being the minister of the law, and armed with the power of enforcing it.

It appears, then, that the term *superiority* (like the terms *duty* and *sanction)* is implied by the term *command*. For superiority is the power of enforcing compliance with a wish: and the expression or intimation of a wish, with the power and the purpose of enforcing it, are the constituent elements of a command.

• • • • • •

1. There are laws, it may be said, which *merely* create *rights:* And, seeing that every command imposes a *duty,* laws of this nature are not imperative.

But, as I have intimated already, and shall shew completely hereafter, there are no laws *merely* creating *rights.* There are laws, it is true, which *merely* create *duties:* duties not correlating with correlating rights, and which, therefore, may be styled *absolute.* But every law, really conferring a right, imposes expressly or tacitly a *relative* duty, or a duty correlating with the right. If it specify the rememdy to be given, in case the right shall be infringed, it imposes the relative duty expressly. If the remedy to be given be not specified, it refers tacitly to pre-existing law, and clothes the right which it purports to create with a remedy provided by that law. Every law, really conferring a right, is, therefore, imperative: as imperative, as if its only purpose were the creation of a duty, or as if the relative duty, which it inevitably imposes, were merely absolute.

• • • • • •

2. According to an opinion which I must notice *incidentally* here, though the subject to which it relates will be treated *directly* hereafter, *customary laws* must be excepted from the proposition "that laws are a species of commands."

By many of the admirers of customary laws (and, especially, of their German admirers), they are thought to oblige legally (independently of the sovereign or state), *because* the citizens or subjects have observed or kept them. Agreeably to this opinion, they are not the *creatures* of the sovereign or state, although the sovereign or state may abolish them at pleasure. Agreeably to this opinion, they are positive law (or law, strictly so called), inasmuch as they are enforced by the courts of justice: But, that notwithstanding, they exist *as positive law* by the spontaneous adoption of the governed, and not by position or establishment on the part of political superiors. Consequently, customary laws, considered as positive law, are not commands. And, consequently, customary laws, considered as positive law, are not laws or rules, properly so called.

An opinion less mysterious, but somewhat allied to this, is not uncommonly held by the adverse party: by the party which is strongly opposed to customary law; and to all law made judicially, or in the way of judicial legislation. According to the latter opinion, all judge-made law, or all judge-made law established by *subject* judges, is purely the creature of the judges by whom it is established immediately. To impute it to the sovereign legislature, or to suppose that it speaks the will of the sovereign legislature, is one of the foolish or knavish *fictions* with which lawyers, in every age and nation, have perplexed and darkened the simplest and clearest truths.

I think it will appear, on a moment's reflexion, that each of these opinions is groundless: that customary law is *imperative,* in the proper signification of the term; and that all judge-made law is the creature of the sovereign or state.

At its origin, a custom is a rule of conduct which the governed observe spontaneously, or not in pursuance of a law set by a political superior. The custom is transmuted into positive law, when it is adopted as such by the courts of justice, and when the judicial decisions fashioned upon it are enforced by the power of the state. But before it is adopted by the courts, and clothed with the legal sanction, it is merely a rule or positive morality: a rule generally observed by the citizens or subjects; but deriving the only force, which it can be said to possess, from the general disapprobation falling on those who transgress it.

Now when judges transmute a custom into a legal rule (or make a legal rule not suggested by a custom), the legal rule which they establish is established by the sovereign legislature. A subordinate or subject judge is merely a minister. The portion of the sovereign power which lies at his disposition is merely delegated. The rules which he makes derive their legal force from authority given by the state: an authority which the state may confer expressly, but which it commonly imparts in the way of acquiescence. For, since the state may reverse the rules which he makes, and yet permits him to enforce them by the power of the political community, its sovereign will "that his rules shall obtain as law" is clearly envinced by its conduct, though not by its express declaration.

• • • • • •

Like other significations of desire, a command is express or tacit. If the desire be signified by *words* (written or spoken), the command is express. If the desire be signified by conduct (or by any signs of desire which are *not* words), the command is tacit.

Now when customs are turned into legal rules by decisions of subject judges, the legal rules which emerge from the customs are *tacit* commands of the sovereign legislature. The state, which is able to abolish, permits its ministers to enforce them: and it, therefore, signifies its pleasure, by that its voluntary acquiescence, "that they shall serve as a law to the governed."

. . . . . .

LECTURE II

In my first lecture, I stated or suggested the purpose and the manner of my attempt to determine the province of jurisprudence: to distinguish positive law, the appropriate matter of jurisprudence, from the various objects to which it is related by resemblance, and to which it is related, nearly or remotely, by a strong or slender analogy.

In pursuance of that purpose, and agreeably to that manner, I stated the essentials of a law or rule (taken with the largest signification which can be given to the term *properly).*

In pursuance of that purpose, and agreeably to that manner, I proceed to distinguish laws set by men to men from those Divine laws which are the ultimate test of human.

The Divine laws, or the laws of God, are laws set by God to his human creatures. As I have intimated already, and shall shew more fully hereafter, they are laws or rules, *properly* so called.

. . . . . .

Of the Divine laws, or the laws of God, some are *revealed* or promulged, and others are *unrevealed*. Such of the laws of God as are unrevealed are not unfrequently denoted by the following names or phrases: "the law of nature;" "natural law;" "the law manifested to man by the light of nature or reason;" " the laws, precepts or dictates of natural religion."

The *revealed* law of God, and the portion of the law of God which is *unrevealed,* are manifested to men in different ways, or by different sets of signs.

With regard to the laws which God is pleased to *reveal,* the way wherein they are manifested is easily conceived. They are *express* commands: portions of the *word* of God: commands signified to men through the medium of human language; and uttered by God directly, or by servants whom he sends to announce them.

Such of the Divine laws as are *unrevealed* are laws set by God to his human creatures, but not through the medium of human language, or not expressly.

These are the only laws which he has set to that portion of mankind who are excluded from the light of Revelation.

• • • • • •

But if God has given us laws which he has not revealed or promulged, how shall we know them? What are those signs of his pleasure, which we style the *light of nature;* and oppose, by that figurative phrase, to express declarations of his will?

The hypotheses or theories which attempt to resolve this question, may be reduced, I think, to two.

According to one of them, there are human actions which all mankind approve, human actions which all men disapprove; and these universal sentiments arise at the thought of those actions, spontaneously, instantly, and inevitably. Being common to all mankind, and inseparable from the thoughts of those actions, these sentiments are marks or signs of the Divine pleasure. They are proofs that the actions which excite them are enjoined or forbidden by the Deity.

The rectitude or pravity of human conduct, or its agreement or disagreement with the laws of God, is instantly inferred from these sentiments, without the possibility of mistake. He has resolved that our happiness shall depend on our keeping his commandments: and it manifestly consists with his manifest wisdom and goodness, that we should know them promptly and certainly. Accordingly, he has not committed us to the guidance of our slow and fallible *reason*. He has wisely endowed us with *feelings,* which warn us at every step; and pursue us, with their importunate reproaches, when we wander from the path of our duties.

These simple or inscrutable feelings have been likened to the outward senses, and styled the *moral sense:* though, admitting that the feelings exist, and are proofs of the Divine pleasure, I am unable to discover the analogy which suggested the comparison and the name. The objects or appearances which properly are perceived through the senses, are perceived immediately, or without an inference of the understanding. According to the hypothesis which I have briefly stated or suggested, there is always an inference of the understanding, though the inference is short and inevitable. From feelings which arise within us when we think of certain actions, we infer that those actions are enjoined or forbidden by the Deity.

The hypothesis, however, of a *moral sense,* is expressed in other ways.

The laws of God, to which these feelings are the index, are not unfrequently named *innate practical principles,* or *postulates of practical reason:* or they are said to be written on our hearts, by the finger of their great Author, in broad and indelible characters.

Common sense (the most yielding and accommodating of phrases) has been moulded and fitted to the purpose of expressing the hypothesis in question. In all their decisions on the rectitude or pravity of conduct (its agreement or disagreement with the unrevealed law), mankind are said to be determined by *common sense:* this same *common sense* meaning, in this instance, the simple or inscrutable sentiments which I have endeavoured to describe.

Considered as affecting the soul, when the man thinks especially of *his own* conduct, these sentiments, feelings, or emotions, are frequently styled his *conscience*.

According to the other of the adverse theories or hyupotheses, the laws of God, which are not revealed or promulged, must be gathered by man from the goodness of God, and from the tendencies of human actions. In other words, the benevolence of God, with the principle of general utility, is our only index or guide to his unrevealed law.

God designs the happiness of all his sentient creatures. Some human actions forward that benevolent purpose, or their tendencies are beneficent or useful. Other human actions are adverse to that purpose, or their tendencies are mischievous or pernicious. The former, as promoting his purpose, God has enjoined. The latter, as opposed to his purpose, God has forbidden. He has given us the faculty of observing; of remembering; of reasoning: and, by duly applying those faculties, we may collect the tendencies of our actions. Knowing the tendencies of our actions, and knowing his benevolent purpose, we know his tacit commands.

• • • • • •

The theory is this. -- Inasmuch as the goodness of God is boundless and impartial, he designs the greatest happiness of all his sentient creatures: he wills that the aggregate of their enjoyments shall find no nearer limit than that which is inevitably set to it by their finite and imperfect nature. From the probable effects of our actions on the greatest happiness of all, or from the tendencies of human actions to increase or diminish that aggregate, we may infer the laws which he has given, but has not expressed or revealed.

Now the *tendency* of a human action (as its tendency is thus understood) is the whole of its tendency: the sum of its probable consequences, in so far as they are important or material: the sum of its remote and collateral, as well as of its direct consequences, in so far as any of its consequences may influence the general happiness.

Trying to collect its tendency (as its tendency is thus understood), we must not consider the action as if it were *single* and *insulated*, but must look at the *class* of actions to which it belongs. The probable *specific* consequences of doing that single act, of forbearing from that single act, or of omitting that single act, are not the objects of the inquiry. The question to be solved, is this. If acts of the *class* were *generally* done, or *generally* forborne or omitted, what would be the probable effect on the general happiness or good?

Considered by itself, a mishievous act may seem to be useful or harmless. Considered by itself, a useful act may seem to be pernicious.

For example, If a poor man steal a handful from the heap of his rich neighbour, the act, considered by itself, is harmless or positively good. One man's poverty is assuaged with the superflous wealth of another.

But suppose that thefts were general (or that the useful right of property were open to frequent invasions), and mark the result.

Without security for property, there were no inducement to save. Without habitual saving on the part of proprietors, there were no accumulation of captial. Without accumulation of capital, there were no fund for the payment of wages, no division of labour, no elaborate and costly machines: there were none of those helps to labour which augment its productive power, and, therefore, multiply the enjoyments of every individual in the community. Frequent invasions of property would bring the rich to poverty; and, what were a greater evil, would aggravate the poverty of the poor.

If a single and insulated theft seem to be harmless or good, the fallacious appearance merely arises from this: that the vast majority of those, who are tempted to steal, abstain from invasions of property. Such is the quantity of wealth engendered by general security, that the handful subtracted by the thief is as nothing when compared with the bulk.

Again: If I evade the payment of a tax imposed by a good government, the *specific* effects of the mischievous forbearance are indisputably useful. For the money which I unduly withhold is convenient to myself; and, compared with the bulk of the public revenue, is a quantity too small to be missed. But the regular payment of taxes is necessary to the existence of the government. And I, and the rest of the community, enjoy the security which it gives, because the payment of taxes is rarely evaded.

In the cases now supposed, the act or omission is good, considered as single or insulated; but, considered with the rest of its class, is evil. In other cases, an act or omission is evil, considered as single or insulated; but, considered with the rest of its class, is good.

For example, A punishment, as a solitary fact, is an evil: the pain inflicted on the criminal being added to the mischief of the crime. But, considered as part of a system, a punishment is useful or beneficent. By a dozen or score of punishments, thousands of crimes are prevented. With the sufferings of the guilty few, the security of the many is purchased. By the lopping of a paccant member, the body is saved from decay.

It, therefore, is true generally (for the proposition admits of exceptions), that, to determine the true tendency of an act, forbearance or omission, we must resolve the following question. -- What would be the probable effect on the general happiness or good, if *similar* acts, forbearances or omissions were general or frequent?

Such is the *test* to which we must usually resort, if we would try the true *tendency* of an act, forbearance or omission: Meaning, by the true *tendency* of an act, forbearance or omission, the sum of its probable effects on the general happiness or good, or its agreement or disagreement with the principle of general utility.

But, if this be the ordinary test for trying the tendencies of actions, and if the tendencies of actions be the index to the will of God, it follows that most of his commands are general or universal. The useful acts which he enjoins, and the pernicious acts which he prohibits, he enjoins or prohibits, for the most part, not singly, but by classes: not by commands which are particular, or directed to insulated cases; but by laws or rules which are general, and commonly inflexible.

For example, Certain acts are pernicious, considered as a class: or (in other words) the frequent repetition of the act were adverse to the general happiness, though, in this or that instance, the act might be useful or harmless. Further: Such are the motives or inducements to the commission of acts of the class, that, unless we were determined to forbearance by the fear of punishment, they *would* be frequently committed. Now, if we combine these *data* with the wisdom and goodness of God, we must infer that he forbids such acts, and forbids them *without exception*. In the tenth, or the hundredth case, the act might be useful: in the nine, or the ninety and nine, the act would be pernicious. If the act were permitted or tolerated in the rare and anomalous case, the motives to forbear in the others would be weakened or destroyed. In the hurry and tumult of action, it is hard to distinguish justly. To grasp at present enjoyment, and to turn from present uneasiness, is the habitual inclination of us all. And thus, through the weakness of our judgments, and the more dangerous infirmity of our wills, we should frequently *stretch* the exception to cases embraced by the rule.

Consequently, where acts, considered as a class, are useful or pernicious, we must conclude that he enjoins or forbids them, and by a *rule* which probably is inflexible.

Such, I say, is the conclusion at which we must arrive, supposing that the fear of punishment be necessary to incite or restrain.

• • • • • •

The theory, be it always remembered, is this:

Our motives to obey the laws which God has given us, are paramount to all others. For the transient pleasures which we may snatch, or the transient pains which we may shun, by violating the duties which they impose, are nothing in comparison with the pains by which those duties are sanctioned.

The greatest possible happiness of all his sentient creatures, is the purpose and the effect of those laws. For the benevolence by which they were prompted, and the wisdom with which they were planned, equal the might which enforces them.

• • • • • •

Admit these premises, and the following conclusion is inevitable -- the *whole* of our conduct should be guided by the principle of utility, in so far as the conduct to be pursued has not been determined by Revelation For, to conform to the principle or maxim with which a law coincides, is equivalent to obeying that law.

Such is the theory: which I have repeated in various forms, and, I fear, at tedious length, in order that my younger hearers might conceive it with due distinctness.

The current and specious objection to which I have adverted, may be stated thus:

'Pleasure and pain (or good and evil) are inseparably connected. Every positive act, and every forbearance or omission, is followed by *both:* immediately or remotely, directly or collaterally, to ourselves or to our fellow creatures.

'Consequently , if we shape our conduct justly to the principle of general utility, every election which we make between doing or forbearing from an act will be preceded by the following process. *First:* We shall conjecture the consequences of the act, and also the consequences of the forbearance. For these are the competing elements of that *calculation,* which, according to our guiding principle, we are bound to make. *Secondly:* We shall compare the consequences of the act with the consequences of the forbearance, and determine the set of consequences which gives the *balance* of advantage: which yields the larger residue of probable good, or (adopting a different, though exactly equivalent expression) which leaves the smaller residue of probable evil.

'Now let us suppose that we actually tried this process, before we arrived at our resolves. And then let us mark the absurd and mischievous effects which would inevitably follow our attempts.

'Generally speaking, the period allowed for deliberation is brief: and to lengthen deliberation beyond that limited period, is equivalent to forbearance or omission. Consequently, if we performed this elaborate process completely and correctly, we should often defeat its purpose. We should abstain from action altogether, though utility required us to act; or the occasion for acting *usefully* would slip through our fingers, whilst we weighed, with anxious scrupulosity, the merits of the act and the forbearance.

'But feeling the necessity of resolving promptly, we should *not* perform the process completely and correctly. We should guess or conjecture hastily the effects of the act and the forbearance, and compare their respective effects with equal precipitancy. Our premises would be false or imperfect; our conclusions, badly deduced. Labouring to adjust our conduct to the principle of general utility, we should work inevitable mischief.'

• • • • • •

Their objection is founded on the following assumption. -- That, if we adjusted our conduct to the principle of general utility, every election which we made between doing and forbearing from an act would be preceded by a *calculation:* by an attempt to conjecture and compare the respective probable consequences of action and forbearance.

Or (changing the expression) their assumption is this. -- That, if we adjusted our conduct to the principle of general utility, our conduct would always be determined by an immediate or direct resort to it.

And, granting their assumption, I grant their inference. I grant that the principle of utility were a halting and purblind guide.

But their assumption is groundless. They are battering (and most effectually) a misconception of their own, whilst they fancy they are hard at work demolishing the theory which they hate.

For, according to that theory, our conduct would conform to *rules* inferred from the tendencies of actions, but would not be determined by a direct resort to the principle of general utility. Utility would be the test of our conduct, ultimately, but not immediately: the immediate test of the rules to which our conduct would conform, but not the immediate test of specific or individual actions. Our rules would be fashioned on utility; our conduct, on our rules.

Recall the true test for trying the tendency of an action, and, by a short and easy deduction, you will see that their assumption is groundless.

If we would try the tendency of a specific or individual act, we must not contemplate the act as if it were single and insulated, but must look at the class of acts to which it belongs. We must suppose that acts of the class were generally done or omitted, and consider the probable effect upon the general happiness or good.

• • • • • •

But these conclusions (like most conclusions) must be taken with limitations.

There certainly are cases (of comparatively rare occurrence) wherein the specific considerations balance or outweigh the general: cases which (in the language of Bacon) are "immersed in matter": cases perplexed with peculiarities from which it were dangerous to abstract them; and to which our attention would be directed, if we were true to our presiding principle. It were mischievous to depart from a rule which regarded any of these cases; since every departure from a rule tends to weaken its authority. But so important were the *specific* consequences which would follow our resolves, that the evil of observing the rule might surpass the evil of breaking it. Looking at the reasons from which we had inferred the rule, it were absurd to think it inflexible. We should, therefore, dismiss the *rule;* resort directly to the *principle* upon which our rules were fashioned; and calculate *specific* consequences to the best of our knowledge and ability.

For example, If we take the principle of utility as our index to the Divine commands, we must infer that obedience to established government is enjoined generally by the Deity. For, without obedience to "the powers which be," there were little security and little enjoyment. The ground, however, of the inference, is the *utility* of government: And if the protection which it yields be *too costly,* or if it vex us with *needless* restraints and load us with *needless* exactions, the principle which points at submission as our general duty may counsel and justify resistance. Disobedience to an estalished government, let it be never so bad, is an evil: For the mischiefs inflicted by a bad government are less than the mischiefs of anarchy. So momentous, however, is the difference between a bad and a good government, that, *if it would lead to a good one,* resistance to a bad one would be useful. The anarchy attending the transition, were an extensive, but a passing evil: The good which would follow the transition, were extensive and lasting. The peculiar good would outweigh the generic evil: The good which would crown the change in the insulated and eccentric case, would more than compensate the evil which is inseparable from rebellion.

Whether resistance to government be useful or pernicious, be consistent or inconsistent with the Divine pleasure, is, therefore, an *anomalous* question. We must try it by a direct resort to the ultimate or presiding *principle,* and not by the Divine *rule* which the principle clearly indicates. To consult the rule, were absurd. For, the rule being general and applicable to ordinary cases, it ordains obedience to government, and excludes the question.

The members of a political society who revolve this momentous question, must, therefore, dismiss the rule, and calculate specific consequences. They must measure the mischief wrought by the actual government; the chance of getting a better, by resorting to resistance; the evil which must attend resistance, whether it prosper or fail; and the good which may follow resistance, in case it be crowned with success. And, then, by comparing these, the elements of their moral calculation, they must solve the question before them to the best of their knowledge and ability.

• • • • • •

But, though the principle of utility would afford no certain solution, the community would be fortunate, if their opinions and sentiments were formed upon it. The pretensions of the opposite parties being tried by an intelligible test, a peaceable compromise of their difference would, at least, be possible. . . .

But, if the parties were led by their ears, and not by the principle of utility; if they appealed to unmeaning abstractions, or to senseless fictions; if they mouthed of "the rights of man," or "the sacred rights of sovereigns"; "of" unalienable liberties," or "eternal and immutable justice;" of an "original contract or covenant," or "the principles of an inviolable constitution"; neither could compare its object with the cost of a violent pursuit, nor would the difference between them admit of a peaceable compromise. A sacred or unalienable right is truly and indeed *invaluable:* For, seeing that it means nothing, there is nothing with which it can be measured. Parties who rest their pretensions on the jargon to which I have adverted, must inevitably push to their objects through thick and thin, though their objects be straws or feathers as weighed in the balance of utility. Having bandied their fustian phrases, and "bawled till their lungs be spent," they must even take to their weapons, and fight their difference out.

7

Kelsen
On the Basic Norm of a Legal System
Pure Theory of Law

The Dynamic Aspect of Law

The Reason for the Validity of a Normative Order: The Basic Norm

a) The Meaning of the Search for the

Reason for Validity

If the law as a normative order is conceived as a system of norms that regulates the behavior of men, the question arises: What constitutes the unity of a multitude of norms -- why does a certain norm belong to a certain order? And this question is closely tied to the question: Why is a norm valid, what is the reason for its validity?

A norm referring to the behavior of a human being is ''valid'' means that it is binding -- that an individual ought to behave in the manner determined by the norm. It has been pointed out in an earlier context that the question why a norm is valid, why an individual ought to behave in a certain way, cannot be answered by ascertaining a fact, that is, by a statement that something is; that the reason for the validity of a norm cannot be a fact. From the circumstance that something *is* cannot follow that something *ought* to be; and that something *ought* to be, cannot be the reason that something *is*. The reason for the validity of a norm can only be the validity of another norm. A norm which represents the reason for the validity of another norm is figuratively spoken of as a higher norm in relation to a lower norm. It looks as if one could give as a reason for the validity of a norm the circumstance that it was established by an authority, human or divine; for example, the statement: "The reason for the validity of the Ten Commandments is that God Jehovah issued them on Mount Sinai"; or: "Men ought to love their enemies, because Jesus, Son of God issued this command in his Sermon on the Mount." But in both cases the reason for the validity is not that God or his son issued a certain norm at a certain time in a certain place, but the tacitly presupposed norm that one ought to obey the commands of God or his son. To be true: In the syllogism whose major premise is the *ought* - statement asserting the validity of the higher norm: "One ought to obey God's commands," and whose conclusion is the ought-statement asserting the validity of the lower norm:

"One ought to obey God's Ten Commandments," the assertion that God had issued the Ten Commandments, an 'is-statement," as the minor premise, is an essential link. The Major premise and the minor premise are both conditions of the conclusion. But only the major premise, which is an *ought* - statement, is the *conditio per quam* in relation to the conclusion, which is also an *ought* - statement; that is, the norm whose validity is stated in the major premise is the reason for the validity of the norm whose validity is stated in the conclusion. The *is* - statement functioning as minor premise is only the *conditio sine qua non* in relation to the conclusion; this means: the fact whose existence is asserted in the minor premise is not the reason for the validity of the norm whose validity is asserted in the conclusion.

The norm whose validity is stated in the major premise ("One ought to obey God's commands") is included in the supposition that the norms, whose reason for validity is in question, originate from an authority, that is, from somebody competent to create valid norms; this norm bestows upon the norm-creating personality the "authority" to create norms. The mere fact that somebody commands something is no reason to regard the command as a "valid" norm, a norm binding the individual at whom it is directed. Only a competent authority can create valid norms; and such competence can only be based on a norm that authorizes the issuing of norms. The authority authorized to issue norms is subject to that norm in the same manner as the individuals are subject to the norms issued by the authority.

The norm which represents the reason for the validity of another norm is called, as we have said, the "higher" norm. But the search for the reason of a norm's validity cannot go on indefinitely like the search for the cause of an effect. It must end with a norm which, as the last and highest, is presupposed. It must be *presupposed,* because it cannot be "posited," that is to say: created, by an authority whose competence would have to rest on a still higher norm. This final norm's validity cannot be derived from a higher norm, the reason for its validity cannot be questioned. Such a presupposed highest norm is referred to in this book as basic norm. All norms whose validity can be traced back to one and the same basic norm constitute a system of norms, a normative order. The basic norm is the common source for the validity of all norms that belong to the same order -- it is their common reason of validity. The fact that a certain norm belongs to a certain order is based on the circumstance that its last reason of validity is the basic norm of this order. It is the basic norm that constitutes the unity in the multitude of norms by representing the reason for the validity of all norms that belong to this order.

• • • • • •

c) The Reason for the Validity of a Legal Order

The norm system that presents itself as a legal order has essentially a dynamic character. A legal norm is not valid because it has a certain content, that is, because its content is logically deducible from a presupposed basic norm, but because it is created in a certain way -- ultimately in a way determined by a presupposed basic norm. For this reason alone does the legal norm belong to the legal order whose norms are created according to this basic norm. Therefore any kind of content might be law. There is no human behavior which, as such, is excluded from being the content of a legal norm. The validity of a legal norm may not be denied for being (in its content) in conflict with that of another norm which does not belong to the legal order whose basic norm is the reason for the validity of the norm in question. The basic norm of a legal order is not a material norm which, because its content is regarded as immediately self-evident, is presupposed as the highest norm and from which norms for human behavior are logically deduced. The norms of a legal order must be created by a specific process. They are posited, that is, positive, norms, elements of a positive order. If by the constitution of a legal community is understood the norm or norms that determine how (that is, by what organs and by what procedure -- through legislation or custom) the general norms of the legal order that constitute the community are to be created, then the basic norm is that norm which is presupposed when the custom through which the constitution has come into existence, or the constitution-creating act consciously performed by certain human beings, is objectively interpreted as a norm-creating fact; if, in the latter case, the individual or the assembly of individuals who created the constitution on which the legal order rests, are looked upon as norm-creating authorities. In this sense, the basic norm determines the basic fact of law creation and may in this respect be described as the constitution in a logical sense of the word (which will be explained later) in contradistinction to the constitution in the meaning of positive law. The basic norm is the presupposed starting point of a procedure: the procedure of positive law creation. It is itself not a norm created by custom or by the act of a legal organ; it is not a positive but a presupposed norm so far as the constitution-establishing authority is looked upon as the highest authority and can therefore not be regarded as authorized by the norm of a higher authority.

If the question as to the reason for the validity of a certain legal norm is raised, then the answer can only consist in the reduction to the basic norm of this legal order, that is, in the assertion that the norm was created -- in the last instance -- according to the basic norm. In the following pages we would like to consider only a national legal order, that is, a legal order limited in its validity to a specific space, the so-called territory of the state, and which is regarded as "sovereign," that is, as not subordinated to any higher legal order. We shall discuss the problem of the validity of the norms of a national legal order, at first without considering an international legal order superordinated to or included in it.

The question of the reason for the validity of a legal norm belonging to a specific national legal order may arise on the occasion of a coercive act; for example, when one individual deprives another of his life by hanging, and now the question is asked why this act is legal, namely the execution of a punishment, and not murder. This act can be interpreted as being legal only if it was prescribed by an individual legal norm, namely as an act that "ought" to be performed, by a norm that presents itself as a judicial decision. This raises the questions: Under what conditions is such an interpretation possible, why is a judicial decision present in this case, why is the individual norm created thereby a legal norm belonging to a valid legal order and therefore ought to be applied? The answer is: Because this individual norm was created in applying a criminal law that contains a general norm according to which (under conditions present in the case concerned) the death penalty ought to be inflicted. If we ask for the reason for the validity of this criminal law, then the answer is: the criminal law is valid because it was created by the legislature, and the legislature, in turn, is authorized by the constitution to create general norms. If we ask for the reason of the validity of the constitution, that is, for the reason of the validity of the norms regulating the creation of the general norms, we may, perhaps, discover an older constitution; that means the validity of the existing constitution is justified by the fact that it was created according to the rules of an earlier constitution by way of a constitutional amendment. In this way we eventually arrive at a historically first constitution that cannot have been created in this way and whose validity, therefore, cannot be traced back to a positive norm created by a legal authority; we arrive, instead, at a constitution that became valid in a revolutionary way, that is, either by breach of a former constitution or for a territory that formerly was not the sphere of validity of a constitution and of a national legal order based on it. If we consider merely the national legal order, not international law, and if we ask for the reason of the validity of the historically first constitution, then the answer can only be (if we leave aside God or ''nature'') that the validity of this constitution -- the assumption that it is a binding norm -- must be *presupposed* if we want to interpret (1) the acts performed according to it as the creation or application of valid general legal norms; and (2) the acts performed in application of these general norms as the creation or application of valid individual legal norms. Since the reason for the validity of a norm can only be another norm, the presupposition must be a norm: not one posited (i.e., created) by a legal authority, but a presupposed norm, that is, a norm presupposed if the subjective meaning of the constitution-creating facts and the subjective meaning of the norm-creating facts established according to the constitution are interpreted as their objective meaning. Since it is the basic norm of a legal order (that is, an order prescribing coercive acts), therefore this norm, namely the basic norm of the legal order concerned, must be formulated as follows: Coercive acts sought to be performed under the conditions and in the manner which the historically first constitution, and the norms created according to it, prescribe. (In short: One ought to behave as the constitution prescribes.) The norms of a legal order, whose common reason for their validity is this basic norm are not a complex of valid norms standing coordinatedly side by side, but form a hierarchical structure of super- and subordinate norms. This structure of the legal order will be discussed later.

• • • • • •

f) Legitimacy and Effectiveness

The function of the basic norm becomes particularly apparent if the constitution is not changed by constitutional means but by revolution; when the existence -- that is, the validity -- of the entire legal order directly based on the constitution, is in question.

It was said earlier that a norm's sphere of validity, particularly its temporal sphere of validity may be limited; the beginning and end of its validity may be determined by the norm itself or by a higher norm regulating the creation of the lower one. The norms of a legal order are valid until their validity is terminated according to the rules of this legal order. By regulating its own creation and application, the legal order determines the beginning and end of the validity of the legal norms. Written constitutions usually contain special rules concerning the method by which they can be changed. The principle that a norm of a legal order is valid until its validity is terminated in a way determined by this legal order or replaced by the validity of another norm of this order, is called the principle of legitimacy.

This principle is applicable to a national legal order with one important limitation only: It does not apply in case of a revolution. A revolution in the broader sense of the word (that includes a coup d'efat) is every not legitimate change of this constitution or its replacement by an other constitution. From the point of view of legal science it is irrelevant whether this change of the legal situation has been brought about by the application of force against the legitimate government or by the members of that government themselves, whether by a mass movement of the population or by a small group of individuals. Decisive is only that the valid constitution has been changed or replaced in a manner not prescribed by the constitution valid until then. Usually a revolution abolishes only the old constitution and certain politically important statutes. A large part of the statutes created under the old constitution remains valid, as the saying goes; but this expression does not fit. If these statutes are to be regarded as being valid under the new constitution, then this is possible only because they have been validated expressly or tacitly by the new constitution. We are confronted here not with a creation of new law but with the reception of norms of one legal order by another; such as the reception of the Roman Law by the German Law. But such reception too is law creation, because the direct reason for the validity of the legal norms taken over by the new revolutionary established constitution can only be the new constitution. The content of these norms remains unchanged, but the reason for their validity, in fact the reason for the validity of the entire legal order, has been changed. As the new constitution becomes valid, so simultaneously changes the basic norm, that is, the presupposition according to which are interpreted as norm-creating and norm-applying facts the constitution-creating fact and the facts established according to the constitution. Suppose the old constitution had the character of an absolute monarchy and the new one of a parliamentary democracy. Then the basic norm no longer reads: "Coercive acts ought to be carried out under the conditions and in the manner as determined by the old, no longer valid, constitution," and hence by the general and individual norms created and applied by the constitutionally functioning monarch and the organs delegated by him; instead, the basic norm reads: "Coercive acts ought to be carried out under the conditions and in the manner determined by the new constitution," and hence by the general and individual norms created and applied by the parliament elected according to that constitution and by the organs delegated in these norms. The new basic norm does not make it possible -- like the old one -- to regard a certain individual as the absolute monarch, but makes it possible to regard a popularly elected parliament as a legal authority. According to the basic norm of a national legal order, the government, which creates effective general and individual norms based on an effective constitution is the legitimate government of the state.

The change of the basic norm follows the change of the facts that are interpreted as creating and applying valid legal norms. The basic norm refers only to a constitution which is actually established by legislative act or custom, and is effective. A constitution is "effective" if the norms created in conformity with it are by and large applied and obeyed. As soon as the old constitution loses its effectiveness and the new one has become effective, the acts that appear with the subjective meaning of creating or applying legal norms are no longer interpreted by presupposing the old basic norm, but by presupposing the new one. The statutes issued under the old constitution and not taken over are no longer regarded as valid, and the organs authorized by the old constitution no longer as competent. If the revolution is not successful there would be no reason to replace the old basic norm by a new one. Then, the revolution would not be regarded as procedure creating new law, but -- according to the old constitution and the criminal law based on it and regarded as valid -- would be interpreted as high treason. The principle applied here is the principle of effectiveness. The principle of legitimacy is limited by the principle of effectiveness.

g) Validity and Effectiveness

This limitation reveals the repeatedly emphasized connection (so important for a theory of positive law) between the validity and the effectiveness of law. The correct determination of this relationship is one of the most important and at the same time most difficult problems of a positivistic legal theory. It is only a special case of the relationship between the "ought" of the legal norm and the "is" of natural reality. Because the act by which a positive legal norm is created, too, is an "is-fact" (German: *Seinstatsache)* just as the effectiveness of the legal norm. A positivistic legal theory is faced by the task to find the correct middle road between two extremes which both are untenable. The one extreme is the thesis that there is no connection between validity as something that ought to be and effectiveness as something that is; that the validity of the law is entirely independent of its effectiveness. The other extreme is the thesis that validity and effectiveness are identical. An idealistic theory of law tends to the first solution of this problem, a realistic theory to the second. The first is wrong for it is undeniable that a legal order in its entirety, and an individual legal norm as well, lose their validity when they cease to be effective; and that a relation exists between the *ought* of the legal norm and the *is* of physical reality also insofar as the positive legal norm, to be valid, must be created by an act which exists in the reality of being. The second solution is wrong because it is equally undeniable that there are many cases -- as has been shown before -- in which legal norms are regarded as valid although they are not, or not yet, effective. The solution proposed by the Pure Theory of Law is this: Just as the norm (according to which something *ought* to be) as the meaning of an act is not identical with the act (which actually *is),* in the same way is the validity of a legal norm not identical with its effectiveness; the effectiveness of a legal order as a whole and the effectiveness of a single legal norm are -- just as the norm-creating act -- the condition for the validity; effectiveness is the condition in the sense that a legal order as a whole, and a single legal norm, can no longer be regarded as valid when they cease to be effective. Nor is the effectiveness of a legal order, any more than the fact of its creation, the reason for its validity. The reason for the validity -- that is, the answer to the question why the norms of this legal order ought to be obeyed and applied -- is the presupposed basic norm, according to which one ought to comply with an actually established, by and large effective, constitution, and therefore with the by and large effective norms, actually created in conformity with that constitution. In the basic norm the fact of creation and the effectiveness are made the condition of the validity -- "effectiveness" in the sense that it has to be added to the fact of creation, so that neither the legal order as a whole nor the individual legal norm shall lose their validity. A condition cannot be identical with that which it conditions. Thus, a man, in order to live, must have been born; but in order that he remain alive other conditions must also be fulfilled, for example, he must receive nutrition. If this condition is not fulfilled, he will lose his life. But life is neither identical with birth nor with being nourished.

In the normative syllogism leading to the foundation of the validity of a legal order, the major premise is the ought-sentence which states the basic norm: "One ought to behave according to the actually established and effective constitution"; the minor premise is the is-sentence which states the facts: "The constitution is actually established and effective"; and the conclusion is the ought-sentence: "One ought to behave according to the legal order, that is, the legal order is valid." The norms of a positive legal order are valid *because* the fundamental rule regulating their creation, that is, the basic norm, is presupposed to be valid, not because they are effective; but they are valid only *as long as* this legal order is effective. As soon as the constitution loses its effectiveness, that is, as soon as the legal order as a whole based on the constitution loses its effectiveness, the legal order and every single norm lose their validity.

However, a legal order does not lose its validity when a single legal norm loses its effectiveness. A legal order is regarded as valid, if its norms are *by and large* effective (that is, actually applied and obeyed). Nor does a single legal norm lose its validity if it is only exceptionally not effective in single cases. As mentioned in another connection, the possibility of an antagonism between that which is prescribed by a norm as something that ought to be and that which actually happens must exist; a norm, prescribing that something *ought* to be, which, as one knows beforehand *must* happen anyway according to a law of nature, is meaningless -- such a norm would not be regarded as valid. On the other hand, a norm is not regarded as valid which is never obeyed or applied. In fact, a legal norm may lose its validity by never being applied or obeyed -- by so-called *desuetude*. *Desuetudo* may be described as negative custom, and its essential function is to abolish the validity of an existing norm. If custom is a law-creating fact at all, then even the validity of statutory law can be abolished by customary law. If effectiveness in the developed sense is the condition for the validity not only of the legal order as a whole but also of a single legal norm, then the law-creating function of custom cannot be excluded by statutory law, at least not as far as the negative function of *desuetudo* is concerned.

The described relation between validity and effectiveness refers to general legal norms. But also individual legal norms (judicial decisions, administrative decrees) that prescribe an individual coercive act lose their validity if they are permanently unexecuted and therefore ineffective, as has been shown in the discussion of a conflict between two legal decisions.

Effectiveness is a condition for the validity -- but it is not validity. This must be stressed because time and again the effort has been made to identify validity with effectiveness; and such identification is tempting because it seems to simplify the theoretical situation. Still, the effort is doomed to failure, not only because even a partly ineffective legal order or legal norm may be regarded as valid, and an absolutely effective norm which cannot be violated as invalid because not being regarded as a norm at all; but particularly for this reason: If the validity, that is, the specific existence of the law, is considered to be part of natural reality, one is unable to grasp the specific meaning in which the law addresses itself to reality and thereby juxtaposes itself to reality, which can be in conformity or in conflict with the law only if reality is not identical with the validity of the law. Just as it is impossible in determining validity to ignore its relation to reality, so it is likewise impossible to identify validity and reality. If we replace the concept of reality (as effectiveness of the legal order) by the concept of of power, then the problem of the relation between validity and effectiveness of the legal order coincides with the more familiar problem of the relationship between law and power or right and might. And then, the solution attempted here is merely the scientifically exact formulation of the old truism that right cannot exist without might and yet is not identical with might. Right (the law), according to the theory here developed, is a certain order (or organization) of might.

h) The Basic Norm of International Law

We shall now also consider the international legal order in relation to national legal orders; and we shall assume -- as it is frequently assumed -- that international law is valid for a state only if its government on the basis of an effective constitution has recognized international law; then our answer given so far to the question as to why law is valid, is still the same: the reason for the validity of law is a presupposed basic norm referring to an effective constitution. For in this case, international law is only a part of the national legal order, regarded as sovereign -- and the reason for the validity of the national legal order is the basic norm referring to the effective constitution. The basic norm, as the reason for the validity of the constitution, is at the same time the reason for the validity of international law, recognized on the basis of the constitution.

The situation is different, however, if international law is not regarded as part of the national legal order, but as a sovereign legal order, superordinated to all national legal orders, limiting them in their spheres of validity; if, in other words, one does not assume the primacy of the national legal orders, but the primacy of the international legal order. The latter does, in fact, contain a norm that represents the reason for the validity of the individual national legal orders. Therefore the reason for the validity of the individual national legal order can be found in positive international law. In that case, a positive norm is the reason for the validity of this legal order, not a merely presupposed norm. The norm of international law that represents this reason for the validity usually is described by the statement that, according to general international law, a government which, independent of other governments, exerts effective control over the population of a certain territory, is the legitimate government; and that the population that lives under such a government in this territory constitutes a "state" in the meaning of international law, regardless of whether this government exerts this effective control on the basis of a previously existing constitution or of one established by revolution. Translated into legal language: A norm of general international law authorizes an individual or a group of individuals, on the basis of an effective constitution, to create and apply as a legitimate government a normative coercive order. That norm, thus, legitimizes this coercive order for the territory of its actual effectiveness as a valid legal order, and the community constituted by this coercive order as a "state" in the sense of international law -- regardless of whether the government came to power in a "legitimate" way (in the sense of the previous constitution) or by revolution. According to international law, this power is to be regarded as *legal* power. This means that international law legitimizes a successful revolution as a law-creating procedure. If a positive norm of international law is recognized as the reason for the validity of a national legal order the problem of the basic norm is shifted, because the reason for the validity of the national legal orders, then, is no longer a norm only presupposed in juristic thinking but a positive norm of international law; and then the question arises as to the reason for the validity of the international legal order to which the norm belongs on which the validity of the individual national legal order is founded -- the norm in which this legal order finds its direct, although not its ultimate, reason for the validity. This reason of validity, then, can only be the basic norm of international law, which, therefore, is the indirect reason for the validity of the national legal order. As a genuine basic norm, it is a presupposed -- not a positive norm. It represents the presupposition under which general international law is regarded as the set of objectively valid norms that regulate the mutual behavior of states. These norms are created by custom, constituted by the actual behavior of the "states," that is, of those individuals who act as governments according to national legal orders. These norms are interpreted as legal norms binding the states, because a basic norm is presupposed which establishes custom among states as a law-creating fact. The basic norm runs as follows: "States -- that is, the governments of the states -- in their mutual relations ought to behave in such a way"; or: "Coercion of state against state ought to be exercised under the conditions and in the manner, that conforms with the custom constituted by the actual behavior of the states." This is the "constitution" of international law in a transcendental-logical sense.

One of the norms of international law created by custom authorizes the states to regulate their mutual relations by treaty. The reason for the validity of the legal norms of international law created by treaty is this custom-created norm. It is usually formulated in the sentence: *pacta sunt servanda*.

The presupposed basic norm of international law, which institutes custom constituted by the states as a law-creating fact, expresses a principle that is the basic presupposition of all customary law: the individual ought to behave in such a manner as the others usually behave (believing that they ought to behave that way), applied to the mutual behavior of states, that is, the behavior of the individuals qualified by the national legal orders as government organs.[1]

No affirmation of a value transcending positive law is inherent in the basic norm of international law, not even of the value of peace guaranteed by the general international law created by custom and the particular international law created by treaty. International law and -- if its primacy is assumed -- the subordinated national legal orders are not valid "because" and "insofar as" they realize the value that consists in peace; they may realize this value if and so far as they are valid; and they are valid if a basic norm is presupposed that institutes custom among states as a law-creating fact regardless of the content of the norms thus created. If the reason for the validity of national legal orders is found in a norm of international law, then the latter is understood as a legal order superior to the former and therefore as the highest sovereign legal order. If the states -- that is, the national legal orders -- are nevertheless referred to as "sovereign," then this "sovereignty" can only mean that the national legal orders are subordinated *only* to the international legal order.

i) The Theory of the Basic Norm and the Theory of Natural Law

If the question as to the reason for the validity of positive law, that is, the question why the norms of an effective coercive order ought to be applied and obeyed, aims at an ethical-political justification of this coercive order, which means at a firm standard according to which a positive legal order may be judged as "just" and therefore as valid or "unjust" and therefore as invalid, then the basic norm of the Pure Theory of Law does neither yield such a justification nor such a standard. For positive law -- as pointed out -- is justified only by a norm or normative order with which positive law according to its contents, may or may not conform, hence be just or unjust. The basic norm, presented by the Pure Theory of Law as the condition for the objective validity of law, establishes the validity of *every* positive legal order, that is, of every coercive order created by acts of human beings and by and large effective. According to the Pure Theory of Law, as a positivistic legal theory, no positive legal order can be regarded as not conforming with its basic norm and hence as not valid. The content of a positive legal order is entirely independent from its basic norm. For -- the point must be stressed -- only the validity, not the content of a legal order can be derived from the basic norm. Every by and large effective coercive order can be interpreted as an objectively valid normative order. The validity of a positive legal order cannot be denied because of the content of its norms. This is an essential element of legal positivism; and it is precisely in its theory of the basic norm that the Pure Theory of Law shows itself as a positivistic legal theory. The Pure Theory describes the positive law as an objectively valid normative order and states that this interpretation is possible only under the condition that a basic norm is presupposed according to which the subjective meaning of the law-creating acts is also their objective meaning. The Pure Theory, thereby characterizes this interpretation as possible, not necessary, and presents the objective validity of positive law only as conditional -- namely conditioned by the presupposed basic norm. The fact that the basic norm of a positive legal order *may* but *need not* be presupposed means: the relevant interhuman relationships may be, but need not be, interpreted as ''normative,'' that is, as obligations, authorizations, rights, etc. constituted by objectively valid norms. It means further: they can be interpreted without such presupposition (i.e., without the basic norm) as power relations (i.e., relations between commanding and obeying or disobeying human beings) -- in other words, they can be interpreted sociologically, not juristically.[2] Since the basic norm, as shown, as a norm presupposed in the foundation of the validity of positive law, is only the transcendental-logical condition of this normative interpretation, it does not perform an ethical-political but only an epistemological function.

A consistent theory of natural law differs from a positivistic theory of law in that the natural-law theory seeks the reason for the validity of positive law in a natural law, different from positive law, and hence in a normative order with which the positive law, according to its contents, may or may not conform; so that the positive law, if not in conformity with natural law, must be regarded as invalid. Therefore, according to a true theory of natural law, not *any* by and large effective coercive order may be interpreted as objectively valid normative order. The possibility of a conflict between natural law and positive law includes the possibility of regarding such a coercive order as invalid. Only to the extent that the content of positive law may or may not conform with natural law and may therefore not only be just but also unjust and therefore invalid -- only to that extent can natural law serve as ethical-political standard and therefore as a possible ethical-political justification of positive law. This is precisely the essential function of natural law. If a legal theory that presents itself as natural-law doctrine formulates the norm or normative order which functions as the reason for the validity of positive law in such a way that a conflict between the so-called natural law and positive law is excluded (for example, by asserting that nature commands to obey every positive legal order, regardless of the kind of behavior this order demands), then such a legal theory divests itself of its character as a theory of natural law, that is, a theory of justice. It thereby abandons the function, essential to natural law, as an ethical-political value standard and therefore as a possible justification of positive law.

According to a positivistic theory of law the validity of positive law rests on a basic norm, which is not a positive but a presupposed norm, hence not a norm of the positive law whose validity is founded on the basic norm; and according to the natural-law doctrine, the validity of positive law likewise rests on a norm that is not a norm of positive law and functions as a value standard of this law. In this fact one might see a certain limitation imposed upon the principle of legal positivism and one might describe the difference between a positivistic theory of law and a theory of natural law as relative rather than absolute. But the difference between the two is large enough to exclude the view (which ignores this difference) that the positivistic theory of a basic norm, as advanced by the Pure Theory of Law, is a theory of natural law.

j) The Basic Norm of Natural Law

Since the Pure Theory of Law, as a positivistic legal theory, by its doctrine of the basic norm of positive law does not provide a standard for justice or injustice of positive law and therefore does not provide its ethical-political justification, it has frequently been criticized as unsatisfactory. What is much sought is a criterion by which positive law may be judged as just or unjust -- most of all: justified as just. The natural-law theory can provide such a criterion only if the norms of the natural law presented by that theory -- the norms that prescribe a certain behavior as just -- have the absolute validity they claim to have; this means: if they exclude the validity of norms which prescribe the opposite behavior as just. However, the history of the natural-law theory shows that this is not the case. As soon as the natural-law theory undertakes to determine the content of the norms that are immanent in nature (may be deduced from nature) it gets caught in the sharpest contrasts. The representatives of that theory have not proclaimed *one* natural law but *several* very different natural laws conflicting with each other. This is particularly true for the fundamental questions of property and form of government. According to one natural-law theory only individual property, according to another only collective property; according to one only democracy, according to another only autocracy are "natural," that is, "just." Any positive law that conforms with the natural law of one theory and therefore is judged "just" is in conflict with the natural law of the other theory and therefore is judged "unjust." Natural-law theory as it actually was developed -- and it cannot be developed differently --is far from providing the criterion expected of it.

Similarly, it is an illusion to assume that a natural-law theory gives an absolute answer to the question as to the reason for the validity of positive law. Such a theory sees the reason for the validity of positive law in the natural law, that is, in an order established by nature as a highest authority standing above the human legislator. In this sense natural law, too, is "posited," that is, positive law -- posited, hoever, not by a human but by a superhuman will. True, a natural-law theory can assert -- although it cannot prove as a fact -- that nature commands men to behave in a certain way. But since a fact cannot be the reason for the validity of a norm, a positive law, conforming with natural law, can be interpreted as valid only if the norm is presupposed that says: "One ought to obey the commands of nature." This is the basic norm of natural law. The natural-law theory, too, can give only a conditional answer to the question as to the reason for the validity of positive law. If the natural-law theory asserts: "The norm that one ought to obey the commands of nature is self-evident," the theory errs. This assertion is untenable. Not only in general because there can be no self-evident norms of human behavior; but also in particular, because this norm, much less than any other, can be said to be self-evident. From the point of view of science, nature is a system of causally determined elements. Nature has no will and therefore cannot enact norms. Norms can be assumed as immanent in nature only if the will of God is assumed to be manifested in nature. To say that God in nature as a manifestation of his will commands men to behave in a certain way, is a metaphysical assumption, which cannot be accepted by science in general and by legal science in particular, because scientific cognition cannot have as its object a fact which is assumed to exist beyond all possible experience.

Notes

1 The theory held by many authors (and at one time also myself) that the norm of *pacta sunt servanda* is the basis of international law is to be rejected because it can be maintained only with the aid of the fiction that the custom established by the conduct of states is a tacit treaty.

In earlier publications I used as an example for the fact that the presupposition of the basic norm is possible but not necessary: An anarchist emotionally rejects the law as a coercive order; he objects to the law; he wants a community free of coecion, a community constituted without a coercive order. Anarchism is a political attitude, based on a certain wish. The sociological interpretation, which does not presuppose a basic norm, is a theoretical attitude. Even an anarchist, if he were a professor of law, could describe positive law as a system of alid norms, without having to approve of this law. Many textbooks in which the capitalist legal order is described as a system of norms constituting obligations, authorizations, rights, jurisdictions, are written by jurists who politically disapprove of this legal order.

2 Therefore, the doctrine of the basic norm is not a doctrine of recognition as is sometimes erroneously understood. According to the doctrine of recognition positive law is valid only if it is recognized by the individuals subject to it, which means; if these individuals agree that one ought to behave according to the norms of the positive law. This recognition, it is said, actually takes place, and if this cannot be proved it is assumed, fictitiously, as a tacit recognition. The theory of recognition, consciously or unconsciously, presupposes the ideal of individual liberty as self-determination, that is, the norm that the individual ought to do only what he wants to do. This is the basic norm of this theory. The difference between it and the theory of the basic norm of a positive legal order, as taught by the Pure Theory of Law, is evident.

The Natural-Law Doctrine Before The Tribunal of Science

The natural-law doctrine undertakes to supply a definitive solution to the eternal problem of justice, to answer the question as to what is right and wrong in the mutual relations of men. The answer is based on the assumption that it is possible to distinguish between human behavior which is natural, that is to say which corresponds to nature because it is required by nature, and human behavior which is unnatural, hence contrary to nature and forbidden by nature. This assumption implies that it is possible to deduce from nature, that is to say from the nature of man, from the nature of society, and even from the nature of things certain rules which provide an altogether adequate prescription for human behavior, that by a careful examination of the facts of nature we can find the just solution of our social problems. Nature is conceived of as a legislator, the supreme legislator.

This view presupposes that natural phenomena are directed toward an end or shaped by a purpose, that natural processes or nature conceived of as a whole are determined by final causes. It is a thoroughly teleological view, and as such does not differ from the idea that nature is endowed with will and intelligence. This implies that nature is a kind of superhuman personal being, an authority to which man owes obedience. At the lowest stage of human civilization this interpretation of nature manifests itself in so-called animism. Primitive man believes that natural things -- animals, plants, rivers, the stars in the sky -- are animated, that spirits or souls dwell within or behind these phenomena, and that consequently these things react toward man like personal beings according to the same principles that determine the relations of man to his fellow men. It is a social interpretation of nature, for primitive man considers nature to be a part of his society. Since the spirits or souls animating the natural phenomena are believed to be very powerful and able to harm as well as to protect man, they must be worshipped. Animism is consequently a religious interpretation of nature. At a higher state of religious evolution, when animism is replaced by monotheism, nature is conceived of as having been created by God and is therefore regarded as a manifestation of his all powerful and just will. If the natural-law doctrine is consistent, it must assume a religious character. It can deduce from nature just rules of human behavior only because and so far as nature is conceived of as a revelation of God's will, so that examining nature amounts to exploring God's will. As a matter of fact, there is no natural-law doctrine of any importance which has not a more or less religious character. Grotius, for example, defines the law of nature as a dictate of rational nature by which certain acts are forbidden or enjoined "by the author of nature, God." He states that the law of nature proceeding from the "essential traits implanted in man can rightly be attributed to God, because of His having willed that such traits exist in us." Hobbes declares that the law of nature is a dictate of reason, but the dictates of reason are "conclusions, or theorems concerning what conduces to the conservation and defense of themselves; whereas law properly is the word of him that by right has command over others. But yet if we consider the same theorems, as delivered in the word of God, that by right commands all things, then are they properly called laws.'' Following Hobbes, Pufendorf states that if the dictates of reason -- that is, the principles of natural law -- are to have the force of law it must ''under all circumstances be maintained that the obligation of natural law is of God.'' Only thus can it be assumed that the law deduced from nature is an eternal and immutable law, in contradistinction to positive law which, created by man, is only a temporary and changeable order; that the rights established by natural law are sacred rights inborn in man because implanted in man by a divine nature; and that positive law can neither establish nor abolish these rights, but only protect them. This is the essence of the natural-law doctrine.

The first objection which must be made from the point of view of science is that this doctrine obliterates the essential difference which exists between scientific laws of nature, the rules by which the science of nature describes its object, and the rules by which ethics and jurisprudence describe their objects, which are morality and law. A scientific law of nature is the rule by which two phenomena are connected with each other according to the principle of causality, that is to say, as cause and effect. Such a rule is, for example, the statement that if a metallic body is heated it expands. The relation between cause and effect, whether it is considered as a relation of necessity or of mere probability, is not attributed to any act of human or superhuman will. If we speak of morality or law, on the other hand, we refer to norms prescribing human behavior, norms which are the specific meaning of acts of human or superhuman beings. Such a norm is, for instance, the moral norm issued by Christ enjoining that one help a fellow man in need, or a legal norm issued by a legislator prescribing punishment for a murderer. Ethics describes the situation which exists under moral norms by the statement: If a man is in need, his fellow men ought to help him; jurisprudence describes the situation under the legal norm: If a man commits murder, he ought to be punished. It is evident that a rule of morality or a rule of law connects the condition with its consequence not according to the principle of causality, but according to a totally different principle. A law of nature is a statement to the effect that if there is A, there *is* B, whereas a rule of morality or a rule of law is a statement to the effect that if there is A, there *ought* to be B. It is the difference between the ''is'' and the ''ought,'' the difference between causality and normativity (or imputation).

If we presuppose a general norm prescribing a certain type of human behavior, we may characterize concrete behavior which is in conformity with the presupposed norm as good, right, correct, and behavior which is not in conformity with the presupposed norm, as wrong, bad, incorrect.

These statements are called value judgments, the term being used in an objective sense. Value, in this sense of the term, is conformity with a presupposed norm. It is a positive value, in contradistinction to a negative value, which is nonconformity with a presupposed norm. Since the statement that the concrete behavior of a definite individual is good or bad (or, what amounts to the same, has a positive or negative value) means that his behavior is in conformity or not in conformity with a presupposed general norm, we may express this value judgment by the statement that the individual ought or ought not to behave as he actually does. Without presupposing a general norm prescribing (or forbidding) something, we cannot make a value judgment in the objective sense of this term. The value attributed to an object is not given with the properties of this object without reference to a presupposed norm. The value is not inherent in the object judged as valuable, it is the relation of this object to a presupposed norm. We cannot find the value of a real thing or of actual behavior by analyzing these objects. Value is not immanent in natural reality. Hence value cannot be deduced from reality. It does not follow from the fact that something is, that it ought to be or to be done, or that it ought not to be or not to be done. The fact that in reality big fish swallow small fish does not imply that the behavior of the fish is good, nor yet that it is bad. There is no logical inference from the "is" to the "ought," from natural reality to moral or legal value.

If we compare the rules by which ethics or jurisprudence describe their objects (rules referring to moral or legal norms) with the rules by which natural science describes its object, that is, causal rules, we must take into consideration the fact that the norms to which the rules of morality and the rules of law refer are, as previously stated, the meaning of acts of a moral or legal authority. So far as this authority is a human being, these norms are subjective in character, that is, they express the intention of their author. That which such a human authority prescribes or forbids depends on the end at which he aims. That at which somebody aims as an end is also called a value, but in a subjective sense of this term; and if it is an ultimate end, not a means to an end, it is called a highest value. There are great variances of opinion about ultimate ends or highest values in this subjective sense of the term, and frequently one highest value is in conflict with another, as, for instance, personal freedom with social security, the welfare of the single individual with the welfare of the whole nation, in situations where the one can be reached only at the expense of the other. Then arises the question which end is preferable, or which value is superior and which is inferior -- which is in truth the highest value? This question cannot be answered in the same way as the question whether iron is heavier than water or water heavier than wood. This latter question can be resolved by experience in a rational scientific way, but the question as to the highest value in the subjective sense of the term can be decided only emotionally, by the feelings or the wishes of the deciding subject. One subject may be led by his emotions to prefer personal freedom; another, social security; one, the welfare of the single individual; the other, the welfare of the whole nation. By no rational consideration can it be proved that the one is right or the other wrong. Consequently there are, as a matter of fact, very different systems of morality and very different systems of law, whereas there is only one system of nature. What according to one system of morality is good may, under another system of morality, be bad; and what under one legal order is a crime may be under another legal order perfectly right. This means that the values which consist in conformity or nonconformity with an existing moral or legal order are relative values. Only if the authority issuing the norms is supposed to be God, an absolute and transcendental being, is there an exclusive moral and legal system, and then the values which consist in compliance with these norms are supposed to be absolute values.

The natural-law doctrine presupposes that value is immanent in reality and that this value is absolute, or, what amounts to the same thing, that a divine will is inherent in nature. Only under this presupposition is it possible to maintain the doctrine that the law can be deduced from nature and that this law is absolute justice. Since the metaphysical assumption of the immanence of value in natural reality is not acceptable from the point of view of science, the natural-law doctrine is based on the logical fallacy of an inference from the "is" to the "ought." The norms allegedly deduced from nature are -- in truth -- tacitly presupposed, and are based on subjective values, which are presented as the intentions of nature as a legislator. By identifying the laws of nature with rules of law, pretending that the order of nature is or contains a just social order, the natural-law doctrine, like primitive animism, conceives of nature as a part of society. But it can be easily proved that modern science is the result of a process characterized by the tendency of emancipating the interpretation of nature from social categories. Before the tribunal of science, the natural-law doctrine has no chance. But it may deny the jurisdiction of this tribunal by referring to its religious character.

II

The natural-law doctrine is characterized by a fundamental dualism of positive and natural law. Above the imperfect positive law created by man, a perfect (because absolutely just) natural law exists, established by a divine authority. Consequently positive law is justified and valid only so far as it corresponds to the natural law. If, however, the positive law is valid only so far as it corresponds to the natural law; if it is possible -- as the natural-law doctrine asserts -- to find the rules of natural law by an analysis of nature; if, as some writers assert, the law of nature is even self-evident, then the positive law is quite superfluous. Faced by the existence of a just ordering of society, intelligible in nature, the activity of positive-law makers is tantamount to a foolish effort to supply artificial illumination in bright sunshine. This is another consequence of the natural-law doctrine. But none of the followers of this doctrine had the courage to be consistent. None of them has declared that the existence of natural law makes the establishment of positive law superfluous. On the contrary. All of them insist upon the necessity of positive law. In fact, one of the most essential functions of all natural-law doctrines is to justify the establishment of positive law or the existence of the state competent to establish the positive law. In performing this function most of the doctrines entangle themselves in a highly characteristic contradiction. On the one hand they maintain that human nature is the source of natural law, which implies that human nature must be basically good. On the other hand they can justify the necessity of positive law with its coercive machinery only by the badness of man. The only philosopher who avoids this contradiction is Hobbes, who proceeds from the assumption that man is by his very nature bad. Consequently, the natural law which he deduces from this nature is practically nothing else but the principle that a state endowed with the unlimited power to establish positive law is necessary and that, by natural law, men are obliged to obey unreservedly the positive law established by the state -- a line of argument which amounts to the negation of natural law by natural law. If, however, natural law is considered to be a system of substantive rules, not a formalistic authorization of any positive law, then the contradiction between a human nature from which this natural law is deduced and a human nature which makes positive law necessary is inevitable. Thus Pufendorf emphasizes that there is "no more fitting and direct way to learn the law of nature than through careful consideration of the nature, condition, and desires of man himself." If there is a law of nature as a dictate of reason which can be deduced from the nature of man, it is necessary that man "be sociable, that is, be willing to join himself with others like him, and conduct himself toward them in such way that, far from having any cause to do him harm, they may feel that there is reason to preserved and increase his good fortune." But Pufendorf is aware that this is not the actual nature of man. He admits that man is "at all times malicious, petulant, and easily irritated, as well as quick and powerful to do injury." He admits "that the mass of men order their lives not by reason, but on impulse." He does not go as far as Hobbes in his pessimistic evaluation of human nature, but he states:

> There is, indeed, such perversity in most men, that, whenever they think they will secure a greater good from the violation than from the observance of laws, they violate them readily.

Consequently he states that it is not possible to believe "that mere respect for natural law, which forbids every manner of injury, could have been able to make it possible for all mankind to live secure in natural liberty."

> For the wickedness of man's character and his proneness to injure others can in no way be restrained more effectively, than by thrusting in his face the immediate evil which will await him upon his attacking another, and by removing every hope of impunity.

Hence, the nature of man necessarily leads to the establishment of the state, and that means to positive law.

> Yet, such is the stupidity of most men and the violence of their passions, that only a very few accord all these matters the consideration due them. Therefore, there remained no more effective remedy to curb the wickedness of men than what is supplied by states. . . .

If the mass of men according to their nature do not order their lives by reason, if most men by their very nature are stupid and wicked, how can the law of nature, the dictates of reason, the absolutely just order of social life, be deduced from the nature of man? It is not from the nature of man as it actually is that Pufendorf -- and all other writers -- deduce what they consider to be the natural law; it is from the nature of man as it should be, and as it would be if it would correspond to the natural law. It is not the law of nature which is deduced from the nature, the real nature, of man -- it is the nature of man, an ideal nature of man, which is deduced from a natural law presupposed in some way or another.

8

Lon L. Fuller

On the Problem of the Grudge Informer

By a narrow margin you have been elected Minster of Justice of your country, a nation of some twenty million inhabitants. At the outset of your term of office you are confronted by a serious problem that will be described below. But first the background of this problem must be presented.

For many decades your country enjoyed a peaceful, constitutional and democratic government. However, some time ago it came upon bad times. Normal relations were disrupted by a deepening economic depression and by an increasing antagonism among various factional groups, formed along economic, political, and religious lines. The proverbial man on horseback appeared in the form of the Headman of a political party or society that called itself the Purple Shirts.

In a national election attended by much disorder the Headman was elected President of the Republic and his party obtained a majority of the seats in the General Assembly. The success of the party at the polls was partly brought about by a campaign of reckless promises and ingenious falsifications, and partly by the physical intimidation of night-riding Purple Shirts who frightened many people away from the polls who would have voted against the party.

When the Purple Shirts arrived in power they took no steps to repeal the ancient Constitution or any of its provisions. They also left intact the Civil and Criminal Codes and the Code of Procedure. No official action was taken to dismiss any government official or to remove any judge from the bench. Elections continued to be held at intervals and ballots were counted with apparent honesty. Nevertheless, the country lived under a reign of terror.

Judges who rendered decisions contrary to the wishes of the party were beaten and murdered. The accepted meaning of the Criminal Code was perverted to place political opponents in jail. Secret statutes were passed, the contents of which were known only to the upper levels of the party hierarchy. Retroactive statutes were enacted which made acts criminal that were legally innocent when committed. No attention was paid by the government to the restraints of the Constitution, of antecedent laws, or even of its own laws. All opposing political parties were disbanded. Thousands of political opponents were put to death, either methodically in prisons or in sporadic night forays of terror. A general amnesty was declared in favor of persons under sentence for acts "committed in defending the fatherland against subversion." Under this amnesty a general liberation of all prisoners who were members of the Purple Shirt party was effected. No one not a member of the party was released under the amnesty.

The Purple Shirts as a matter of deliberate policy preserved an element of flexibility in their operations by acting at times through the party "in the streets," and by acting at other times through the apparatus of the state which they controlled. Choice between the two methods of proceeding was purely a matter of expediency. For example, when the inner circle of the party decided to ruin all the former Socialist-Republicans (whose party put up a last-ditch resistance to the new regime), a dispute arose as to the best way of confiscating their property. One faction, perhaps still influenced by prerevolutionary conceptions, wanted to accomplish this by a statute declaring their goods forfeited for criminal acts. Another wanted to do it by compelling the owners to deed their property over at the point of a bayonet. This group argued against the proposed statute on the ground that it would attract unfavorable comment abroad. The Headman decided in favor of direct action through the party to be followed by a secret statute ratifying the party's action and confirming the titles obtained by threats of physical violence.

The Purple Shirts have now been overthrown and a democratic and constitutional government restored. Some difficult problems have, however, been left behind by the deposed regime. These you and your associates in the new government must find some way of solving. One of these problems is that of the "grudge informer."

During the Purple Shirt regime a great many people worked off grudges by reporting their enemies to the party or to the government authorities. The activities reported were such things as the private expression of views critical of the government, listening to foreign radio broadcasts, associating with known wreckers and hooligans, hoarding more than the permitted amount of dried eggs, failing to report a loss of identification papers within five days, etcetera. As things then stood with the administration of justice, any of these acts, if proved, could lead to a sentence of death. In some cases this sentence was authorized by "emergency" statutes; in others it was imposed without statutory warrant, though by judges duly appointed to their offices.

After the overthrow of the Purple Shirts, a strong public demand grew up that these grudge informers be punished. The interim government, which preceded that with which you are associated, temporized on this matter. Meanwhile it has become a burning issue and a decision concerning it can no longer be postponed. Accordingly, your first act as Minister of Justice has been to address yourself to it. You have asked your five Deputies to give thought to the matter and to bring their recommendations to conference. At the conference the five Deputies speak in turn as follows:

FIRST DEPUTY. "It is perfectly clear to me that we can do nothing about these so-called grudge informers. The acts they reported were unlawful according to the rules of the government then in actual control of the nation's affairs. The sentences imposed on their victims were rendered in accordance with principles of law then obtaining. These principles differed from those familiar to us in ways that we consider detestable. Nevertheless they were then the law of the land. One of the principal differences between that law and our own lies in the much wider discretion it accorded to the judge in criminal matters. This rule and its consequences are as much entitled to respect by us as the reform which the Purple Shirts introduced into the law of wills, whereby only two witnesses were required instead of three. It is immaterial that the rule granting the judge a more or less uncontrolled discretion in criminal cases was never formally enacted but was a matter of tacit acceptance. Exactly the same thing can be said of the opposite rule which we accept that restricts the judge's discretion narrowly. The difference between ourselves and the Purple Shirts is not that theirs was an unlawful government -- a contradiction in terms -- but lies rather in the field of ideology. No one has a greater abhorrence than I for Purple Shirtism. Yet the fundamental difference between our philosophy and theirs is that we permit and tolerate differences in viewpoint, while they attempted to impose their monolithic code on everyone. Our whole system of government assumes that law is a flexible thing, capable of expressing and effectuating many different aims. The cardinal point of our creed is that when an objective has been duly incorporated into a law or judicial decree it must be provisionally accepted even by those that hate it, who must await their chance at the polls, or in another litigation, to secure a legal recognition for their own aims. The Purple Shirts, on the other hand, simply disregarded laws that incorporated objectives of which they did not approve, not even considering it worth the effort involved to repeal them. If we now seek to unscramble the acts of the Purple Shirt regime, declaring this judgment invalid, that statute void, this sentence excessive, we shall be doing exactly the thing we most condemn in them. I recognize that it will take courage to carry through with the program I recommend and we shall have to resist strong pressures to public opinion. We shall also have to be prepared to prevent the people from taking the law into their own hands. In the long run, however, I believe the course I recommend is the only one that will insure the triumph of the conceptions of law and government in which we believe.''

SECOND DEPUTY. ''Curiously, I arrive at the same conclusion as my colleague, by an exactly opposite route. To me it seems absurd to call the Purple Shirt regime a lawful government. A legal system does not exist simply because policemen continue to patrole the streets and wear uniforms or because a constitution and code are left on the shelf unrepealed. A legal system presupposes laws that are known, or can be known, by those subject to them. It presupposes some uniformity of action and that like cases will be given like treatment. It presupposes the absence of some lawless power, like the Purple Shirt Party, standing above the government and able at any time to interfere with the administration of justice whenever it does not function according to the whims of that power. All of these presuppositions enter into the very conception of an order of law and have nothing to do with political and economic ideologies. In my opinion law in any ordinary sense of the word ceased to exist when the Purple Shirts came to power. During their regime we had, in effect, an interregnum in the rule of law. Instead of a government of laws we had a war of all against all conducted behind barred doors, in dark alleyways, in palace intrigues, and prison-yard conspiracies. The acts of these so-called grudge informers were just one phase of that war. For us to condemn these acts as criminal would involve as much incongruity as if we were to attempt to apply juristic conceptions to the struggle for existence that goes on in the jungle or beneath the surface of the sea. We must put this whole dark, lawless chapter of our history behind us like a bad dream. If we stir among its hatreds, we shall bring upon ourselves something of its evil spirit and risk infection from its miasmas. I therefore say with my colleague, let bygones be bygones. Let us do nothing about the so-called grudge informers. What they did do was neither lawful nor contrary to law, for they lived, not under a regime of law, but under one of anarchy and terror."

• • • • • •

THIRD DEPUTY. "I have a profound suspicion of any kind of reasoning that proceeds by an 'either-or' alternative. I do not think we need to assume either, on the one hand, that in some manner the whole of the Purple Shirt regime was outside the realm of law, or, on the other, that all of its doings are entitled to full credence as the acts of a lawful government. My two colleagues have unwittingly delivered powerful arguments against these extreme assumptions by demonstrating that both of them lead to the same absurd conclusion, a conclusion that is ethically and politically impossible. If one reflects about the matter without emotion it becomes clear that we did not have during the Purple Shirt regime a 'war of all against all.' Under the surface much of what we call normal human life went on -- marriages were contracted, goods were sold, wills were drafted and executed. This life was attended by the usual dislocations -- automobile accidents, bankruptcies, unwitnessed wills, defamatory misprints in the newspapers. Much of this normal life and most of these equally normal dislocations of it were unaffected by the Purple Shirt ideology. The legal questions that arose in this area were handled by the courts much as they had been formerly and much as they are being handled today. It would invite an intolerable chaos if we were to declare everything that happened under the Purple Shirts to be without legal basis. On the other hand, we certainly cannot say that the murders committed in the streets by members of the party acting under orders from the Headman were lawful simply because the party had achieved control of the government and its chief had become President of the Republic. If we must condemn the criminal acts of the party and its members, it would seem absurd to uphold every act which happened to be canalized through the apparatus of a government that had become, in effect, the alter ego of the Purple Shirt Party. We must therefore, in this situation, as in most human affiars, discriminate. Where the Purple Shirt philosophy intruded itself and perverted the administration of justice from its normal aims and uses, there we must interfere. Among these perversions of justice I would count, for example, the case of a man who was in love with another man's wife and brought about the death of the husband by informing against him for a wholly trivial offense, that is, for not reporting a loss of his identification papers within five days. This informer was a murderer under the Criminal Code which was in effect at the time of his act and which the Purple Shirts had not repealed. He encompassed the death of one who stood in the way of his illicit passions and utilized the courts for the realization of his murderous intent. He knew that the courts were themselves the pliant instruments of whatever policy the Purple Shirts might for the moment consider expedient. There are other cases that are equally clear. I admit that there are also some that are less clear. We shall be embarrassed, for example, by the cases of mere busybodies who reported to the authorities everything that looked suspect. Some of these persons acted not from desire to get rid of those they accused, but with a desire to curry favor with the party, to divert suspicions (perhaps ill-found) raised against themselves, or through sheer officiousness. I don't know how these cases should be handled, and make no recommendation with regard to them. But the fact that these troublesome cases exist should not deter us from acting at once in the cases that are clear, of which there are far too many to permit us to disregard them."

FOURTH DEPUTY. "Like my colleague I too distrust 'either-or' reasoning, but I think we need to reflect more than he has about where we are headed. This proposal to pick and choose among the acts of this deposed regime is thoroughly objectionable. It is, in fact, Purple Shirtism itself, pure and simple. We like this law, so let us enforce it. We like this judgment, let it stand. This law we don't like, therefore it never was a law at all. This governmental act we disapprove, let it be deemed a nullity. If we proceed this way, we take toward the laws and acts of the Purple Shirt government precisely the unprincipled attitude they took toward the laws and acts of the government they supplanted. We shall have chaos, with every judge and every prosecuting attorney a law unto himself. Instead of ending the abuses of the Purple Shirt regime, my colleague's proposal would perpetuate them. There is only one way of dealing with this problem that is compatible with our philosophy of law and government and that is to deal with it by duly enacted law, I mean, by a special statute directed toward it. Let us study this whole problem of the grudge informer, get all the relevant facts, and draft a comprehensive law dealing with it. We shall not then be twisting old laws to purposes for which they were never intended. We shall furthermore provide penalites appropriate to the offense and not treat every informer as a murderer simply because the one he informed against was ultimately executed. I admit that we shall encounter some difficult problems of draftsmanship. Among other things, we shall have to assign a definite legal meaning to 'grudge' and that will not be easy. We should not be deterred by these difficulties, however, from adopting the only course that will lead us out of a condition of lawless, personal rule."

FIFTH DEPUTY. "I find a considerable irony in the last proposal. It speaks of putting a definite end to the abuses of the Purple Shirtism, yet it proposes to do this by resorting to one of the most hated devices of the Purple Shirt regime, the ex post facto criminal statute. My colleague dreads the confusion that will result if we attempt without a statute to undo and redress 'wrong' acts of the departed order, while we uphold and enforce its 'right' acts. Yet he seems not to realize that his proposed statute is a wholly specious cure for this uncertainty. It is easy to make a plausible argument for an undrafted statute; we all agree it would be nice to have things down in black and white on paper. But just what would this statute provide? One of my colleagues speaks of someone who had failed for five days to report a loss of his identification papers. My colleague implies that the judicial sentence imposed for that offense, namely death, was so utterly disporportionate as to be clearly wrong. But we must remember that at that time the underground movement against the Purple Shirts was mounting in intensity and that the Purple Shirts were being harassed constantly by people with false identification papers. From their point of view they had a real problem, and the only objection we can make to their solution of it (other than the fact that we didn't want them to solve it) was that they acted with somewhat more rigor than the occasion seemed to demand. How will my colleague deal with this case in his statute, and with all of its cousins and second cousins? Will he deny the existence of any need for law and order under the Purple Shirt regime? I will not go further into the difficulties involved in drafting this proposed statute, since they are evident enough to anyone who reflects. I shall instead turn to my own solution. It has been said on very respectable authority that the main purpose of the criminal law is to give an outlet to the human instinct for revenge. There are times, and I believe this is one of them, when we should allow that instinct to express itself directly without the intervention of forms of law. This matter of the grudge informers is already in process of straightening itself out. One reads almost every day that a former lackey of the Purple Shirt regime has met his just reward in some unguarded spot. The people are quietly handling this thing in their own way and if we leave them alone, and instruct our public prosecutors to do the same, there will soon be no problem left for us to solve. There will be some disorders, of course, and a few innocent heads will be broken. But our government and our legal system will not be involed in the affair and we shall not find ourselves hopelessly bogged down in an attempt to unscramble all the deeds and misdeeds of the Purple Shirts."

As Minister of Justice which of these recommendations would you adopt?

Selected Bibliography

Books:

BRECHT, Arnold. *Political Theory: The Foundations of Twentieth Century Political Thought*. Princeton: Princeton University Press, 1959.

COGLEY, J. [and others]. *Natural Law and Modern Society*. New York: The World Publishing Co., 1962.

COHEN, Morris. *Reason and Nature*. 2nd edition. New York: Free Press, 1953, 1959.

d'ENTRÈVES, A. P. *Natural Law*. Revised edition. London: Hutchinson University Library, 1951, 1972.

FINNIS, John. *Natural Law and Natural Rights*. Oxford: Clarendon Press, 1980.

FULLER, Lon L. *The Morality of Law*, Revised edition. London and New Haven: Yale University Press, 1969.

GRANT, George. *Philosophy in the Mass Age*. Vancouver: Copp Clark, 1966.

_________. *Technology and Empire: Perspectives on North America*. Toronto: House of Anansi, 1968.

_________. *Time as History*. Toronto: Canadian Broadcasting Corporation, 1969.

_________. *English Speaking Justice. Sackville: Mount Allison University, 1974.*

HARDING, A. L. ed. Origins of the Natural Law Tradition. New York and London: Kennikat Press, 1954, 1971.

HART, H. L. A. *The Concept of Law*. Oxford: Clarendon Press, 1961.

HOOK, Sidney. ed. *Law and Philosophy: A Symposium*. New York: New York University Press, 1964.

JARVIE, I. C. *Concepts and Society*. London: Routledge and Kegan Paul, 1972.

JENNINGS, Sir Ivor. *The Law and the Constitution*. 5th edition. London: University of London Press, 1959.

KENNEDY, W. P. M. *Some Aspects of the Theories and Workings of Constitutional Law*. New York: Macmillan, 1932.

MIDGLEY, L. C. *Beyond Human Nature: The Contemporary debate over Natural Moral Law*. Utah: Brigham Young University Press, 1968.

O'CONNOR, D. J. *Aquinas and Natural Law*. Toronto and London: Macmillan and Co. Ltd., 1967.

OPPENHEIM, Felix E. *Moral Principles in Political Philosophy*, 2nd edition. New York: Random House, 1968, 1976.

ROMMEN, H. *The Natural Law*. tr. by Thomas R. Hanley St. Louis and London: B. Hender Book Co., 1947.

SABINE, George H. *A History of Political Theory*. 4th edition Illinois: Dryden Press, 1937, 1973; esp. Part II.

SAYRE, Paul. ed. *Interpretations of Modern Legal Philosophies*. New York: Oxford University Press, 1947.

SCOTT, Frank. *Essays on the Constitution: Aspects of Canadian Law and Politics*. Toronto: University of Toronto Press, 1977.

SIMON, Y. *The Tradition of Natural Law*. Vakan Kuic, ed. New York: Fordham University Press, 1965.

SHUMAN, Samuel I. *Legal Positivism*. Detroit: Wayne State University Press, 1963.

STONE, Julius. *Human Law and Human Justice*. California: Stanford University Press, 1965.

STRAUSS, Leo. *Natural Right and History*. Chicago: University of Chicago Press, 1953.

TARNOPOLSKY, Walter. *The Canadian Bill of Rights*. 2nd, revised edition. Toronto: McClelland and Stewart, 1975.

TUCK, Richard. *Natural Right Theories*. Cambridge: Cambridge University Press, 1979.

WEILER, Paul. *In the Last Resort: A Critical Study of the Supreme Court of Canada*. Toronto: Carswell/Methuen, 1974.

WILD, John. *Plato's Modern Enemies and the Theory of Natural Law*. Chicago: University of Chicago Press, 1953.

Articles:

BLACK, Edwin R. and Cairns, Alan C. "A Different Perspective on Canadian Federalism." J. Peter Meekison, ed. *Canadian Federalism: Myth or Reality*. 3rd edition. Toronto: Methuen, 1977.

BOURKE, Vernon J. "Natural Law, Thomism and Professor Nielsen." *Natural Law Reform,* Vol. 5 (1960), pp. 116ff. This article is a response to Kai Nielsen's article below.

BROWN, S. M. "Inalienable Rights." *Philosophical Review,* Vol. 64 (1955), pp. 192-211.

CAIRNS, Alan C. "The Judicial Committee and its Critics." *Canadian Journal of Political Science,* Vol. 4 (1971), pp. 301-345.

________. "The Living Canadian Constitution." J. Peter Meekison, ed. *Canadian Federalism: Myth or Reality*. 3rd edition. Toronto: Methuen, 1977.

CROPSEY, Joseph. "Political Life and a Natural Order." In his *Political Philosophy and the Issues of Politics.* Chicago: University of Chicago Press, 1977.

DONAGAN, Alan. "The Scholastic Theory of Moral Law in the Modern World." A. Kenney, ed. *Aquinas*. London: Macmillan, 1969.

EWART, Lewis. "Natural Law and Expediency in Medieval Political Theory." *Ethics,* Vol. 50 (1939-41), pp. 144-163.

FAY, C. "Human Evolution: A Challenge to Thomistic Ethics." *International Philosophical Quarterly,* Vol. 2 (1960), pp. 50-80.

FRANKENA, W. K. "Natural and Inalenable Rights." *Philosophical Review,* Vol. 64 (1955), pp. 212-232.

FULLER, Lon L. "Human Purpose and Natural Law." *Journal of Philosophy,* Vol. 53 (1956), pp. 697-705. This is part of a symposium on natural law.

JAFFA, Harry V. "In Defense of the 'Natural Law Thesis'." In his *Equality and Liberty: Theory and Practice in American Politics*. New York: Oxford University Press, 1965. This is a response to Felix Oppenheim.

KOSSEL, Clifford G. "The moral View of Thomas Aquinas." *Encyclopedia of Morals*. Vergilius Fern, ed. New York: Philosophical Library, 1956, pp. 12ff.

LECLERCQ. "Natural Law and the Unknown." *Natural Law Forum,* Vol. 7 (1962), pp. 26-43.

NAGEL, Ernst. "Fact, Value and Human Purpose." *Natural Law Forum,* Vol. 4, no. 1 (1959), pp. 26-43.

NELSON, A. D. "Ethical Relativism and the Study of Political Values." *Canadian Journal of Political Science,* Vol. 11 (1978), pp. 3-31.

NIELSEN, Kai. "An Examination of the Thomistic Theory of Natural Law." *Natural Law Forum,* Vol. 4 (1959), pp. 63-71. Vernon Bourke's article above is a reply to Professor Nielsen.

OPPENHEIM, Felix. "The Natural Law Thesis: Affirmation or Denial." *American Political Science Review,* Vol. 51 (1957), pp. 41-53. Harry Jaffa's article above is a response to Oppenheim.

PLAMENATZ, John. Lamont, W. D. Acton, H. B., "Rights." A Symposium. *PAS,* Vol. 24 (1950), pp. 75-110.

SELZNICK, Philip. "Natural Law and Sociology." *Natural Law Forum,* Vol. 6 (1961), pp. 84-108.

STANLEY, G. F. G. "Act or Pact: Another Look at Confederation." *Canadian Historical Association Report,* (1956), pp. 1-25.

WATKINS, F. M. "Natural Law and the Problem of Value-Judgement." O. Garceau, ed. *Political Research and Political Theory.* Massachusetts: Harvard University Press, 1968.